# THE CHRISTIAN EDUCATOR'S
# HANDBOOK ON
# FAMILY LIFE
# EDUCATION

# THE CHRISTIAN EDUCATOR'S
# HANDBOOK ON
# FAMILY LIFE
# EDUCATION

*edited by*

## KENNETH O. GANGEL & JAMES C. WILHOIT

**Baker Books**

A Division of Baker Book House Co
Grand Rapids, Michigan 49516

© 1996 by Kenneth O. Gangel and James C. Wilhoit

Published by Baker Books
a division of Baker Book House Company
P.O. Box 6287, Grand Rapids, MI 49516-6287

Paperback edition published 2000

Printed in the United States of America

**Library of Congress Cataloging-in-Publication Data**

The Christian educator's handbook on family life education / edited by
   Kenneth O. Gangel & James C. Wilhoit.
      p.     cm.
   Originally published: 1996.
   Includes biographical references and indexes.
   ISBN 0-8010-2247-9 (pbk.)
     Family—Religious life. 2. Church work with families. 3. Christian
education. I. Title: Handbook on family life education. II. Gangel,
Kenneth O. III. Wilhoit, Jim.
   BV4526.2 .C4416   2000
   261.8'3585—dc21                          00-033686

For information about academic books, resources for Christian leaders, and all new releases available from Baker Book House, visit our web site:
http://www.bakerbooks.com

# CONTENTS

"Who we will be" and "how we will live" announces a special edition of *Newsweek*, with even larger letters announcing the issue's feature: "The 21st Century Family" (*Newsweek*, 1990, Winter/Spring). The cover promises to deliver information on Made-to-Order Babies, Living in a Stepfamily, Doubts about Day Care, Making Your Money Grow, The House of the Future, and Dr. Spock's Good Advice.

As interesting and helpful as that special edition of *Newsweek* was, it cannot compete with the book you have just opened. In these pages you will hear from twenty-four family experts, including pastors like Tony Evans and Leith Anderson; elementary/secondary teachers like Barb Alexander and Jane Schimmer; college and seminary professors like Beth Brown, Jim Slaughter, Daryl Eldridge, and Jim Davies; media experts like Kerby Anderson and Coleen Cook; and counselors like David Carder and the Newmans. We have selected authors from a wide range of denominational traditions and theological perspectives within the evangelical camp.

This fourth volume of *The Christian Educator's Handboook* series is not about family life directly but, rather, about how churches and other ministry organizations can carry out programs of family life education. As we discuss it in these chapters, family life education is much broader than counseling and, ultimately, much more valuable than crisis intervention. Our authors talk about how to preempt problems before they become full-blown crises.

Though we did not plan it this way, this particular volume of our series could not be released at a better time. Recent information reveals that 1995 was a pivotal year in the next boom to hit education.

> Five years ago the U.S. Census Bureau predicted that school enrollment would drop by about one percent by the year 2025. But current congestion in the classroom suggests otherwise. Six million more children are attending school now than were ten years ago. From 1980 to 1993, kindergarten enrollment alone shot up by 22 percent. . . . All this has sent demographers back to their calculators. By 2025 the school population will grow from 49 million to 58 million children—an 18 percent hike—according to new figures released by the Educational Research Service, an independent firm (Hancock & Gordon, 1995, p. 58).

Once besieged by hordes of teenagers, the church now must cope with both ends of the life cycle as burgeoning demographics mandate ministry to senior adults and young children.

At the same time we are experiencing what one author calls "a total breakdown of American values, common sense, and parent and community responsibility to protect and nurture children" (Edelman, 1995, p. 7). In a provocative article, she attacks our nation's "numbing and reckless reliance on violence to resolve problems, feel powerful, or be entertained" (p. 7).

One of Edelman's steps captures the spirit of this book: "Adults must stop our hypocrisy and break the code of silence about the breakdown of spiritual values, parental and community responsibility for children" (p. 11). She goes on to say,

> . . . *we need to improve the religious education and programs we provide for parents.* How are we supporting them in the challenging work of nurturing peaceful, spiritually grounded children in the midst of today's violent and materialistic culture? Do we provide classes so that parents can learn to nurture, guide, and discipline their children without resorting to violence or abuse? Do our congregations house family resource centers to connect parents with the various forms of support they need? Do we help parents find the spiritual centering they need, the faithful insights into what

it means to be a parent, to steady them through trying moments? (Can parents turn to our congregations for literacy training programs?) (p. 14)

A quick run through the Contents will demonstrate that this is not a book about children alone nor about parenting. We have attempted to approach our subject from numerous different perspectives, always with the focus on how ministry programs can build stronger families. Lyle Schaller wrote at the beginning of this decade:

> Perhaps the most significant implication is the attractiveness to church-shoppers of the parish that can deliver on the promise that their "distinctive role is to strengthen the family." Fulfilling that promise has become one of the two guaranteed routes to numerical growth today (the other is high quality, memorable, motivational and persuasive biblical preaching) (1990, p. 14).

Martin Luther once reminded parents that "on the Day of Judgment God will demand of them the children he has given and committed to them"(Edelman, 1995, p. 16). Those words were spoken in 1520; they need renewed emphasis today. Those of us who lead church ministries must be able to provide biblical and effective family life education or we will lose the battle with those generations already in our churches and those yet to come.

We express deep appreciation to all the authors for their fine work on this project and special acknowledgment to Karen Grassmick, Christy Sullivan, and Cheri Bowen for assisting in manuscript preparation.

Kenneth O. Gangel, Dallas, Texas
James C. Wilhoit, Wheaton, Illinois

# PART ONE

# FOUNDATIONS FOR FAMILY LIFE EDUCATION

# TOWARD A BIBLICAL THEOLOGY OF FAMILY
*James R. Slaughter*

We live in a supersonic, supercharged, fast-paced culture in which change is the expected norm. Every day new technological and sociological advances burst on the scene. We welcome creative ideas to enhance our status, refresh our bodies, and stimulate our brains. We question traditional models in every sphere of life from relaxation to religion, with an apparent insatiability for ingenuity and novelty. Should we be surprised that the traditional model of family comes under fire today, or that our society attacks long-established family values and structures?

Scanzoni and Scanzoni note the immense increase in the incidents of cohabitation in America today, unmarried adults in the same or adjacent age groups living together in some kind of personal relationship (1976, pp. 156–159). They also point out the rise of homosexual "marriages," and affirm that an overt ongoing relationship of two economically and sexually interdependent women, or a similar relationship between two males, could legitimately be called a marriage (p. 183). Such departure from traditional standards raises serious concerns about our understanding of "family," and motivates Schreur and Schreur to identify and describe five family fears, four of which relate directly to the issue of models and values: (1) the fear that our children will make life-dominating mistakes; (2) the fear that our children will not "turn out right"; (3) the fear that we are failing as a family; (4) the fear that a family member will die or be seriously injured or sick; (5) the fear that our children will not share our family's values and faith (1994, pp. 38–39).

In addition to this concern for our understanding of family and our questioning of traditional models and values, we see all around us serious imperfections of family life. Most of our families are scarred to some extent by death, disease, alcoholism, drug addiction, violence, spouse-battering, child abuse, lack of communication, quarreling between or among generations, and quarreling with in-laws (Wright, 1989, p. 20). A well-known psychiatrist boldly asserts that by far the most issues adults bring into counseling are directly related to their fathers (Minirth, Newman, & Warren, 1992, p. 12). This crisis in the parenting task has prompted the establishment of an organization called "National Fatherhood Initiative," which called a National Summit on Fatherhood in 1994.

In our world of changing systems and values, perhaps there has never been a greater need to investigate what the Bible has to say about family and family relationships. This chapter will provide an opportunity to consider a biblical overview of family. The material will be restricted to what Scripture says about family and therefore could be called a biblical theology. By necessity, however, it must remain brief and selective, serving its limited role as the foundation for this book. But these paragraphs can also become a launch pad for further study and insight into that unique, personal, fundamental unit of our world's social system.

## THE TERMINOLOGY OF FAMILY

Old Testament writers often used the Hebrew word *bayit* ("house") to reflect the idea of family (Ruth 4:11), or the word, *mishpaha,* usually translated "clan" (Gen. 24:38; Jud. 9:1). A secondary form of the latter occurs as *shiphghah* and is used of central relationships such as servants (Gen. 30:7, 10, 12). These terms, usually translated as "family" or "clan," may embrace a wide range of meanings and relationships.

The New Testament represents the idea of household, family, or race by the word *oikos:* "House of Israel" (Matt. 10:6; 15:24; Acts 2:36; Heb. 8:8, 10); "House of David" (Luke 1:27, 69; 2:4) referring to the royal race of David. The term occurs especially in the story of the birth of Christ. The New Testament refers also to the "House of Jacob" (Luke 1:33; Acts 7:46), and the "House of Judah" (Heb. 8:8).

The Greek word *oikia* became the common New Testament designation for "family" in the sense of "household" as in Matt. 10:12b and Mark 6:4 (TDNT, 1975, p. 131).

## THE NATURE OF FAMILY

It may be best to define the nature of "family" in terms of the nature of human beings who make up family—in particular, the man and the woman from whom offspring come. Genesis 1:26-27 (cf. Gen. 5:1-2), describes both male and female as being created in God's image (Cassuto, 1978, pp. 57-58). Though the phrase "in the image of God" could refer, at least in part, to human ability to think abstractly, or authority to rule (Gen. 1:28), human beings seem more uniquely like God in their capacity to enjoy other beings (God and people) on a deeply intimate plane of relationship. Intimacy is something not demonstrated in the animal kingdom or in the angelic world but is the exclusive domain of God and humans. Maston uses the word "communication" in place of intimacy, but nevertheless sees relationship as the overarching focus or principle of "image," and consequently of family:

The image referred to something of a deeper and spiritual nature. God is a person; man and woman created in the image of God are persons. A person can think, feel, will. A person is conscious of self and of other selves or persons. Possibly most important from the perspective of . . . the family is the fact that a person has the capacity and even the necessity for communication with other persons. . . . In the truest sense there is no person without other persons. Even our God is three in one: Father, Son, and Holy Spirit (1975, pp. 33-40).

Some see the idea of "covenant" as being family's overarching principle, and a starting place for the development of intimacy: "We agree [with others] that the concept of covenant is the fundamental and essential element in developing a theology of the family" (Balswick and Balswick, 1989, pp. 20-21).

Perhaps the greatest longing of every human heart is the deep desire to know and be known by another person. On the highest level, men and women find this longing met through the intimacy of their relationship with God. On the human level, the longing is met through intimacy with other people. Such a construct finds support in Jesus' own words in response to the lawyer's question in Matthew 22, "Teacher, which is the greatest commandment in the Law?" Jesus replied:

> Love the Lord your God with all your heart and with all your soul and with all your mind. This is the first and greatest commandment. And the second is like it: Love your neighbor as yourself. All the Law and the Prophets hang on these two commandments (Matt. 22:35-40).

The commitment to love unselfishly opens up a world of intimacy as human beings enter into relationship with God and with each other. This capacity for intimate relationship given by God with the bestowal of His image has become the hallmark of humanness. It defines the overarching principle of "family," for which community the man and the woman would become a source. From the intimacy of the man and the woman would come offspring with whom they would enter uniquely into relationship as family.

The biblical-theological development of the idea of family is reflected in the following statement: *A God-defined, God-designed family creates an atmosphere of unique intimacy that promotes growth through a matrix of dynamic relationships.* The Bible promotes family as a nurturing environment. God desires to provide a climate in which He enables people to grow to their full potential as their longing to know and be known by Him and by others is fulfilled.

## FOUNDATIONS OF FAMILY

The establishment of the family is predicated on the relationship of the first man and woman, described in the opening chapters of the Old Testament (Gen. 1-2). The man and the woman, having been made in the image of God, were the crowning achievement in the creation sequence. Genesis 2:18-25 describes the fundamental details of their relationship and identifies the components of biblical marriage. Verses 18-23 recount God's provision of the woman for the man and constitute a backdrop or foundation for what will follow. On the basis of the material in verses 18-23, the author identifies the components of biblical marriage: "For this reason a man will leave his father and mother and be united to his wife, and they will become one flesh" (v. 24). A brief epilogue follows in verse 25: "The man and his wife were both naked, and they felt no shame."

## Man's Need for a Companion

Though God had continually pronounced the creation good throughout the various stages of His handiwork (Gen. 1:10, 12, 18, 21, 25, 31), Genesis 2:18 records that He now considered something in His creation "not good" (*lo'tob,* an emphatic negative). The man's aloneness was not good in God's eyes. It limited him in ways that would hinder his fulfillment of God's design and purposes for his life, especially in his important responsibility to populate and cultivate the earth. Therefore, the Lord created a woman out of the man's need for community, for relationship. By himself the man could never do what God had for him to do, or be what God wanted him to be. But together with the woman, his suitable helper, the man would be able to carry out God's work and purposes for him.

## God's Provision of Someone Suitable

The term "suitable helper" (*ezer kenegdo*) describes the woman as the man's partner, emphasizing two aspects of their relationship—that they are similar in some ways, and that they are different in others. The woman would be essentially like the man, yet mysteriously unlike him. The word "suitable" points out the fact that the man and the woman were similar. The text which follows reveals the nature of their similarity as being human. Verses 19-20 describe the naming of the animals (or animal groups), which demonstrated vividly to the man his distinctiveness from members of the animal kingdom: "But for Adam no suitable helper was found" (v. 20). There was no creature like him. Not only was there no creature that looked like him, but there was none like him with the capacity for relationship. There was no one to talk to, no one to make love to, no one to pray with—no one who could enjoy intimacy with him. But the woman was "suitable" for him. She looked like him, with a few wonderful exceptions. More than that, being made in the image of God, she was capable of relating to Adam on a plane of intimate involvement. With man and woman together, humanity was complete.

### God's Provision of a Helper

The fact that the woman was in some ways unlike the man is represented by the word "helper" (*ezer*). Adam was limited. He certainly could never bear children by himself (a part of God's plan for his life), and it is likely that alone with his maleness he would be unable to relate to God in the most meaningful way. Had Adam been sufficient in himself he would not have needed a helper. Adam needed a woman to come alongside him, answering his limitations with the contribution of her strengths as a female.[1] Together they would enable one another to do what they could never do on their own, and to be what they could never be by themselves. That they were suitable for one another physically would enable them to produce offspring through sexual union, thus to begin fulfilling the mandate of Genesis 1:28: "Be fruitful and increase in number; fill the earth and subdue it" (cf. Gen. 3:20; 4:1-2).

Sexuality appears to be a crucial element in God's original design for coupleness and in the foundation and purposes for family. God created a woman for the man, indicating that His design for marriage was the coupling of male and female. They would be perfectly suited (physically, emotionally, spiritually, and psychologically) to relate on this most intimate plane of human relationship. Sexual intimacy between people of the same gender is prohibited by God in His Word (Lev. 18:22; 20:13; Rom. 1:21-27; 1 Cor. 6:9, 10).[2] Contrary to the drift of our culture, the Bible denounces the practice of homosexuality as a perversion and everywhere affirms marriage as being a uniquely male-female relationship (see chapter 24).

The exclamatory statement by Adam in Genesis 2:23 introduces an emotional nuance to God's presentation of the woman to the man: "This is now bone of my bones and flesh of my flesh; she shall be called woman, for she was taken out of man." The sentence represents Adam's cry of excitement over the companion God has brought to him. They would belong together and find fulfillment in one another.

## COMPONENTS OF MARRIAGE

The author's commentary in Genesis 2:24 builds on the foundation of the maleness-femaleness theme of verses 18-23 by identifying the components of marriage: "For this reason a man will leave his father and mother and be united to his wife, and they will become one flesh." The words describe a new male-female relationship, and suggest a deeply personal, intimate element in addition to the procreative possibilities of their union. The man and woman will unite in a permanent commitment, becoming one uniquely and mysteriously through their sexual relationship.

### Leaving Families of Origin

God calls a man and woman who unite in marriage to leave their families of origin (i.e., father and mother). The sense would be that the woman follows her husband in leaving parents behind to establish with him a new and distinctive family unit. Leaving presumably entails both a physical and an emotional move. In order to ensure autonomy of the new family relationship and freedom to establish independent family dynamics, the couple moves out from under their parents' roofs.

An appropriate emotional leaving enables a couple to move away from their parents physically. They no longer depend on their parents for a sense of identity, for the establishment of objectives and goals, or for making decisions.[3] Leaving families of origin physically and emotionally facilitates the establishment of a healthy new marriage and family as husband and wife look to God for direction in their life together.

### Uniting with Each Other

The word "unite" (*dabaq*) in verse 24 carries with it the idea of welding tightly, or joining permanently. It is used in Job 41:15 to describe Leviathan's shields, which are joined together so tightly that not even air can come between them. Thus, the union of the man and the woman produces a relationship so committed and permanent that nothing can come between them. As Norman Wright puts it, biblical marriage is "an unconditional commitment of the total person for total life" (1974, p.4). Genesis 2:24 argues for monogamy in marriage; one marriage partner in a lifelong relationship. God's ideal plan for a husband and wife rules out deeply intimate relationships with someone of the opposite sex, especially physical intimacy.[4] This original design with its emphasis on permanence also militates against divorce.

## Becoming One Flesh

Verse 24 identifies the third component of biblical marriage as becoming "one flesh." There can be little doubt that the meaning of the phrase refers to a unique human relationship established by having sexual intercourse. The Apostle Paul used the same terminology in 1 Corinthians 6:15-16 to warn Christians about the evil of sexual immorality:

> Do you not know that your bodies are members of Christ himself? Shall I take the members of Christ and unite them with a prostitute? Never! Do you not know that he who unites himself with a prostitute is one with her in body? For it is said, "The two will become one flesh."

Paul also related the oneness of marriage to the oneness between Christ and the believer (Eph. 5:22-33). As a person becomes one with Christ by grace through faith, a man and woman become one with each other through sexual intercourse. Becoming one with Christ and becoming one flesh with another person are mysteries which we cannot fully understand. But the text seems to imply that when a man and woman unite sexually they together become one in a unique and personal way.

## INTIMACY IN MARRIAGE

Following the foundation of Genesis 2:18-23 and the components of marriage in verse 24, the author adds an epilogue with a statement about intimacy in verse 25: "The man and his wife were both naked but felt no shame." This verse enhances the personal, emotional sense of the husband-wife bond by emphasizing the absence of shame in their nakedness. Nakedness represented something wonderful about Eden. Sin had not entered the picture at this time, so there was nothing to produce guilt or disgrace. In the same way no sense of embarrassment or unworthiness existed, only an open transparency that reflected the truth about the two partners. They enjoyed an honest vulnerability that was natural, good, and mutually appreciated.

Unfortunately, this relationship of open, honest, vulnerable intimacy was disrupted and seriously damaged by the couple's sin as described in Genesis 3. Their disobedience to God resulted in a judgment that would affect their relationship forever. She would be cursed with "desire" for her husband, and with his rulership over her (Gen. 3:16). Some interpret "desire" as a deep (often sexual) yearning of the wife for her husband (Stigers, 1976, p. 80). However, this interpretation does not fit the context of judgment, since such desire is fulfilling and commendable. According to its use in the next chapter of Genesis (4:7), "desire" probably refers to a prompting to evil: "[Sin's] desire is for you [Cain], but you must master it" (Ross, 1988, p. 146). Part of Eve's judgment would be the craving to control her husband just as sin had desired to control Cain in Genesis 4.

Adam, on the other hand, would seek to dominate his wife, another part of the curse. The word "rule" likely has a harsh application in Genesis 3:16 (Ross, 1988, pp.146-47). It cannot be weakened to mean leadership alone, because it forms part of a judgment oracle for sin. Loving leadership of the husband for the wife, coupled with loving submission of the wife, brought glory to God and produced fulfillment for the man and the woman. The fall changed the dynamics of the relationship, particularly because of the effects of the judgment pronounced on Eve. The harmony of headship and submission would be disrupted by the woman's desire to control her husband and by his efforts to dominate her. These dynamics represent exactly the opposite of what God initiated before the Fall.[5]

Into this fallen environment children entered through the union of the man and his wife (Gen. 4:1). The birth of Cain and Abel, sons of Adam and Eve, enlarged the circle of the first family and was the first step toward fulfilling the command to be fruitful and increase in number.

The tragedy of Abel's murder by his brother Cain points out the presence of sin in the world and its power to destroy throughout the ranks of humankind. This sorrowful event notwithstanding, the Bible affirms the family as God's provision for a nurturing environment. The intimacy produced in such a bond creates a warm, nurturing environment for bearing and raising children.

God's covenant love for the man and woman makes possible the love a couple enjoys. Loving headship and submission, God's plan for marriage from the beginning, may be restored, though imperfectly due to sin, in the marriage relationship founded on faith in Christ (Eph. 5:22-33; 1 Peter 3:1-7). Out of this intimate relationship come children who receive from their parents the opportunity to grow to maturity in an environment of love, acceptance, and encouragement. This group of people—man, woman, and children— forms the family, the most fundamental social system. It is the building block for society's structure. Through family God would fulfill certain purposes by which He would bring people into intimate covenant relationship with Himself and with other human beings.

## THE PURPOSES OF FAMILY

### A Soteriological Purpose
*Family as agency for salvation.* The presence of numerous genealogies in the Scriptures highlights the importance of family in the biblical community. The consistent occurrence of genealogies throughout the Book of Genesis reflects an emphasis on family that is hard to miss.

MAJOR GENEALOGIES OF GENESIS

| | |
|---|---|
| Adam's Line | Gen. 5 |
| Noah's Line | Gen. 10 |
| Noah's Son's Lines | Gen. 11:10-26 |
| Terah's Line | Gen. 11:26–25:11 |
| (including Abraham) | |
| Ishmael's Line | Gen. 25:12-18 |
| Isaac's Line | Gen. 25:19-35 |
| Esau's Line | Gen. 36 |
| Jacob's Line | Gen. 37–50 |
| (including Joseph) | |

The New Testament includes the two genealogies of Jesus, one in Matthew 1:1-16, the other in Luke 3:23-38. Matthew traces Jesus' roots through His father, Joseph, while Luke follows them through Mary, His mother.

These Old Testament and New Testament genealogies would be crucial in both Hebrew and Christian communities for identifying the person of Messiah.[6] The Savior would be offered to the world by the Heavenly Father through the agency of family. Harris notes, "By means of genealogical records, God has given us a connected history from Adam to Christ" (*The Zondervan Pictorial Encyclopedia of the Bible,* 1975, vol. 2, p. 673). The Old and New Testament genealogies represent a funneling of possibilities for the identification of Messiah from the broadest of options to the most narrow.

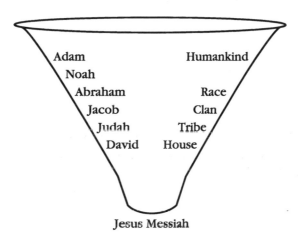

Jesus Messiah

Bible authors take great care to establish the family background of Jesus in order to demonstrate his credentials; He qualifies as a legal, genealogical heir to the Messianic throne. Jesus draws attention to the Messianic implications of His own lineage when He responds to the questions of the Pharisees:

> "What do you think about the Christ? Whose son is he?" "The son of David," they replied. He said to them, "How is it then that David speaking by the Spirit, calls him Lord? For he says, 'The Lord said to my Lord: sit at my right hand until I put your enemies under your feet.' If then David calls him Lord, how can he be his son?" (Matt. 22:42-45)

No one could say a word in reply to this statement, and from that day they dared ask Jesus no more questions (v. 46), indicating that the religious leaders knew the Messianic implications of Psalm 2 which the Lord quoted, and that He was applying it to Himself as both descendent of David and Lord of Heaven. They dared not debate Him on this issue lest his identity as Messiah should become more clear.

### A Procreational Purpose
*Family as agency for populating and subduing the earth.*

> God blessed [the man and the woman] and said to them, "Be fruitful and increase in number; fill the earth and subdue it. Rule over the fish of the sea and the birds of the air and over every living creature that moves on the ground" (Gen. 1:28).

Family would provide a vehicle for bearing and raising children, populating the earth, and subduing the creation. In this sense Maston calls husbands and wives "God's deputy creators" who receive a sacred privilege and bear a sacred responsibility (1975, p. 39). God charges humankind with the responsibility of harnessing and utilizing creation resources for the glory of God.

### A Demonstrative Purpose
*Family as agency for illustrating God's relationship to His covenant people.* The Bible consistently uses two metaphors to demonstrate the loving relationship between Yahweh and Israel and between Christ and the church. One is the figure of the husband-wife relationship, the other the figure of a loving father.

The Old Testament utilizes the marriage of the prophet Hosea to show the reality, depth, and regenerative power of true love. God himself directed Hosea to marry a woman who eventually ran away from him in favor of other lovers. This situation strikingly paralleled the waywardness of Israel in Hosea's day. They abandoned the Lord to serve earthly kings and to worship false gods. But Hosea's love for his wife was true and powerful, the same kind of love God has for His errant people. The prophet's efforts to find his bride, woo her back, and nourish her to health represented a perfect picture of Yahweh's unconditional love for his people Israel, whom He would seek out, woo back, and nourish to health as a nation.

The Apostle Paul used the marriage figure in a similar way to demonstrate Christ's sacrificial love for the church (Eph. 5:22-33). In his instruction to husbands and wives, Paul commanded husbands, "Love your wives, just as Christ loved the church and gave himself up for her" (v. 25). Christ sacrificed Himself to make the church holy and radiant, without stain or blemish. In this same way husbands must love their wives as their own bodies, nourishing them and cherishing them (vv. 27-30). The word "nourish" (NIV, "feed") is the Greek word *ektrephō,* which reflects the idea of enabling to grow. The husband enables his wife to grow to her full potential physically, mentally, spiritually, and socially, helping her achieve goals in these areas of her life.

When the husband cherishes his wife, he injects a romantic element into their relationship. The word "cherish" (*thalpō*) means to keep warm. It was often used in connection with metallurgy, but here the apostle applied it metaphorically to a husband's love for his wife. To cherish a woman means to make her feel loved.

In response to the husband's sacrificial love, the wife submits herself to him as an act of service to the Lord (v. 22). The verb "submit" (*hypotassō*) implies that the wife yields herself voluntarily to her husband. In her submission she acts as his "suitable helper" and a complementary partner to encourage, support, defend, advise, and confront.

The loving, sacrificial husband together with his responsive wife demonstrate the loving, sacrificial headship of Christ for His church and the Spirit-filled response of a believing community who give themselves to Him.

A second metaphor used to show God's love for His people may be seen in Jesus' use of the term "Father" to refer to God. The Lord's parable of the prodigal son (Luke 15:11-32) might more accurately be called the parable of the loving father. In this story Jesus portrayed God as a loving and gracious father who offers compassion and seeks reconciliation with wayward children. It would be hard to miss the point that God seeks reconciliation with those who distance themselves from Him by their sin. Jesus often referred to God as "Father," as in John 14:2, "In my father's house are many rooms . . .," and in John 14:6, "No one comes to the Father except through me" (cf. John 15:1, the Father as vine dresser, and all of John 17 in which Jesus in His high priestly prayer addressed God as Father).

The idea of God as father occurs in the Old Testament as well as the New. For example, God instructed Moses to tell Pharaoh,

"This is what the Lord says: 'Israel is My firstborn son, and I told you, let my son go so he may worship Me'" (Ex. 4:22). One of the most tender references to the father-child relationship between God and his people occurs in Hosea 11:1, 3-4:

> When Israel was a child, I loved him, and out of Egypt I called My son. . . . It was I who taught Ephraim to walk, taking them by the arms; but they did not realize it was I who healed them. I led them with cords of human kindness, with ties of love; I lifted the yoke from their neck and bent down to feed them.

The figure of the father demonstrates the loving compassion of God for His people, and the tenderness which characterizes His care and leading.

### An Educational Purpose

*Family as agency for the transmission of spiritual truth.* Time constraints and feelings of inadequacy often tempt parents to relinquish the teaching of their children to professionals. But the Bible promotes family as the primary sphere for the spiritual training of children. When Israel camped in the plains of Moab, poised for the invasion of Canaan, Moses instructed parents that the responsibility for training children lay squarely on their shoulders. When Canaan was conquered, parents were to remember these words and obey them:

> Hear, O Israel: The Lord our God, the Lord is one. Love the Lord your God with all your heart and with all your soul and with all your strength. These commandments that I give you today are to be upon your hearts. Impress them on your children. Talk about them when you sit at home and when you walk along the road, when you lie down and when you get up. Tie them as symbols on your hands and bind them on your foreheads. Write them on the doorframes of your houses and on your gates (Deut. 6:4-9).

The text emphasizes two major truths about parental training of children. First, if parents are to teach their children the truth about a relationship with God, they themselves must have hearts burning with passion for Him. They must love God with all their heart, soul, and strength; in other words, with every aspect of their being. The word "love" in this Old Testament passage is translated from the Hebrew *aheb,* often used to emphasize passion in married love. The Book of Hosea uses this word frequently of Hosea's love for his wife. In Deuteronomy 6 the same idea of passion applies to the love God's people are to have for Him. Before parents will be able to teach their children about God in an effective way, they must have hearts filled with passion for the Lord and must be attentive to His commands.

Second, spiritual truth is taught best through casual conversation about God and His word, through the normal experiences of everyday life. Parents must "impress" these commands on their children. The Hebrew word *shanan* means "to whet," as in sharpening a knife or razor. The speaker may have intended to emphasize the action of drawing a razor over a whetstone time and time again to produce a keen edge. If this is the correct figure, the meaning would have to do with constancy. The translation of the *New American Standard Version* may come close to the idea: "Teach them diligently to your sons." Children will learn best through constant exposure to their parents' instruction about God and His word.

The instruction to tie God's commands to forehead and hands and on doorposts and gates has been taken literally by some later Jewish readers. The words probably are best understood metaphorically, however (Walvoord and Zuck, BKCOT, 1985, p. 275). Use of the imagery of "heads" and "hands" probably emphasizes the importance of spiritual truth guiding one's thoughts and behavior. "Doorposts" and "gates" likely represent the idea of spiritual truth governing one's life in both the private and public sectors.

Discipline is another aspect of the educational purpose of family, as Hebrews 12 points out:

Endure hardship as discipline; God is treating you as sons. For what son is not disciplined by his father? If you are not disciplined ... then you are illegitimate children and not true sons (vv. 7-8).

The Proverbs frequently address the parental responsibility of discipline in the child training process (Prov. 3:1-12; 19:18; 29:15, 17).

Many passages in Scripture describe the father's role in the instruction of children: "Listen my sons to a father's instruction" (Prov. 4:1); "Fathers, do not exasperate your children; instead, bring them up in the training and instruction of the Lord" (Eph. 6:4); "Fathers, do not embitter your children or they will become discouraged" (Col. 3:21). But also important is the mother's role in the training process: "Keep your father's commands and do not forsake your mother's teaching" (Prov. 6:20); "The sayings of King Lemuel—an oracle his mother taught him" (Prov. 31:1); "I have been reminded of your sincere faith, which first lived in your grandmother Lois and in your mother Eunice and, I am persuaded, now lives in you also" (2 Tim. 1:5).

## A Nurturing Purpose

*Family as an agency for nourishing children through a healthy process of growth.* The outcry over the abuse of children in our society today may be heard in every corner of the land. The serious dysfunction in many families creates a dangerous situation for children. But the Bible clearly speaks to this issue, it affirms that by God's design families are to provide a safe environment in which children may grow.

Luke 2:52 provides the only biblical glimpse of Jesus near His teenage years. The passage reveals a great deal about the family environment in which Jesus grew up, including implications regarding the success of his father and mother in the parenting task. Luke records that after the incident of Jesus' teaching the elders in the temple Jesus grew in wisdom and stature and in favor with God and people. The Lord found within the environment created by His parents a relationship that facilitated growth—mental and emotional growth (wisdom); physical growth (stature); spiritual growth (favor with God); and social growth (favor with people). The passage describes what would appear to be God's design for growth of children in the family.

Parents must take care to create an environment in the family that promotes consistent stimulation of mental faculties and an opportunity for education. Emotional growth would include the impartation of a healthy self-image. Wisdom would be the ability to use knowledge in a mature way, making good decisions, thus living life skillfully.

Parents should also provide an environment for growing healthy bodies. They should instruct their children in personal hygiene, in nutrition, and in the importance of regular exercise and sleep. Attending promptly to children's medical needs is a parental responsibility for this aspect of growth.

Parents also encourage spiritual growth in children. They do this by setting a personal example in their own devotional walks and by consistent teaching about God and His Word. Regular fellowship with a church congregation would presumably fall within this growth category.

Parents who enable their children to grow socially will establish relationships with other families in the community. A consistent ministry of hospitality makes it possible to enjoy others in a social context. Involvement in local community affairs provides the occasion to expand the boundaries of friendships and to witness for Christ.

Ephesians 6:4 offers crucial information for parents as they seek to nourish their children through a healthy process of growth: "Fathers, do not exasperate your children; instead, bring them up in the training and instruction of the Lord." The key to understanding this verse lies in the interpretation of the phrase, "of the Lord." People may be tempted to interpret "of the Lord" as the *content* of parental instruction—that is, teaching children about the Lord. More likely the phrase refers to the *context* of parental instruction—that is, teaching children the way Christ would teach them (Abbott, 1974, p. 178).

Parents may exasperate (make their children angry ) in a number of ways, including absence (either physical or emotional), abuse (psychological, physical or sexual), imposing excessive or impossible demands, and disciplining in a harsh, angry way. Parents who treat children in such a way as to exasperate them have violated the biblical instruction of Ephesians 6:4. Instead, they must raise ("nourish") their children personally, tenderly, lovingly, and reasonably, with understanding, compassion, and grace. Their training may include confrontation when necessary and the expression of firm conviction, but it never leaves room for distance, harshness, unkindness, or mean excesses.[8]

In Ephesians 6:1-3 the apostle calls children to obey their parents in the Lord. "In the Lord" makes reference to the fact that a child's obedience to parents is pleasing in the Lord's sight (cf. Col. 3:20; Walvoord and Zuck, BKCNT, 1983, p. 178).

## CONCLUSION

The God-designed and God-defined family creates an atmosphere of unique intimacy which promotes growth through a matrix of dynamic relationships. God's original plan involved a man and woman in committed, intimate relationship. This husband and wife would establish an environment of loving intimacy in which their children would be nurtured and enabled to grow to their full potential.

Sin has influenced God's original design, however, and families exist in a variety of shapes and sizes today. Many single-parent families arise because of the death of a spouse or because of separation or divorce. Sometimes children are raised by members of the extended family such as aunts and uncles or even grandparents. Some families include a couple or single adult and an adopted child. Though the faces of "family" may change, the Word of God remains a source of relevant instruction for making family the intimate, nurturing matrix of relationships God wants it to be.

### Notes

1. The term "helper" implies no sense of inferiority. The Scriptures refer to God Himself as man's "helper," one who comes alongside to supply what is lacking (Ex. 18:4; Deut. 33:7; Ps. 115-9-11; etc.)

2. Prohibitions against homosexual practices may be found in both Old and New Testament portions of Scripture. The fact that Paul in Romans 1 linked homosexual behavior to the rebellion of worshiping the creation rather than the Creator makes it difficult to interpret homosexuality as a merely cultural phenomenon and therefore acceptable by today's standards.

3. The Bible consistently exhorts children to "obey" their parents. But instruction to adult children is to "honor" their older parents (Ex. 20:12 and Matt. 15:3-9).

4. W. White notes that aside from specific, rare instances the extent of polygamy or bigamy in the Old Testament is small. In the Books of Samuel, Kings and Chronicles there is no reported polygamy on the part of commoners who lived during the age of the monarchy of Israel. Though polygamy did exist at times, actual situations in which it oc-

curred are hardly shown to be happy and are described clearly as sources of continual bickering, envy, and other sinful behavior. (*The Zondervan Pictorial Encyclopedia of the Bible.* Grand Rapids: Zondervan Publishing House, 1975 ed. S.V. "Family," 2:498.)

5. For an excellent discussion of male-female relationships prior to the Fall see Raymond C. Ortlund, "Male-Female Equality and Male Headship" in *Recovering Biblical Manhood and Womanhood.* Edited by John Piper and Wayne Grudem. Wheaton: Crossway Books, 1991, pp. 95–112.

6. Other important Bible genealogies include those of Ezra (Ezra 7:1-5), those of Joshua, the high priest (Neh. 12:10-11), and a remarkable list of names in 1 Chronicles 1–9.

7. References to Messiah's birth and lineage may be found in such texts as Isaiah 7:14, 9:6-7, 11:1.

8. Cf. Paul's emphasis in Colossians 3:21.

## For Further Reading

Balswick, J., & Balswick, J. (1989). *The family: A Christian perspective on the contemporary home.* Grand Rapids: Baker Book House. A work well balanced between the theological and sociological aspects of family, this book offers a good look at the dynamics of current family life. Topics include marriage, parenting, sexuality, communication, and others.

Clark, S. (1980). *Man and woman in Christ.* Ann Arbor, MI: Servant Books. An extremely comprehensive volume which examines the roles of men and women in light of Scripture and the social sciences. Especially helpful are its discussions of maleness and femaleness, and a Christian approach to men's and women's roles in today's social structure.

Crabb, L. (1991). *Men and women: Enjoying the difference.* Grand Rapids: Zondervan Publishing House. In this volume Crabb explores the fundamental problem in marriages today which he identifies as selfishness. As he helps readers deal with this problem, he suggests avenues for being other-centered rather than self-centered in the marriage relationship.

Maston, T.B. (1983). *The Bible and family relations.* Nashville: Broadman Press. A standard in the field, this work represents a sound, comprehensive biblical theology of family. It sticks to biblical issues offering numerous passages for further research.

31

Piper, J., & Gruden, W. (1991). *Recovering biblical manhood and womanhood: A response to evangelical feminism.* Wheaton, IL: Crossway Books. This excellent anthology addresses crucial contemporary issues relating to the roles of men and women in society and especially in the church. Along with male-female issues are sections dealing with family and parenting.

Sell, C. (1981, revised 1995). *Family ministry: Enriching families through the church.* Grand Rapids: Zondervan Publishing House. Sell's long-awaited revision constitutes the most thorough work available on Christian family and the church's ministry to families (until the publication of this present volume).

# THE SOCIOLOGICAL FRAMEWORK OF THE CONTEMPORARY FAMILY IN NORTH AMERICA
*Daryl Eldridge*

Family life seems more fragile than ever. Many blame the ills of our society on the deterioration of the traditional family. Others claim that the changes in the traditional family are simply the result of complex economic and social changes. It is easy to look with nostalgia at the "golden age" of the family and wish we could return to the days of "Donna Reed" and "Father Knows Best." But, as one writer accurately points out, "Leave It to Beaver" was not a documentary (Coontz, 1992, p. 29). The American family was never as perfect as Norman Rockwell portrayed. Regardless, in the last forty years the American family has been undergoing a transformation. Longing for the way things used to be does not help us understand these complex changes or identify what can be done to strengthen families.

## FAMILY IN TRANSITION: A LOOK AT THE DEMOGRAPHICS

Falwell views the transition in the American family as a revolution. He writes, "It is not a revolution of guns, insurrections, and rioting in the streets. . . . It is a revolution which will determine the fate and the future of the American family" (Falwell, 1992, p. 1). Falwell is not alone in his assessment. The dramatic alterations in marriage and family relationships that have transpired over the past generation concern others, including those outside evangelical circles. The following trends give us a snapshot of these changes.

## Cohabitation

The leveling off of the divorce rate is not due to the increase in lasting marriages, but to fewer marriages. More people are skipping marriage altogether, opting to "live together" instead. Since 1960, the number of unmarried households in the U.S. has grown by more than 300 percent, with most of the growth occurring since 1970. In that year there were only 500,000 cohabitating couples (Melville, 1988, p. 11). Today, there are more than 2.5 million (Frazier, 1994, p. 106). Some may view cohabitation as a viable protection against the pain of divorce. Yet, people who live together without a marriage license are more likely to separate than those who tie the knot. The resulting emotional and psychological trauma is every bit as great as those who go through a divorce.

Furthermore, cohabitation before marriage is unsuccessful in preventing divorce. Those who live together prior to marriage are more likely to get a divorce than those who live separately before voicing their vows (Barna, 1993, p. 22). Those who divorce are more likely to cohabitate than to remarry. Less marriage and more cohabitation is the trend for the postmodern world. Cohabitation will become more culturally acceptable and may be given the same legal protection now afforded marriage (Frazier, 1994, p. 106).

## Living Alone

Because of widowhood, divorce, and more young adults choosing to postpone marriage, over 20 million Americans now live by themselves. The figure is almost twice the number of people who lived in one-person households just twenty years ago (Melville, 1988, p. 11). This is the fastest-growing household category in the Western world. In the 1950s, one-person households represented just 10 percent of the country's homes. Today they represent more than 25 percent (Frazier, 1994, p. 109). In many major urban centers, single adults comprise 50 percent of the households. Particularly alarming is the fact that an ever-increasing number of people choose never to marry (Frazier, p. 95).

## Marrying Later

On average, Americans get married two years later than they did twenty years ago. The median marriage age for males is 25.7, for females, it is at an all-time high of 23.1 (Melville, 1988, p. 11).

However, postponing marriage does not mean postponing sexual activity, which is common among unmarried people.

## Divorce

While the nation's divorce rate has reached a plateau over the past few years, it remains the highest in American history. Some researchers cite that 50 percent of the couples who say, "Till death do us part," will break their marital vows. This statistic is more complex than it appears. Couples on their second or third marriage are more likely to divorce than those in first-time marriages. Barna's research indicates that about 25 percent of adults who marry eventually become divorced (1993, p. 68). Children of divorced parents are more likely to divorce in later life. The frightening reality is that an enormous pool of "children of divorce" are entering adulthood. Despite the variance in statistical figures, no researcher refutes the premise that divorce is on the rise.

While cohabitation, divorce, and single households increase, Americans are still a marrying people. Nine out of every ten adults will wear a wedding band at some point in their lives (Barna, 1993, p. 22). Americans do not believe that marriage as an institution is inadequate; rather they believe their partners are inadequate. Most married people who divorce will remarry. Americans keep looking for the perfect mate to meet their emotional and psychological needs. Many adults will experience two or three marriages looking for the ideal mate, a process termed serial monogamy or sequential marriage (Barna, 1993, p. 61).

Interestingly, people who belong to denominations that tend to campaign most vigorously against divorce are more likely to experience a marital breakup. While evangelicals represent 12 percent of the adult population, they comprise 16 percent of the divorced population (Barna, 1993, p. 70).

## Dual Wage Earners

Today, the majority of American women work outside the home. In addition, the number of children with mothers who work is greater than that of children with mothers at home. The two-parent family in which only the father worked for wages represents only 25 percent of families with children, down from 44 percent in 1975 (Coontz, 1992, p. 18). This is due in part to the decline in the value of the dollar since 1971, just when baby boomers were entering the job market. While many women would like to stay home, they feel their income is an economic necessity. Not surprisingly, research indicates the most common source of marital stress is financial hardship (Barna, 1993, p. 58).

### Single-Parent Families and Unmarried Mothers

Over the past twenty years the number of single-parent households has tripled. Before they reach the age of eighteen, roughly two out of three children will live with only one parent (Barna, 1993, p. 23). More than one in five births in the U.S. is outside of marriage, and 75 percent of those births are to women not in consensual unions. More than a third of the out-of-wedlock births are to teenagers (Frazier, 1994, p. 106).

In the United States, this problem is most acute in the African-American community, where more than 50 percent of black children now grow up in single-parent households. Seventeen percent of white children at the age of seventeen live with only one biological parent. For blacks, that figure is 80 percent (Frazier, 1994, p.106).

As expected, the median income for a single-parent family headed by a woman is drastically lower than for married-couple families. The poverty rate for single-parent families is six times higher than among married-couple families (Barna, 1993, 110). Twenty percent of American children live in poverty, and on any given night there are 100,000 homeless children in America (Coontz, 1992, p. 2). It is tough enough for a two-parent family to face the challenges of rearing children; attempting to raise children alone takes its toll on the parent and the children.

### Smaller Households

Since 1970, the average household size has declined from 3.14 to 2.63 persons. More pregnant women opt to remain single. More couples are childless by choice. People delay marriage, which depresses the fertility rate. More people choose never to marry. This trend will dramatically affect housing arrangements as the cost of housing continues to rise.

### Reconstituted and Multigenerational Families

More stepfamilies, more households headed by grandparents, more young adults (especially males) staying home with their parents are definite trends. Researchers estimate that 30 percent of all children born today will live with a stepparent before reaching adulthood. The high rate of marital dissolution and the increase in life expectancy has created a new phenomenon of family reconstitution. Grandparents are now assuming responsibility for their children, grandchildren, and parents. More than three million children now live with their grandparents, up 40 percent in just ten years (Frazier, 1994, p. 112).

## Other Trends

In the coming years we can expect more interracial families. Gay and lesbian "marriages" also will become more accepted and common. With minorities comprising a larger portion of the American landscape, their cultural values will greatly affect the character of American families.

The diversity of American households has challenged educators, sociologists, and politicians to redefine the meaning of family. It has also challenged Christian educators to examine the theology of family and its role in God's redemptive plan (see chapter 1).

## THE FAMILY OF GOD

The hot word for the 1990s is "dysfunctional." Lest we become too preoccupied with bashing today's family, we should be reminded that this generation does not have a corner on family problems. From the very beginning, the family has been in crisis. Eve lied to her husband. Adam in turn would not accept responsibility for his behavior and blamed their troubles on his wife. They were ashamed of their nakedness, not a good way to start a healthy sexual relationship. One of their children murdered his brother. Their story has all the makings of a daytime soap opera.

Or consider the following: Abraham sleeping with his concubine, Hagar; Lot's incestuous relationship with his daughters; Jacob's sons selling their brother, Joseph, into slavery; David and Bathsheba; Hosea and Gomer, his adulterous wife; Amnon raping his sister Tamar; and the man in the Corinthian church who was sleeping with his stepmother. When you add to this list the number of parents with rebellious and difficult children, the Bible forms a virtual "Who's Who" of dysfunctional families. In fact, we are hard pressed to find many biblical families that could serve as a role model for today's family.

The Bible contains many different forms of family life. In it one finds polygamy (name any of the patriarchs); stepfamilies (King Solomon may have had the largest blended family in history); families without children (Abraham and Sarah); single-parent families (Elisha providing oil for the widow and her son); adopted children (Moses); interracial marriages (Samson and his Philistine wife); and intact biological families such as Moses, Zipporah and their two sons.

Throughout the ages, the family has been in crisis, incapable to heal itself. Nor can we expect the government to solve the ills of the family. Restoring and redeeming the family begins with the Church. As Clapp writes:

> The family is not God's most important institution on earth. . . . The church is God's most important institution on earth. The church is the social agent that most significantly shapes and forms the character of Christians. And the church is the primary vehicle of God's grace and salvation for a waiting, desperate world (1993, p. 67).

Jesus created a new family, a third race, neither Gentile or Jew, but "in Christ." Our Lord neither denied nor eliminated the biological family; He provided the means for the human family to become part of His divine family. The dysfunctional family can be healed only by joining the household of God (Eph 2:19). Through God's Spirit, the church is the extended family for those who receive Him. It is only in the power of God's Spirit, within the church, that the nuclear family can resist the social forces that attempt to remake the family. As the church approaches the next millennium, it must assume its role in redeeming and strengthening the family.

## STRENGTHENING FAMILIES

### Helping Married Families

The first thing the church can do to strengthen families is to support those who are married. The traditional family is not dead.

Couples need affirmation and encouragement as they chart their course through turbulent marital waters. Simply advocating that families stay together through it all, however, does little to help families establish strong relationships. Families need to understand the traits that comprise healthy families. The healthy family:

1. communicates and listens,
2. affirms and supports its members,
3. teaches respect for others,
4. develops a sense of trust,
5. has a sense of play and humor,
6. exhibits a sense of shared responsibility,
7. teaches a sense of right and wrong,
8. has a strong sense of family in which rituals and traditions abound,
9. has a balance of interaction among members,
10. has a shared religious core,
11. respects the privacy of its members,
12. values service to others,
13. fosters table time and conversation,
14. shares leisure time,
15. admits to and seeks help with problems (Curran, 1983, pp. 23–24).

If the church is to counterbalance the godless influences in our culture, it must provide marriage enrichment opportunities, financial and parenting seminars, and other ministries that encourage and help families develop these traits.

## Multigenerational Activities

The church can provide an extended family network through multigenerational activities. Young adults need older mentors. Senior adults need the touch of children and youth. The church can provide activities for families of all types to relate and have fun together.

## Premarital Training

Our culture does little to prepare young adults for marriage and child rearing. The church must help young adults prepare for the responsibilities of marriage. More emphasis should be given to preventative marital medicine than emergency treatment.

Youth need encouragement to keep high moral standards through such programs as "True Love Waits." Children and youth can benefit from instruction on God's teachings about the family, marriage, and sexuality.

### Retraining Young Adults

Young adults who grew up in broken and dysfunctional homes need retraining on what it means to be a family. Healthy older couples could take young single adults and young couples into their homes, where they can learn social and relationship skills.

### Financial Assistance

Because financial hardship is the number one stress in families in today's culture, the contemporary church must help families with financial and employment assistance. Family ministries might include financial planning seminars, job bulletin boards, helping retool adults who have lost their jobs, and training mothers who want to work at home.

### Support Systems

Blended families, singles, widows, and others need a caring support system. Small group ministries and support groups can help adults become functional Christians. The church can also provide help for unwed pregnant teenagers.

### Divorce Seminars

Persons who are experiencing divorce, including the children of divorced parents, need help in dealing with the emotional, psychological, and financial trauma facing their families. Divorce recovery workshops provide excellent outreach as well as ministry opportunities.

### Life Purpose Course

A healthy family has a mission or purpose beyond itself. The church needs to help families discover and write a personal family purpose statement. Families also need help in balancing the many demands on their lives, based on God's purpose for their family. Church families need to capture a vision for their homes as mission bases from which they offer salt and light to a lost and dying world.

## CONCLUSION

The diversity of family forms and the issues facing today's family are here to stay. We cannot turn back the clock. We also cannot expect families or the government to solve the social and spiritual ills of the family. The hope for the family lies in the church. The church must continue to proclaim biblical principles that guide families. At the same time, the family of God must respond compassionately and sensitively to the variety of modern families. The church cannot ignore sin, nor lower its moral standards. Yet, the church must recognize the needs and value of each family. The divorced, the separated, the single parent, as well as married couples with or without children, need the healing and redeeming power found in Jesus Christ and His church. The church as a spiritual extended family can provide a caring support system that will strengthen families. As McKay states:

> The religious institution, carrying the label of God's family, offers each of us an essential identity in a world in which we feel disconnected and alone. Through our families and our extended families of all kinds, we have the means to inoculate ourselves against the narcissism that has been so injurious to our society. It is a sickness we must eradicate (1991, p. 137).

### For Further Reading

Barna, G. (1993). *The future of the American family.* Chicago: Moody Press. A description of the crisis in the American family, where the family is headed, and what we can do to facilitate the development of stronger families.

Clapp, R. (1993). *Families at the crossroads: Beyond traditional and modern options.* Downers Grove, IL: InterVarsity Press. A look at how postmodern influences and capitalism have affected the American family. Clapp proposes that the church is the primary family.

Coontz, S. (1992). *The way we never were.* New York: HarperCollins Publishers. Exposes many of the "memories" of traditional family life as myths.

Curran, D. (1983). *Traits of a healthy family.* Minneapolis: Winston Press. Examines fifteen qualities of healthy families and how these qualities can be enhanced.

Falwell, J. (1992). *The new American family: The rebirth of the American dream.* Dallas: Word Publishing. Refutes the media's claims about the demise of the American family and offers ways for Christians to become involved in saving the traditional family.

Frazier, S. (1994). *Psychotrends: What kind of people are we becoming?* New York: Simon & Schuster. A psychological interpretation of the trends affecting today's family.

McKay, B. (1991). *Whatever happened to the family: A psychologist looks at sixty years of change.* Cleveland: United Church Press. An examination of the state of the family in contemporary society and the future for the American family.

Melville, K. (1988). *Marriage and family today (4th ed.).* New York: Random House. A comprehensive summary of the research on the state of the American family.

Miles, M. (1990). *Families growing together: Church programs for family learning.* Wheaton, IL: Victor Books. Practical suggestions on how the church can strengthen and enrich family life.

Sell, C. (1981). *Family ministry: The enrichment of family life through the church.* Grand Rapids: Zondervan Publishing House. An overview of the principles, practices, and processes for a family ministry program in the local church.

# MINISTERING TO FAMILIES IN A MULTICULTURAL SOCIETY
*Anthony T. Evans*

The face of America is rapidly changing, and every church needs to stay on the cutting edge by learning about the changes and effectively responding to them. Social change comes in all forms, but one of its main features is the population growth of culturally different people groups. Essential to effective ministry in this and future decades is the need to develop new techniques that will be successful in making a positive impact on these changing cultural patterns. As we approach the end of the twentieth century, progressive congregations can expect to be rejected by those who fear change and demand that the old traditional practices be kept.

Effective family ministry requires much prayer and intensive thought. Amid demolition by societal pressures and the ungodly disposition of human nature, the family must yet serve as the foundation of society. Society as a whole stands or falls on the basis of the family structure. It is no small task in today's world to nurture one's own family, let alone to develop and assist others.

## ESTABLISHING ONESELF THROUGH ESSENTIAL PRINCIPLES

### Biblical Ministry
Those who wish to minister to minority families must be keenly aware and adamant in two areas of concern. First, although cultural differences must factor into the manner and matter of minis-

tering to minority families, appeasing a culture must not be the driving force or the essence of the ministry itself. To do so would result in theologies that do not affirm the truth of Scripture but rather make Scripture subservient to cultural trends.

The preaching and teaching of the church must be distinctly biblical and other-worldly in order to provide clarity as to what God expects. Too much cultural dressing makes the gospel simply another religious philosophy. When cultural relevance fails to reach people's reality, the Bible can become merely an appropriate salve for the particular ailments of a certain people group.

In many respects ministering to an ethnic family is no different from ministering to families not classified in such a group. Most families have in common the same set of hopes, the same desire for a better life for their children, and the same types of struggles. Almost all families are concerned with money matters, such as livelihood, retirement income, and money for college. Such matters are common to nearly all families because they share a common venue of life.

On the other hand, though some of society's maladies are universal, others seem somewhat more indigenous to particular people groups. In order for a ministry to be effective to families from various people groups, that ministry must be sensitive not only to the predilections and dispositions of the macro-culture but just as sensitive to the idiosyncrasies of micro-cultures (the smaller social groupings within a society). Christian educators must agree that both groups' concerns are equally important and treat them that way.

**Integrated Ministry**

Secondly, if ministry is to function properly in any cultural environment, it must be integrative. An integrated ministry is one in which the leadership understands interrelationships. No one can compartmentalize the life of any one individual, let alone an entire race or nationality. All the parts and facets of a person's life connect, establishing a network of events, responsibilities, and relationships.

The life of a parent does not consist only of taking care of the children, as important as that is. Likewise, the life of a child does not consist merely of interaction with parents. It contains complicated interaction with peers, school, fads, and music. An effective ministry must see the connections. A youth ministry must endeavor to inform teenagers of what their parents' lives are like and how they can possibly affect them. An integrated parenting ministry must seek to explain the world in which their children live.

The absence of crosstalk in ministry negates integration. Without integration, there is no growth. Where there is no growth, one finds despair and confusion in abundance. People exposed to ministry that does not integrate the various aspects of life and faith into a holistic picture will eventually question the relevance of that ministry to their lives.

"I have a dream," said Dr. Martin Luther King, Jr. He dreamed that racial reconciliation would one day be the norm instead of an exception to the rule for all God's creation. The passion for his dream may have come from the life he lived and the scars left from the racial wars he fought; but his belief that the dream could come true was made possible because of the church.

This chapter offers a resource tool to assist church leaders in their endeavor to minister effectively to families from different cultural backgrounds. Christians must take the lead in the area of reconciliation; then the Bible could be established as the standard society should follow; the church would establish the moral tone for society at large; specific programs will provide models for society at large; and, most important, the oneness of the body of Christ will be demonstrated.

## PREPARING ONESELF THROUGH EDUCATION

Unity in the midst of diversity for today assumes change from yesterday in hopes of a better tomorrow. If sincere change is to take place, we must start with the basics. This means having a proper understanding of essential terms before we can have relevant application.

### Culture

Culture, one of several key terms, is defined as "the totality of socially transmitted behavior patterns, arts, beliefs, institutions, and all other products of human work and thought characteristics of a community or population" (*The American Heritage Dictionary*, 1985, p. 348).

## Minority Group

"A minority group is a subordinate group whose members have significantly less control or power over their own lives than the members of a dominant or majority group" (Schaefer, 1988, p. 8).

John Axelson defines five other related terms. Concerning "racial minority," he says:

> The term racial minority is often used in reference to members of those groups who are readily identified by distinctive physical characteristics that are perceived as different from those of members of the dominant group in a society. Skin color, hair type, body structure, shape of head or nose or eyes, and color of eyes are often singled out as different (1983, pp. 152–153).

An "ethnic minority" is "usually identified by cultural practices, such as language, accent, religion, customs, beliefs, and styles of living. Ethnic characteristics, essentially, can be traced to national origins or geographic regions" (Axelson, 1983, p. 153).

Axelson also treats "numerical minority."

> Although the term minority literally means numbering less than half, it does not customarily refer to numerical size when it is used to describe groups of people.... In the South and in many urban areas of the North and Southwest, Blacks and Hispanics form the majority of the population, but they are still a minority people if the politically and economically more powerful group perceives and treats them as inferiors (1983, p.153).

## Prejudice

Prejudice involves attitude, thoughts, and beliefs. Axelson says:

> In the literal sense, prejudice is defined as a preconceived judgment or opinion without just grounds or sufficient knowledge.... It is an irrational attitude or behavior directed against an individual or a group, or their supposed characteristics. Groups that become targets of prejudice are most often categorized by racial, geographic, or ethnic background, religious beliefs, socioeconomic class, sex, or age.

Some of these prejudices are so intense that they are considered "isms" or doctrinaire (racism, classism, ageism, sexism). Unlike discrimination, which involves action, prejudice involves attitudes, thoughts, and beliefs, not actions (p.155).

## Discrimination

According to Axelson, "discrimination is a process of social control that serves to perpetuate or maintain social distance; it is often institutionalized and rationalized. The practice of discrimination may include isolation and segregation or may include personal acts growing out of prejudice" (p. 168).

## APPLYING ONESELF THROUGH PRACTICAL SOLUTIONS

The specific suggestions that follow are not exhaustive, but perhaps they may encourage you to begin making a difference where you can. The idea is not to do everything, but to do something. Start where you are with an individual, church, or organization you know and see where God takes you. If we start ministering *together* without possessing either a superior attitude or a victim mentality, we will discover the unity that Christian service brings to a community in which Christians try to empower one another.

## General Principles
1. The biblical mandate to be involved in racial reconciliation is a command that God expects all His children to obey.
2. Be open to learning, because everyone has something to teach.
3. Affirm another's culture as highly as you would your own.
4. Getting rid of stereotypes means changing one's own perspective and perceptions of others' differences.
5. Talk through prejudices with the goal of decreasing the negative and accentuating the positive.
6. Because of the existence of the sin nature, remember that all God's children have the potential for showing prejudice and discrimination.
7. Get beyond the guilt, anger, and blame by forgiving yourself

and others. Do it, if for no other reason, because God forgave you for the many times you failed Him.

8. How much change one sees depends on how much effort one invests.

9. Three main hindrances to success in cultural reconciliation are miscommunication, personal perceptions, and lack of public affirmation of the good seen in another's culture.

10. Above all, remember that Christ says the greatest demonstration that He is Lord over our lives is the love we unconditionally show one another.

## Specific Suggestions

First, hire *additional staff from diverse backgrounds* to be a part of your counseling team. A counseling program needs to be sensitive to the surrounding neighborhood, especially if the community is racially mixed. Looking out across a wider arena of ministry, evangelical congregations can build a network among themselves focusing on multiple utilization of African-American, Hispanic, Asian, and Anglo counselors from other churches. Obviously that takes a good bit of cooperation, but that is what the church is all about. Some churches have been successful in establishing a general counseling center in a neutral location that targets people groups served by all the supporting congregations.

Second, a church can *network with other churches* in seminars that allow members of one congregation to utilize their business skills to help others who hope to start or maintain a business. Churches can team up to organize conferences or business expos to encourage economic relationships among diverse churches. A church can develop a job training program in which business people from diverse backgrounds volunteer time to do the training. A church and bank minority business loan program can be started. An exchange program can be set up by which one church offers economic resources and referrals, and the other church offers a list of volunteers to operate it.

Third, in the area of education, churches can develop a part of their Christian Education training manual to *address issues on diversity, sensitivity, and management.* Churches can also partner with museums and other organizations to do a presentation displaying the uniqueness of different cultures. A singles ministry (or some other type of ministry) in one church can team up with a singles ministry in another church to conduct retreats, seminars, or conferences together. *Adopt-A-School* is a program in which a church adopts a school in a different neighborhood or partners with a church in that neighborhood for the purpose of having an on-site adult counselor, encouraging life skills, student interaction, and addressing local needs from a biblical basis.

Fourth, *churches can team up to manage health issues.* If one congregation has developed policies on how to deal with AIDS, for example, it could volunteer that information to another church. Team up to develop and circulate information in your own and other neighborhoods on legal matters relating to health issues or the best insurance coverage for those involved with an activity on the church grounds. Team up with other churches to develop a volunteer medical group that serves as a referral system and ministers to the needs of various churches. Cooperate in a crisis pregnancy center or a support group for rape victims.

Fifth, partnering churches can *create a program that puts out a circular about various services for senior citizens and help them get connected with the services.* Start a pen pal program with some elderly folks in a nursing home in a different ethnic community. Adopt a nursing home whose members are predominantly from a different ethnic background and minister to the whole group. Churches can cooperate to do home and auto repair work for senior citizens in their churches.

A sixth suggestion would be to *focus on the homeless.* Develop a ministry in your church in which volunteers from other churches come to help feed the homeless or join an existing program that targets a neighborhood racially different from your own. Develop a food pantry or program that networks with other ethnic churches to donate food to a homeless ministry. Work with other ethnic churches to create a partnership with HUD or some similar organization for housing the homeless. A group of churches can create a service by which the homeless can find resources that can help them. In our multicultural society, the committee can consist of people from diverse backgrounds.

Finally, why not start an association of concerned mothers from different churches *to address problems youth are facing today?* Adopt a high school outside your neighborhood and start a campus fellowship to encourage kids from diverse backgrounds to get involved in each other's lives. Develop a program to mentor boys and girls in and outside your church with a mentoring team consisting of adults from different racial groups. Take your youth to other churches where they can experience other worship styles and discuss the differences. Invite speakers for different youth functions from different ethnic backgrounds to speak on a broad range of topics.

## CONCLUSION

For years, ministering to families in a multicultural society has brought us to the table for discussion. We have pointed fingers and blamed the problem on others. Some made half-hearted commitments; others have been sincere and put forth good effort for many years. But too much is at stake today to continue to function in such a haphazard fashion. Unless we adopt the proper contemporary format necessary to be effective in ministering in a multicultural society, the Bible will be confined to paper and ink, hopes, dreams, and good intentions.

But God is a God of action. When He spoke of a new mystery in Ephesians 2:11–3:12, Jews and Gentiles becoming one in the body of Christ, He wanted this to be reality, not an unusual exception. Jesus Christ let His self-sacrificing action do the talking for Him. If we sincerely want to have effective ministries in a multicultural society now and in the coming twenty-first century, we need to let our self-sacrificing action do the talking for us.

### For Further Reading

Axelson, J., (1993). *Counseling and development in a multicultural society.* Pacific Grove, CA: Brooks/Cole. A condensed and very concise coverage of some of the unique elements that make up the major cultural groups. Emphasizes methods that need to be sensitive to these elements in order to have a more effective counseling ministry.

Breckenridge, J., and Breckenridge, L. (1995). *What color is your God? Multicultural education in the church.* Wheaton, IL: Victor/BridgePoint. Convinced that greater understanding and reconciliation is possible, the authors evaluate multiculturalism, develop a philosophy of culture, examine relevant biblical materials, communicate a theology of cultural aware-ness, and suggest contextualization models appropriate for African-, Asian-, Hispanic-, and Native-American cultures.

Evans, A. (1990). *America's only hope: Impacting society in the 90's.* Chicago: Moody Press. Addresses the need for local churches to stop fol-lowing behind society's agenda in confronting the moral, racial, and so-cial ills that plague our societies and to start setting the agenda as God has commanded, because the church is really America's only hope.

Lee, G. (1991). *Pastoral management of a Chinese church.* D.Min. dis-sertation, Dallas Theological Seminary. Deals with the history of the Chinese church, its problems, and some of the ways to address them in order to have effective church growth.

Montoya, A. (1987). *Hispanic ministry in North America.* Grand Rapids: Zondervan Publishing House. This book emphasizes the unique cultural elements that exist in the Hispanic culture that call not only for adapta-tion but originality in methods of evangelism, organization and adminis-tration, preaching, and worship.

Ng, Donald (1988). *Asian Pacific American youth ministry.* Valley Forge, PA: Judson Press. This book contains historical and biblical back-ground information, programs, and planning helps, and addresses issues dealing with community identity and beliefs and their comparison to the Christian faith.

Perkins, J., and Tarrants, T. (1994). *He's my brother.* Grand Rapids: Chosen Books. Former Ku Klux Klan members tell their personal stories of racial strife and offer practical and relevant biblical solutions for addressing this issue today.

Perkins, S., and Rice, C. (1993). *More than equals: Racial healing for the sake of the gospel.* Downers Grove: InterVarsity Press. Simple in struc-ture but deep in content. States three simple and yet profound concepts needed to effectively maintain racial reconciliation: admit, submit, and commit. Demands action.

Schaefer, R. (1988). *Racial and ethnic groups.* Glenview, IL: Scott, Foresman and Co. This sociological book contains eye-opening statistics that paint a picture of just how multicultural America has become and outlines this growth's negative and positive effects on education, em-ployment, family life, housing, criminal justice, and politics.

Washington, R., and Kehrein, G. (1993). *Breaking down walls: A model for reconciliation in an age of racial strife.* Chicago: Moody Press. Gives eight practical principles for ministering effectively amid racial differences.

# DEVELOPING A FAMILY-FRIENDLY CHURCH
*Leith Anderson*

During summer vacation our family of six attended a country church along with a neighbor family of four. We filled two pews and increased the Sunday morning worship service attendance by 25 percent, from 40 to a total of 50. Simple logic says they must have noticed we were there. But the only acknowledging of our presence was from the usher who handed us bulletins when I requested them. Otherwise, no one spoke to any of us before, during, or after the worship service.

If the people of that church were asked if they are "family friendly," I believe they would unanimously say, "Yes!" In a sense I suppose they are, although the families to which they are friendly are their own.

It is easy for those on the inside of a church to have a sense of warm acceptance that is missing in the experience of outsiders. In order to be biblical, effective, and relevant a church must be perceived as friendly to insider and outsider families.

Developing a family-oriented church begins with examination of attitudes and assumptions more than with programs.

## WHAT ARE CURRENT PERCEPTIONS?

Surveying the internal and external perceptions of a church is an easy and valuable exercise, although it can be threatening to church leaders and established programs.

Most churches are familiar with internal surveys. The most common form is a questionnaire asking insiders a series of simple questions:

1. Do you think ours is a family-friendly church?
2. List several positive examples of our family friendliness.
3. What could we do to improve?
4. What do you think a family-friendly church should look like?
5. Do outsiders consider ours to be a family-friendly church?
6. Would you like to have more new families as part of our church?

Don't stop with internal questionnaires. They give a helpful but limited perspective. They must be interpreted rather than taken at face value. Your full diagnosis has only begun.

Next, try a focus group of present church members and attendees. Limit the group to twelve and include at least one old-timer, one newcomer, one person who is generally positive about the church, and one person who is usually negative about the church. Seek variety in age, gender, and marital status. Select a neutral outsider—perhaps a Christian educator from a nearby church—to serve as facilitator and moderate discussion on the issue of the friendliness of the church toward families.

Key church leaders should observe the focus group but not participate. Many communities have focus group rooms available for free or for a modest rental charge. These rooms have soundproof observation areas behind one-way glass so that observers can freely talk without being heard or disturbing the focus group discussion.

The location and setup are minimally important. The greatest value is hearing people from the church freely discuss the questions listed above, respond to the results of the written survey, and tell about their own perceptions and experiences in the church.

Equally valuable is a similar focus group of outsiders. At Wooddale Church in Eden Prairie, Minnesota, we recruited outsiders from unchurched coworkers and neighbors of church committee members. They were asked to visit the church on any one of five Sunday mornings before Easter, attend a worship service, place their children in the nursery, attend Sunday school, and otherwise experience the church in ways they felt comfortable. The actual focus group was held on a weeknight a few days after Easter. The purpose of a focus group of the unchurched is to see the people and programs of the church through the eyes of outsiders and then compare perceptions with insiders.

Using these or other methods, write a short summary of inside and outside perceptions of the church. As a further check, ask the insiders to read the insider perceptions and ask some outsiders to read the outsider perceptions. If they respond by saying, "Yes, that pretty much describes the way things are at the church," you know that you have a good understanding of perceptions about the church.

## INCLUSIVE OR EXCLUSIVE?

Exclusive churches may serve the needs of those who are already members, but they are difficult social systems for outsiders to penetrate. Some churches may choose to be exclusive, targeting their ministries on themselves. Other churches want to be open to outsiders and incorporate them as individuals and families into the fellowship and ministry of the congregation.

The questionnaire and focus groups may be all you need to decide if the church is inclusive or exclusive, but additional research may help:

1. From existing church records (or from a survey) determine the year each church member first came to the church. If most came more than ten years ago and if very few came in the past five years, the church probably tends to be exclusive.

2. Another exercise is to gather a committee of persons who know most of the congregation and draw a chart indicating how many church members are related to each other by birth or marriage. If the majority of church members are related to a handful of extended families, the church is probably exclusive and the primary gateway to newcomers is through birth or marriage.

3. A third exercise to determine inclusivity and exclusivity is to

prepare a list of all church leaders (especially the governing board of the church, but also include ministry leaders and informal leaders who may not currently hold a position but still have great influence in the church). Next to each name write the year that person first came to the church. How long does it take for a newcomer to become a leader? Exclusive churches keep newcomers out of leadership and inclusive churches usually have a short time line to leadership.

4. A fourth test calculates the percentage of visitors to the church each Sunday. Inclusive churches tend to have at least 1 to 2 percent or more first-time visitors each week.

5. A fifth calculation is to determine how many visitors become regular attendees and members—50 percent is exceptional, 25 percent is good, 10 percent is OK, less than 5 percent is almost a sure sign of exclusivity.

6. A sixth measure is figuring out how many new members stop attending on a regular basis within their first two years. Inclusive churches have a high percentage of participation of two-year members and exclusive churches have a low percentage because the newcomers have not felt connected.

## SYSTEMS OR INDIVIDUALS?

Family-friendly churches recognize that families are social systems which represent more than the sum of the individual parts. Families are interconnected so that an impact on one person affects everyone else in the family.

Family systems theory is most commonly applied to counseling. Therapists know that individual counseling of the person with a presenting problem is not enough. Help may be sought for the delinquent daughter, the depressed mother, or the alcoholic father. However, the problems are never isolated from the rest of the family system. Even if significant progress is made, an individual often reverts to prior patterns when returned to the family system. Therefore the counselor tries to work with the whole family in order to address dysfunction and establish health.

Family-friendly churches are systems oriented. They recognize the interconnectedness of family members and minister to both individuals and their families. We see a practical example of this in the job descriptions of youth pastors who are expected to minister to "families with teenagers" rather than to just teenagers. The youth pastor with a systems approach will include parents in decisions, activities, discipline, and celebration. Beware of youth pastors who express adversarial relationships with non-youth family members. This is not to say that Sunday school classes for high schoolers should include parents and grandparents or that younger brothers and sisters will be invited to all-night parties. It is much more attitude than curriculum. *The effective youth pastor sees his job as ministering to the entire family, with the teenagers as the primary contact persons.*

## SELF-CENTERED OR OTHERS-CENTERED?

One of the most important factors in developing a family-friendly church is the most difficult to explain and to understand. Is the church as an organization primarily self-centered or others-centered?

Self-centered churches have a high sense of institutional importance and priority. Great emphasis is placed on meeting the budget, counting the number of people at activities, expecting members to change their schedules to fit the church schedule, and telling families to sacrifice their needs in order for the church to meet its institutional goals.

Others-centered churches have comparatively little talk about the institutional needs, problems, and successes of the church. Talk focuses outside itself and deals with the needs of people, especially families. These churches have a willingness to change their programs and schedules to meet the needs of their families.

An example comes from a community high school baccalaureate program. The program was slated for 6 P.M. on a Sunday and conflicted with the church's evening service. What should happen? The self-centered church calls on the high school principal to change the time or date of the baccalaureate service or demands that parishioners choose the church service over the community activity. In other words, the institutional priorities of the church come first. The others-centered church is more likely to cancel or reschedule the Sunday evening service in order to free parishioners to attend the baccalaureate.

One church planned an annual father-son fishing trip for the opening day of the fishing season. It became a strong annual tradition of the congregation. At first glance this seems like a pro-family event. Except, most years the opening day of fishing season was the second Saturday of May, and the weekend trip included Mothers' Day. The church unintentionally communicated that fish were more important than mothers. Sensitivity and sense led to a reconsideration, and the church found another weekend.

Sunday evening church services began as a family-friendly tradition in most parts of North America. It was a weekly time for families to have a time out together after the cows were milked and the chores were finished. Usually the services started about 8 P.M. In the past fifty years the culture has changed and Sunday night has become America's night at home. Restaurants have their lowest patronage and sales on Sunday evenings. Top-rated television shows are aired Sunday nights, and if the President of the United States wants to address the nation at a time when the most citizens are at home to watch, he always prefers Sunday night. The family-friendly church rethinks the tradition of Sunday evening services in order to keep families at home together and so that young children can get to bed early for school the next day. The purposes of Sunday evening services are then accomplished at other times and through other programs.

The others-orientation of family-friendly churches does not criticize members for lack of commitment when they do not place the church's institutional agenda ahead of their family needs. Commitment to Jesus Christ is the standard for both church and home.

## THE POWER OF MODELS

Once the church has been diagnosed, it is ready for a prescription. Perhaps the most powerful prescription for churches serious about developing family friendliness is to find and follow positive models.

### Church Models

*Church models* are those that have an effective ongoing ministry to new and long-term church families. *You can find these* *mentor churches with about twelve hours of research and less than $100 in long-distance telephone calls.* One or two church volunteers can call two or three family-friendly churches anywhere in America to learn about what they are doing. The first churches to call can come from suggestions by the pastor, Christian Education pastor, or the churches listed in chapter 5. Learn as much as possible about each church's approach and program in a fifteen-minute interview. Ask for suggestions on other churches to call. Also ask denominational officials and church members who have moved from another part of the country for suggestions of more churches to phone. Set a goal of finding at least twelve congregations with family ministry ideas that would be good in your church.

*Next, choose the three or four best examples within one day's driving distance and ask if a small group of your church leaders may come to visit and observe.* Gather additional information before the weekend visit. Try to select churches in similar settings (urban, suburban, rural, etc.) and no more than twice the size of your congregation. Often it works better to select model churches of another denomination because the principles are clearer and observers are forced to extract the transferable principles rather than copy a program.

*Finally, take a group of six key church leaders to visit one or more model churches.* These should be people who have great respect and influence in your church, not just those who can get away for three days. Everyone should travel together, and it is better to drive than to fly. The farther away the better, because there will be plenty of time for discussion while traveling back and forth.

This approach is so powerful because of the church-to-church mentoring influence. Churches are systems just like families. Individuals who see a good example are rarely able to return and institute that example alone. Six people of influence will make a profound difference. Seeing is believing. When these leaders see and experience a family-friendly church, they will be able to visualize what it looks like and how to do it in ways that books, articles, lectures, and committees can never match. Also, when you follow the procedure above, it is impossible for the visitors to come home and say, "That can't be done," because they have seen it done in a setting similar to their home church.

## Personal Models

*Personal models* are healthy families within the church. They should be recognized in comfortable and appropriate ways that will show other families how to relate to each other and to the church. Healthy families are not families without problems but families able to deal with their problems in a biblical manner. Dysfunctional families are also families with problems but are unable to handle those problems in a healthy fashion.

Because so many Americans have grown up in dysfunctional families, they have no idea what a healthy family looks or acts like. Example is a most effective teaching strategy. Much of this can be done informally, but it can also be programmed through family-to-family discipling, retreats gathering families together, support groups matching model families with learner families, and classes taught by experienced marriage partners, parents, and grandparents.

When family members don't know how to relate to each other, they are unlikely to sit down together and read a book about family skills. If they have spent time with a healthy Christian family, they are very likely to go home and act out what they have seen.

## ENCOURAGE NETWORKS

Networks are informal associations among people. They are the modern alternative to geographic communities. Earlier generations depended on extended families and neighborhood communities to strengthen families and help in crises. Post World War II mobility has significantly reduced extended family connections. Grandchildren and grandparents may live thousands of miles apart and see each other less than once a year. Many people live in houses or apartments without ever meeting or building a close relationship with a next-door neighbor. The result is a weakening of family life because all the needs must be met inside the family without the traditional outside help. Often the crises are so great that families fall apart and marriages end.

Church networks of families and individuals can more than make up for what has been lost. The goal should be to connect people with other people in as many ways as possible. Teach the importance of networking. Encourage the servicing of each person's private network. Provide ongoing opportunities for strangers to become friends. Examples include support groups, professional assistance (plumbers teaching church members how to do simple repairs; mechanics holding Saturday fix-up hours for cars of single mothers; teachers showing parents how to tutor their own children; etc.), athletics, ministry events (when families work together cleaning up a camp or building a Habitat for Humanity house they establish bonds that last for a lifetime), prayer gatherings (many churches have parents of teenagers pray together for their children while their sons and daughters are out on church activities), and job placement (a bulletin board listing job openings in businesses where members work can provide leads for those who are unemployed).

Understand that networking is more than providing all these programs. In some ways the programs aren't as important as the networking itself. When networks of relationships are established, family members know whom to call when they have a problem. When teenagers begin to become prodigals, a dozen other adults in the church network are connected enough to offer love, perspective, intervention, and even housing. When a couple's conflicts move toward divorce, their network will function as a score of strings pulling them back together again and helping them through their pain. Where there are no networks, problems quickly escalate into tragedy. Where there are no networks, those with experience and strength have few outlets to minister.

It is particularly important to the family-friendly church that the network be open. In other words, it is not just to serve those already in the church but is also available to outsiders. The network should intentionally extend beyond the church to pull others into the church as a means of outreach. We live in a time when community has been lost and millions are searching to replace it. When people hear about churches that provide community for them and for their families, they are drawn to be part of that community.

## USE EXISTING CHANNELS

Family-friendly churches are not developed with free-standing "family-life programs" as much as using existing church channels to encourage a positive family atmosphere. Sunday School classes and electives have been around for generations, but the family-friendly church intentionally uses them to program for life stages with courses on pre-marriage, family devotions, evangelizing and discipling young children, parenting teenagers, enriching marriages, sex education, financial planning, handling problems at school, preparing for retirement, and grandparenting.

Sermon illustrations that promote family life and values are a powerful tool from the mouth of the family-friendly pastor. If stories from the pulpit always demonstrate respect rather than make cheap jokes about marriage; if the pastor explains that the first appointments he writes into his calendar each year are family birthdays and anniversaries; if the pastor never uses an illustration about one of his own children without that child's prior permission; if Mother's and Father's Day prayers and remarks are sensitive to infertile couples—there will be fifty-two Sundays of public reminder about family values.

The family-friendly church repeatedly evaluates all that it is doing and attempts to turn existing programs into good for families before adding new programs. New activities may be pro-family but burden families with additional expectations and give the impression that family life is adjunct rather than integral to the church's ministry.

## For Further Reading

Enroth, R. (1992). *Churches that abuse.* Grand Rapids: Zondervan Publishing House. The negative side of church life skillfully researched by a Christian sociologist. All the traits he describes are anti-family.

Halverson, R. (1994). *The living body.* Gresham, OR: Vision House. The former chaplain of the U.S. Senate reviews with clarity the biblical behavior of godly congregations, pausing at points to criticize the secularism that marks too many contemporary churches.

Means, J. (1993). *Effective pastors for a new century.* Grand Rapids: Baker Book House. Family-friendly churches begin with family-friendly pastors. Means deals with syncretism, pluralism, and ends his book with a focus on relationships.

Shelley, B. and Shelley, M. (1992). *The consumer church.* Downers Grove, IL: InterVarsity Press. The father/son author team describes the modern world in which the church must serve families, emphasizing "the four cultural strands" of evangelical ministry today and the ministry style essential to be effective in today's church.

Zuck, R., ed. (1994). *Vital ministry issues.* Grand Rapids: Kregel. Sixteen contributors provide twenty chapters on crucial aspects of ministry, including leadership style, pastoral functions, preaching, worship, women's roles, and legal issues.

# A SURVEY OF EFFECTIVE FAMILY LIFE EDUCATION PROGRAMS
*Jeffrey S. Gangel*

Through the deafening sounds of battle, you can hear them shouting instructions and calling for supplies. When the smoke clears, you see them scurrying from one bunker to another, delivering weapons and ammunition to the front-line soldiers defending the hill. If anyone knows the needs of the soldiers, they know. If anyone feels the desperation of the situation, they feel it. If anyone understands the value of the ammunitions and supplies, they understand it.

In the battle for biblical families in today's world, God places certain individuals on the front lines to equip husbands, wives, and children for spiritual warfare and service (Eph. 4:11,12). They are the pastoral staff members in our churches. They must continually identify needs, haul in supplies and munitions, and call out instructions and encouragement. Who better to turn to for ideas on family life education? Who better to scope out the family life battle zone in our churches?

## GENERAL SURVEY INFORMATION

A survey sent to select members of PACE (Professional Association of Christian Educators) drew on their experience as Family Life Ministers or Christian Education Directors. The ideas and information they submitted can apply to churches and ministries of any size. This diverse group of fifty-five "front-line equippers" represents seventeen denominations and numerous varieties of independent and interdenominational churches. The churches range in size from 200 to 13,000 and include families from twenty-six states. These churches average a combined professional and lay staff of two and a half who in some way have responsibility for family life education.

The survey asked about programs for marriages, parents, children, and special needs. It asked opinions on para-church family ministries and curriculum resources. It requested information on the most effective family life education programs and opinions on the greatest needs of today's families.

## PLANNING FOR FAMILY LIFE EDUCATION

When staff members gather to evaluate the effectiveness of their family ministries, how do they feel? According to this survey, most feel that significant, positive ministry takes place in their churches on a regular basis. However, four of the fifty-five respondents admitted a distinct weakness in actually carrying out a family life ministry. One person explained, "This church has long professed a strong family emphasis, but we are just beginning to think through its implications. There has been no unified approach to family ministry."

Judging by the lack of written family ministry philosophy statements and family ministry goals, many churches must still be searching for an overall, unified battle plan. Only *three* of the fifty-five churches surveyed have written a family ministry philosophy statement (seven are working on it). Only nine of the churches have a set of family ministry goals (seven are working on it). Can our family life programs produce long-term results when our plans do not prepare for life-long family discipleship?

## EVALUATING THE NEEDS OF FAMILIES

When asked to scope out their church families, the surveyors provided a panoramic view of needs. These eight categories summarize what the church staff members believe families need from the church.

## God and His Word

Families need to be led into a personal relationship with God. They need to know how to worship God as a family whether at church or at home. They need foundational training in the Bible that will shape their values, perspectives, commitments, and actions.

## Encouraging Support

Families need the hope and help that come from God's forgiveness and restoration. They need listening ears, encouraging words, affirming hearts, and supporting hands. And they need this from other families, not just the church staff.

## Practical Skills

Families need to be trained in the "how-to" skills of applying biblical principles. Skills for parenting, communicating, managing money, creating intimacy, setting goals, managing time, and solving problems all provide a solid foundation for family growth and stability.

## Accountability Groups

Families need opportunities to gather with other families for mutual accountability and discipleship. Bringing families together challenges the prevailing isolationism of our day. Sharing needs, hurts, victories, and blessings spurs them on to love and good deeds (Heb. 10:24-25) and produces a desire for change and growth.

## Mentoring and Modeling

Families need to see biblical families in action. As more and more parents bring their dysfunctional experiences into new family settings, more "functional" families need to model the principles of biblical family life. Intergenerational mentoring must fill in gaps left by poor parental and societal modeling. This generation of families must learn from the successes and failures of the previous generation. The previous generation must be willing to share those lessons learned.

## Family Environment

Families need a positive, fun, and safe place to function as family, while learning to be part of the family of light in a world of sin. The church can provide family-oriented activities unpolluted by a self-oriented society. The church should be a refuge for families without becoming a shelter from all contact with a needy world. Families need opportunities to serve together and play together.

### Family Counseling

Families need preventive, biblical counseling in addition to the more common therapeutic counseling. Though most family counseling is crisis-oriented, a preventive approach can save families from years of pain and destruction.

### Accessible Resources

Families need easy access to books, videos, tapes, and other resources that can provide practical training in their own time frame. Churches should help families choose the best materials, invest in a library and/or resource center, and encourage families to make use of such resources.

### STRUCTURING EFFECTIVE FAMILY LIFE PROGRAMS

What overall programming strategies do these ministers believe will be most effective in the fight for Christian families?

The survey asked respondents to mark the family life education programs they were using or had used in the past and then to double-check the programs they felt were most effective. The accompanying charts indicate the percentage of surveyed churches that have tried such programs and then the percentage of those who also marked them as being the "most effective" family life programs for them. The four categories of programs surveyed included those for marriages, parents, children, and special family needs.

### Marriage Enrichment/Education Programs (Chart #1)

The surveyors marked *Premarriage Counseling* most often as an effective family ministry strategy for couples. One church staffer said that they extend that counseling to include two follow-up sessions three months and twelve months after the wedding. What a great idea! But 16 percent of the churches did not have a premarriage counseling ministry. Churches that do not require personal, biblical counseling for couples before marriage are setting them up for unrealistic expectations and future difficulties. Though more churches have tried *Marriage Seminars and Conferences*, the *Small Groups* approach to marriage enrichment seems to be having a greater impact on the churches surveyed.

### Parent Education Programs (Chart #2)

Ninety-three percent of the churches surveyed reported having some kind of *General Parenting Class* or course. This also received the most votes for being a very effective family life program. Others listed specialized parenting classes for parents of *teens*, parents of *preschoolers,* and *new* parents. It seems clear that biblical parenting classes should have a foundational role in any church's family life education ministry.

### Children's Education Programs  (Chart #3)

Most churches have *Sunday School* programs, and the surveyors listed this most often as an effective way to minister to families. But programs like *Children's Clubs* and *Vacation Bible School* also received a number of "most effective" votes. Fewer churches have *Mother's Day Out* types of programs, but some staffers saw effective family ministry going on there. A family ministry strategy must include ministry to children and, perhaps more than we see now, a ministry to parents and children together. Forty percent of the churches surveyed have tried some kind of parent/child program or intergenerational class.

### Special Needs Programs (Chart #4)

These "special family needs" included programs for single parents, blended families, empty nesters, home-school families, challenged children, homeless families, and twelve-step recovery. But three of the most common programs in this category were also the ones listed most often as effective. Those surveyed chose *Financial Counseling*, *Family Counseling*, and *Support Groups*. Though not all churches have the resources to provide many of these special needs programs, these three suggestions provide a significant starting point for any family ministry strategy.


### IMPLEMENTING CREATIVE FAMILY LIFE IDEAS

When the surveyors were asked to share their best family life education programs, they came back with a stockpile of ideas.

The following represent some of the most unusual approaches!

### Sunday School Classes

Think there is nothing new about providing family life education in Sunday School? How about a class that intentionally puts parents and grandparents together to discuss biblical family issues? Another church has created a "Families 'R' Us" class that encourages couples without children, single parents, and parent couples to join together in studying marriage and family topics. In another church of 800, the senior pastor takes the time and effort to teach a marriage and parenting class. The C.E. director says, "Our people have watched our pastor love his family well. They are encouraged by his example and want to learn in a formal setting more of what he does [in his home]." What a testimony to the power of modeling!

### Family Outreach Programs

Churches can find numerous creative outreach ideas if they will think "families." One church offered a dysfunctional family seminar to the community as an outreach and followed up with small groups that met for fifteen weeks. Other churches use their counseling services as an outreach to their communities. Many church child-care and preschool programs serve as an outreach to the community families. One educational leader even had an opportunity to teach a dad's class through a local community education program.

Can parents and children serve together in an outreach capacity? When churches hook up with an international students ministry, they can! In our church, dozens of families became friendship partners with international students attending local universities. What a great way to train children in ministry and reach nations with the gospel!

### Church Family Nights

How can you strengthen individual families and the church family at the same time? One church sets aside a Sunday night each month for "Family Night." During a potluck dinner, table questions direct the discussion between adults and children. After dinner, the families with children gather for enrichment ideas and begin to apply them. The rest of the "church family" receives instruction on what it means to be a church.

Another church holds an annual "Family Vacation Bible School."

It runs for five consecutive nights and focuses on one theme. The parents and children stay together for the hour-and-a-half program, with only the very youngest consigned to the nursery. The program is written and run by the pastoral staff so the volunteer C.E. staff receives a much-needed break!

### Men's Ministries

Many churches have discovered that one key to family ministry hangs on the men's ministry hook. Training men to function as biblical husbands and fathers brings stability, leadership, and hope to the home. One church has even developed a specific "Fathering Ministry" that seeks to provide training, support, encouragement, and accountability through small groups, conferences, special events, resources, and a newsletter.

For churches without the resources to develop their own men's ministry, our survey soldiers recommended organizations like Christian Business Men's Committee and Promise Keepers. Both ministries provide the large gathering and small group contexts needed to combine the challenges to commitment with the support for follow-up.

### Family Mission Statements

How can we help families focus on the proper priorities before the world stands them on end? One church takes families through a five-session training program that helps them form a "family mission statement." This intergenerational approach walks them through the process of determining core values while learning communication and cooperation.

### Pre-Parenting Courses

We have premarriage training, why not pre-parenting training? If engaged couples need help preparing for the responsibilities of marriage, then expectant parents surely need help preparing for the most awesome responsibility in life—rearing a child! Just as doctors and hospitals help expectant parents make the physical preparations, pastors and churches must help them make the spiritual and emotional preparations. The nine-month gestation period is the optimum time for reaching couples who have not had the interest in parent education before and who may not have the time for parent education later. We must equip these new soldiers with proper tools for heading out to the family battlefields!

## ACCESSING RESOURCES FOR FAMILY LIFE EDUCATION

Where can you turn for effective family ministry resources? Our respondents indicated the para-church family ministries and family curricula that were available and most helpful to them at the time of the survey.

With the recent interest in male spirituality, a number of staffers felt that some national men's ministries have been most effective in supporting family life values in their churches. *Promise Keepers*, *Men's Leadership Ministries*, and *Christian Business Men's Committee* all received gestures of approval and appreciation from the churches surveyed. Two established family ministries also received mention: Campus Crusade's *FamilyLife* and *Focus on the Family*. Both of these ministries have much to offer churches who are equipping their family warriors. A few newer ministries also caught the attention of some respondents: *Marriage and Family Intimacy* and *Life Partners*.

The most effective curriculum resources for family life education were divided into two categories: *Marriage* and *Family/Parenting*. "Curriculum resources" here can refer to videos, study guides, or books. The marriage curriculum authors considered most effective were Gary Smalley, Larry Crabb, and Norman Wright. Our C.E. respondents also liked materials produced by *HomeBuilders* and David C. Cook's "Life Topics." Of the family and parenting authors, James Dobson, John Trent, and Gary Ezzo ("Growing Kids God's Way") were considered most effective. Other authors suggested were Chuck Swindoll, Kenneth Gangel, Ross Campbell, Gary Richmond ("Ounce of Prevention"), Ron Rose ("Faith in Families"), and Royce Money (*Ministering to Families*). Resources from Serendipity and the Minirth/Meier Clinics also received mention.

Churches should be grabbing these resources from the supply posts and rushing them into the hands of their families. The needed curriculum is available. We don't lack for weapons and equipment. But sometimes we watch our families fight spiritual battles with their bare fists while biblical resources rust in the armories. Don't let it happen to you!

## CONCLUSION

I believe that the information gathered in these surveys points out two paradigm shifts that will affect the future of family life education. Churches and family ministries must consider these paradigm shifts in order to minister to families into the next century.

First, the battle for the biblical family cannot be won by continually segmenting family members through programming. The family life ministry of the future will include programs that teach families *together* about how to be godly families. This means putting couples with couples, parents with kids, and families with families. We learn family dynamics by creating dynamics in families!

Second, we cannot win the battle for the biblical family by taking pot shots a few times a year. An occasional class here and an annual seminar there do not constitute a family life education ministry. Our families need more and deserve better. Family life ministry of the future will involve a pre-planned strategy of ongoing, year-round, life-situation-oriented training for families. Never has the battle raged more fiercely. Never have Christian families needed more ammunition and instruction. But never have the equippers been more capable. Never have the armories been so well stocked with resources. Fight on, family warriors!

**Many Thanks to These Survey Participants!**
Leroy Armstrong, Concord Missionary Baptist; Dallas, TX
Jim Baird, El Camino Baptist; Tucson, AZ
Stephen Baker, Covenant Community; Redford, MI
Bill Barber, Central Church; Memphis, TN
Richard Batten, South Park Church; Park Ridge, IL
Margaret Bauer, Wesleyan Church of Hamburg; Hamburg, NY
Andrew Beaty, Temple Hill Baptist; Cadillac, MI
Pat Blewett, Cole Community Church; Boise, ID
Gordon Bond, N. Syracuse Christian; Syracuse, NY
Elaine Bonner, Trinity Presbyterian; Asheville, NC
David Borror, Boca Raton Community; Boca Raton, FL
Rick Bushnell, College Heights Christian; Joplin, MO
Wayne Cone, Cypress Bible; Cypress, TX
Kathy Cott, North Avenue Presbyterian; Atlanta, GA
Tim Cox, Colonial Baptist Church; Cary, NC
Jim Fleming, Midland Evangelical Free; Midland, MI

Ted Grove, First Baptist; Charlotte, MI
Timothy Hanley, Cornerstone Presbyterian; Columbia, SC
Daniel Holmquist, The Village Church; Western Springs, IL
Ron Hughes, Lebanon Baptist Church; Roswell, GA
Phil Humphries, Scofield Memorial; Dallas, TX
Tim Johnson, Grace Evangelical Free; Mason City, IA
Ric Joline, Calvary Church; Lancaster, PA
Tim Judkins, Cornerstone Church; San Antonio, TX
Scott Kerr, First Evangelical Free; Lincoln, NE
A. Leon Langston, First Christian Church; Largo, FL
Darlene Larsen, Faith Community; Racine, WI
Cathy Leestma, First Covenant; Oakland, CA
Bruce Lester, Grace Chapel; Denver, CO
Stephen Lizzio, Medinah Baptist; Medinah, IL
Linden McLaughlin, Plano Bible; Plano, TX
Mark McSweeney, Reidsville Alliance; Reidsville, NC
Dwight Mix, Fellowship Bible of NW Arkansas; Lowell, AR
Danny Mize, Quail Springs Church of Christ; Oklahoma City, OK
Carole Neidhardt, South Shores Baptist; Monarch Beach, CA
Susan Payne, Christ Presbyterian; Edina, MN
Mark Posson, Central Christian; Wichita, KS
Terry Powell, Cornerstone Presbyterian; Columbia, SC
Roy Reiswig, First Christian; Phoenix, AZ
Art Ringger, Castleview Baptist; Indianapolis, IN
Jim Schmotzer, Birchwood Presbyterian; Bellingham, WA
Bob Schroeder, Paramount Terrace Christian; Amarillo, TX
Larry Schweizer, Evangelical Free; Naperville, IL
Tim Siemons, Grace Community; Columbia, MD
Mark Steiner, First Baptist; Ft. Collins, CO
Molly Strong, Calvary Christian; Bellevue, NE
Craig Sturm, New Song EFC; Bolingbrook, IL
J. Michael Thomas, Blythefield Hills Baptist; Rockford, MI
Jackie Timmer, Shawnee Park Christian Reformed; Grand Rapids, MI
Karen Van Galder, First Presbyterian; Indianapolis, IN
Richard Viel, Calvary Evangelical Free; Broomfield, CO
Ruth Westerholm, Branford Evangelical Free; Branford, CT
Tim Winkleman, Bethany Evangelical Free; La Crosse, WI
Gary Wrisberg, Evangelical Free; Columbia, MO

## For Further Reading

Guernsey, D. (1982). *A new design for family ministry*. Elgin, IL: David C. Cook. An explanation of the developmental stages of families and how to address their particular needs.

Hebbard, D. (1995). *The complete handbook for family life ministry in the church*. Nashville: Thomas Nelson. A "Congregational Family Needs Analysis" kit can also be obtained from Don Hebbard by writing to Family Ministry Consultants, 4012 Jones Bridge Circle, Atlanta, GA 30092 (404-840-8242).

Miles, S. (1990). *Families growing together*. Wheaton, IL: Victor Books, 1990. An introduction to intergenerational learning that includes examples of such family learning sessions.

Money, R. (1987). *Ministering to families: A positive plan of action*. Wheaton, IL: Victor Books. A guide to family ministry that will help in the administration of family life education programs.

Olson, R., & Leonard, J. (1990) *Ministry with families in flux: The church and changing patterns of life*. Louisville: Westminster/John Knox. As families change, the way churches minister to families must also change. This book will help churches anticipate and address those changes.

Sell, C. (1981, revised 1995). *Family ministry: Enriching families through the church*. Grand Rapids: Zondervan Publishing House. This book addresses the theology and philosophy of family ministry while explaining how to integrate family life programs into the whole of church life.

Stinnett, N., & DeFrain, J. (1986). *Secrets of strong families*. New York: Little, Brown and Co. Though a secular book based on a nationwide survey, the writers discovered religion plays a key role in family strength.

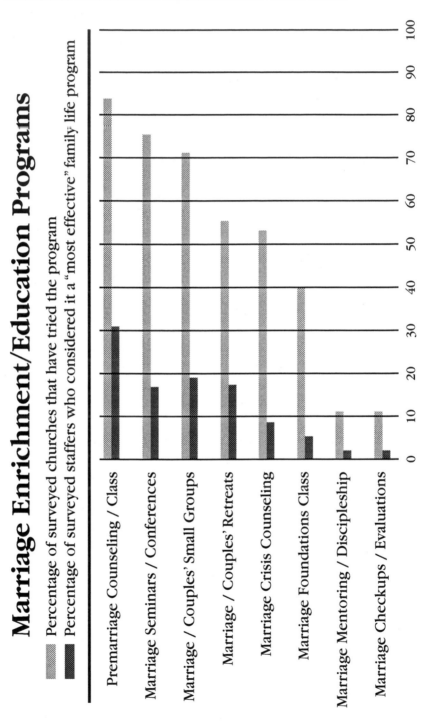

Marriage Enrichment/Education Programs

Percentage of surveyed churches that have tried the program
Percentage of surveyed staffers who considered it a "most effective" family life program

# Parent Education Programs

Percentage of surveyed churches that have tried the program

Percentage of surveyed staffers who considered it a "most effective" family life program

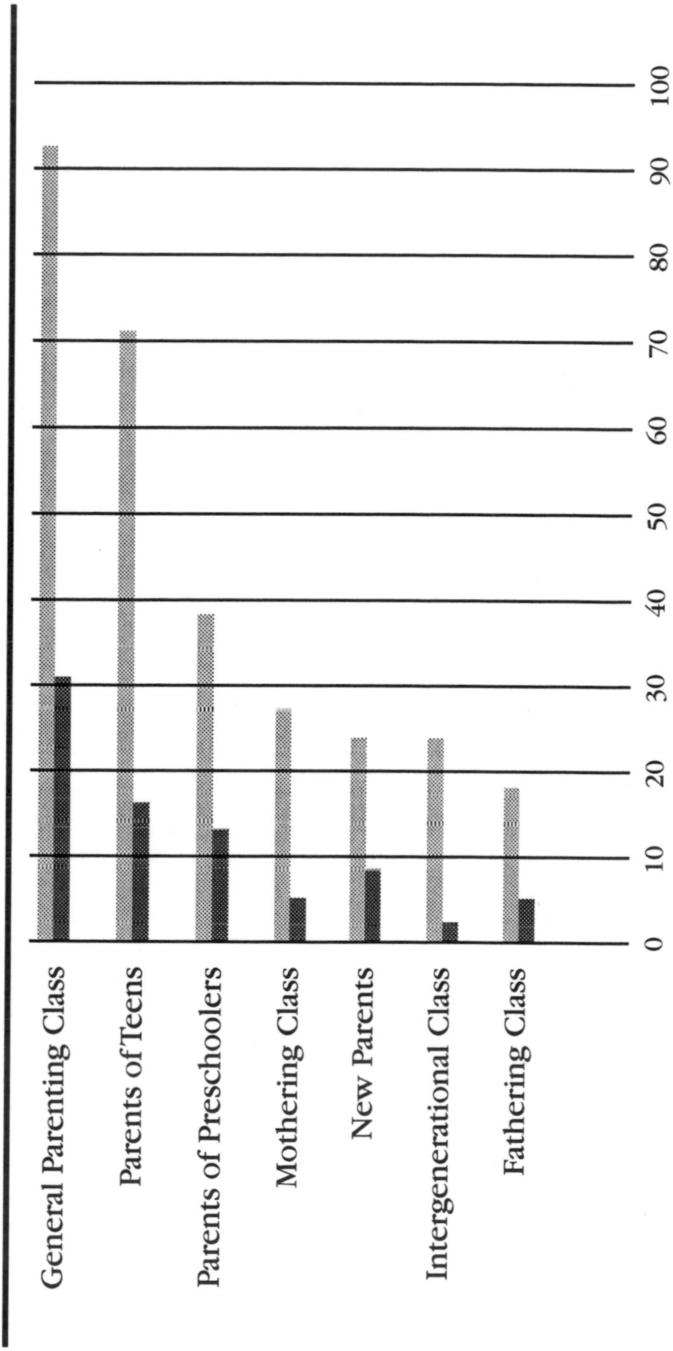

General Parenting Class

Parents of Teens

Parents of Preschoolers

Mothering Class

New Parents

Intergenerational Class

Fathering Class

0 10 20 30 40 50 60 70 80 90 100

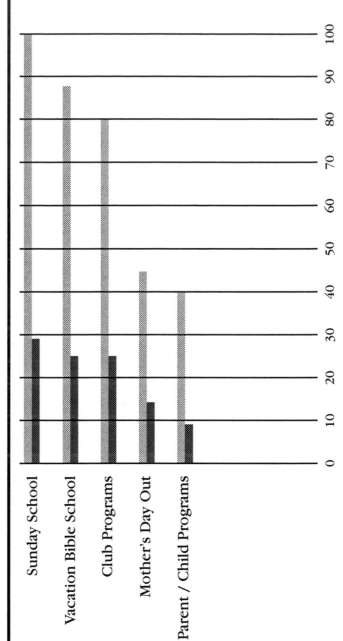

# Children's Education Programs

- Percentage of surveyed churches that have tried the program
- Percentage of surveyed staffers who considered it a "most effective" family life program

# Special Needs Programs

Percentage of surveyed churches that have tried the program

Percentage of surveyed staffers who considered it a "most effective" family life program

# PART TWO

# EDUCATION FOR FAMILY ROLES AND RELATIONSHIPS

# OLDER WOMEN/YOUNGER WOMEN: THE IMPLEMENTATION OF TITUS 2
*M. Lynn Gannett*

During the Sunday School hour, the room was too small to hold the group of recently divorced women. As the church staff member responsible for women's ministries, I had gathered them to listen to their needs as single mothers and discuss ways the church could be supportive. When we noticed Jessica's absence, I heard these unforgettable words: "Jess doesn't need to be here. She's lucky; she has Bev." Then her friend added in a laughing, almost jealous tone, "Too bad she didn't know Bev a few years ago—she'd probably still be married!" Jessica's relationship with Bev was making an impact during a very difficult time. Her friend (along with the other women in the room) longed for such a relationship.

Who is this Bev, and what makes her so special? Bev is an "ordinary" homemaker and a mother of three grown daughters. Quietly doing "extraordinary" things, she impacts young women like Jessica as a result of walking with God for years and learning to respond to passages such as Titus 2.

> Likewise, teach the older women to be reverent in the way they live, not to be slanderers or addicted to much wine, but to teach what is good. Then they can train the younger women to love their husbands and children, to be self-controlled and pure, to be busy at home, to be kind, and to be subject to their husbands, so that no one will malign the Word of God (Titus 2:1-5).

This directive was written to the young man Titus by his mentor, the Apostle Paul. Titus acted on Paul's behalf in Crete, struggling to establish a church in a morally decayed community. He was probably thrilled when this letter arrived instructing him in the strategies of church planting. The letter reads as if Paul anticipated Titus' questions. *How do I know if someone would make a good elder? How do I handle that group of false teachers causing trouble? How can the church help women live lives consistent with the teaching of the Scriptures?* Anticipating this last question, Paul gave Titus a workable method for developing godly women in a pagan society.

Paul's wisdom for establishing a spiritually vibrant church with healthy families also applies to the church today. His strategy— older women ministering to younger women—has a specific goal: "that no one will malign the Word of God" (Titus 2:5). This chapter focuses on how to implement this principle in the local church.

## WOMEN MINISTERING TO WOMEN

It is clear from the New Testament that Jesus, Paul, and the other apostles included women in their audiences. So why was Paul so specific in his instructions that the older *women* were to teach the younger women? Research and common sense suggest some possible reasons for this directive.

First, women experience unique *physical challenges*: menstruation, pregnancy, childbirth or miscarriage, breastfeeding, PMS, and, ultimately, menopause with its hot flashes! As empathetic as a man may want to be, he will never experience the impact these hormonal shifts have on a woman's physical and emotional being. These uniquely female issues provide common experience and opportunity for women to share insight and give needed support.

Second, the differences between men and women go beyond the physical. The title of a popular bestseller, *Men Are from Mars, Women Are from Venus* (Gray, 1992) illustrates that many perceive the genders as worlds apart! Numerous studies of *male and female differences* have examined such areas as socialization, psychoanalysis, brain research, moral development, and cognitive learning styles (Schroeder, 1987).

Catherine Stonehouse (1993) summarizes some of the most recent and significant studies and calls the church to respond by beginning to value the knowledge of experience and by providing support. She concludes:

> There is need for reconnecting the generations in the church. Middle-aged and older men and women who understand the processes of development and are walking with God into maturity have much to offer younger men and women. . . . Young people long for spiritual mothers and fathers, aunts and uncles (p. 116).

## THE CURRENT STATUS OF WOMEN'S MINISTRIES

Ask staff members from an average local church how their women's ministries are going, and you will probably get two thumbs up. Larger churches are hiring staff members to direct programs and to minister directly to women, and even the smallest of churches has some kind of weekly women's gathering. Christian bookstores are filled with study guides from a multitude of publishers, addressing almost every aspect of a woman's life.

Yet does the average woman today feel that some "older woman" is making an investment in her life? Is a mentor teaching her through life and words the intricacies of being a godly wife and mother? Probably not. Why are many women's ministries strong on formal group teaching but weak in the intentional investment of one life into another? Two answers seem to be most prevalent.

First is the *generation gap*. We often think of this terminology in regard to the dissimilarity of the worlds of teenagers and their parents. The world of young women who marry, have children, and establish a home is also quite different from the world in which their mothers and grandmothers were brides. These are the 90s! Chapter 2 of this book outlines the state of the family in today's society.

For example, a lifelong marriage to one man may still be considered an admirable goal but certainly unnecessary. We celebrate the birth of a child but by no means require a detour from a woman's career goals. Young families furnish starter homes equal to those of their parents, thanks to credit cards. Younger women appear more educated, more affluent, and more sophisticated than the previous generation.

Older women sense these changes. Many perceive their experience in marriage and family life as light years away from today's culture. They often feel out of touch with little to offer. Unfortunately, this may be exactly what the younger generation thinks. But perhaps not. Younger women may look with envy at an older woman in the church, desiring to know her secrets. *How did she raise her children to love the Lord? Why does she look so content in her marriage?*

A second reason these relationships struggle to develop is the *lack of training and equipping* of older women to minister. The process just commences with the challenge presented in Titus 2 to teach the younger women. Then follows the often unasked question, "But how?" We cannot assume that our women know how to encourage, to teach in a formal or informal setting, or to disciple a young Christian woman in the faith. Like most laypeople in the church, older women will be eager to minister when they feel equipped with the skills and tools necessary to be effective. It is encouraging to see more emphasis on training, not only in individual churches, but also through local and national organizations and conferences.

If the church is to effectively train women to live according to the Scriptures in today's world using this woman-to-woman approach, it must help the older women surmount these obstacles. One starting place is intergenerational communication and the equipping of women to minister.

## ALL "OLDER" WOMEN RAISE YOUR HANDS!

The concept of "older" and "younger" can be relative. In the forties class of any church there might be a woman sending her "baby" to college sitting next to a woman pregnant with her first child! These women, close in chronological age, are worlds apart in their stage of life. Perhaps chronological age is not always the best way to differentiate between the concepts of older and younger.

### Life Stages

Stage of life might be a more helpful definition. Carol Porter and Mike Hamel (1992) have outlined the following ten stages of a woman's life:

Single Career Woman
Young Married Woman
Mother of Young Children
Mother of School-Age Children
Working Mother
Single Mother
Mother of Teen/College Children
Empty Nest Woman
Caregiver (woman caring for aging parents or husband)
Senior Woman

Each stage brings different challenges: emotional, physical, relational, and spiritual. An "older" woman may be defined by a bride as a woman who has gone through the adjustment of the first few years of marriage. To a mother of teenagers, an "older" woman may be a mother whose children have left home and entered the working world. The "older" woman to the recent widow may be a chronologically younger woman who has already been through the stages of grief after the premature death of her husband.

**Spiritual Maturity**

A key measure in defining the older and the younger, the teacher and the student, is spiritual maturity. Susan Hunt (1992) uses the term *spiritual mothering* and defines the relationship in this way: "When a woman possessing faith and spiritual maturity enters into a nurturing relationship with a younger woman in order to encourage and equip her to live for God's glory" (p. 12).

Hunt points out that biological birth and chronological age are not prerequisites for the task of spiritual mothering. An "older" woman for a new believer may very well be a peer. The issue is a proven walk with God that permeates every aspect of life in such a way that a woman's life is worthy of emulation.

## THE CURRICULUM

Paul lists seven items that constitute the curriculum in this training program. These seven roles or behaviors encompass a young woman's world. Women are to be lovers of their husbands, lovers of their children, self-controlled, pure, busy at home, kind, and subject to their husbands. These issues touch the emotional areas of loving feelings, character qualities, morality, work ethic, relationships, and roles.[1]

Notice that the application of truth to real-life struggles is stressed in this list. How does a Christian woman love a selfish husband? What is the loving thing to do for a child involved in drugs? How does a professional woman define "busy at home"? The church cannot be content with teaching sound doctrine without relating it to the core issues of life.

## EQUIPPING WOMEN TO MINISTER

A key issue in implementing Paul's plan is the availability of older and more spiritually mature women to "teach the younger women." Wes Willis (1985) has helpfully described five contrasting categories in regard to recruiting and training for ministry.

### Unaware or Aware

Leadership's first task is to help older women become aware of the biblical exhortation given to them: to impact the lives of the younger generation. The goal of moving a woman from unaware to aware may be realized effectively in large groups through preaching, teaching, and Bible study.

### Unwilling or Willing

Unfortunately, many older women resist becoming involved in the task of imparting principles of Christian living to the next generation. How do we move them from unwilling to willing? It is unlikely that more teaching or preaching will be as effective as a personal challenge. A pastor, the director of women's ministries, or a key lay leader can approach godly women individually or in a focus group to challenge them with this ministry.

### Immature or Mature

Paul exhorts Titus to teach the older women in Crete for good reason. In New Testament times life in Crete had sunk to such a deplorable moral level that dishonesty, gluttony, and laziness of its inhabitants were rampant. From Paul's admonition (2:3) it sounds as though these women struggled with alcohol abuse and the negative use of their tongues. Their lives were to be *reverent*, "conducting themselves as if they were servants in God's temple, for such, indeed, they are!" (Hendriksen, 1957, p. 364). Once they had dealt with their own lack of control they were ready to train the younger women. "The verb rendered 'train' (*sophronizosin*) offers a cognate of the adjective translated 'self-control' in verse 5 and implies the idea of restoring one to her senses" (Gangel, 1992, p. 22).

There is a prerequisite to teaching! Our concern, like Paul's, is that the older women in our congregations love the Lord, walk in obedience to His Word, and live lives worthy of imitation by the younger women. If the older women are spiritually immature, we are challenged, with Titus, to teach them "what is in accord with sound doctrine" (Titus 2:1).

### Untrained or Trained

People today want to be sufficiently trained to do a good job in the task at hand. Our role as Christian educators is to expand the concept of the teaching ministry to encompass the informal as well as the formal aspects.

Leadership lingo such as "discipling" and "mentoring" can be intimidating to the person who does not know what the terms mean. Women want to understand both the concepts and the processes. Later this chapter will define various levels of involvement. Each requires different gifts, skills, and, therefore, training.

### Resting or Active

The act of modeling never ends. Every disciple of Jesus Christ constantly portrays to a watching world what it means to follow Him. Yet, intense ministry with people can be very draining. The women who give of themselves fervently may need to back off and recharge. Sensitive church leaders will provide a period of rest for those who need it for one reason or another. The opportunity to challenge them again into active status will come soon enough.

## LEVELS OF INVOLVEMENT

The following levels of teaching seek to illustrate that every growing Christian woman, regardless of her spiritual gifts or skills, can be used in some manner in the life of another. The keys are opportunity, challenge, and training.

### Modeling

Educators use the term "modeling" to describe teaching through example. Paul was very specific with Titus: "In everything set them an example by doing what is good" (2:7). We have already noted that Paul exhorted the older women to be reverent or holy in their demeanor (v. 3). What better way for young women to learn how to incarnate sound doctrine than to see other women in action?

Older women need to be challenged with the old teaching adage, "More is caught than taught." How a mature woman relates to her husband, speaks to her children, creates atmosphere and order in her home, and reacts to the trials of life are all circumstances of life that younger women can observe if given the opportunity. The challenge is for older women to allow younger women close enough to see.

Minimally, the church must initiate the process by providing opportunities for the generations to become acquainted. We do this intentionally through socialization, small groups, elective Sunday school classes, committees, women's Bible studies, retreats, and general church life.

### Encouraging

The epistles are filled with "one another" directives, one of the most common being "encourage one another" (e.g., 1 Thes. 4:18; 2 Tim. 4:2; Heb. 3:13). The Greek word translated "encouragement" stems from the root word *parakletos*, meaning "called to one's aid" (Hunt, 1992, p. 117). To some women this comes naturally. Others may need ideas on specific ways to encourage a younger woman: a phone call, a note, providing babysitting, an invitation to dinner, a sincere compliment, or praying daily for specific needs. "Heart-to-Heart" (Kraft, 1992) has designed women's ministries to offer a plan for pairing women for the purpose of encouragement and spiritual development.

### Formal Teaching

Formal Bible teaching continues as the most common form of ministry to women found in churches today. Not only are women included in the teaching ministry of the entire church, but many churches have ministries for women taught by women. The structure differs from church to church, with the most common formats composed of either large group teaching, small group discussions, or a combination of both.

Two elements remain indispensable to the effectiveness of the formal Bible teaching model. First, *adequate child care* is as important as an able teacher! If women are to concentrate without distraction, they need assurance that their children are in a loving, safe environment. The second indispensable element is *relevance*. Our complex and busy world offers women a myriad of opportunities in which to invest their limited time and energy. Decisions are made dependent on the significance of a particular activity in the life of the woman and her family. Therefore, Bible teaching must not only answer the questions, "What does it say?" and, "What does it mean?" but also, "What does it mean to me today?" The application and the relating of the truths of God's Word to life creates relevance. We must teach the Scriptures in such a way that everyday life is touched.[2]

## Mentoring

In Homer's *Odyssey*, Mentor served as a loyal adviser of Odysseus entrusted with the care and education of Telemachus. In business and education, the term "mentoring" refers to a relationship between a seasoned expert and a novice that involves coaching, training, or tutoring.

Is the process of mentoring different from discipling? Although from the Christian perspective there is no real separation between the secular and the sacred, the term "discipling" usually functions in regard to spiritual disciplines, while mentoring comprises a broader meaning. Allen Curry (Gangel and Wilhoit, 1993) clearly establishes the link between the two concepts and illustrates how practices involved in the mentoring process can enhance discipleship programs in the local church. Yet understanding their subtle differences can open the door of involvement to more women.

A mentoring relationship between two women can be very informal and focus on the development of skills as well as spiritual growth (Brestin, 1988). It may begin through a common interest in some aspect of home management or a life challenge, such as the death of a child, overcoming some addictive behavior, re-entering the workplace, or starting graduate school—anything that is common ground.

The beauty of a mentoring relationship is that many women have something to offer another in some area of life. In her book,

*Thank You for Being a Friend*, Jill Briscoe (1980) shares how ten different women impacted her life, including her hospital room-mate who led her to Christ. Some women in our churches will never be able to teach the weekly Bible study, but they can share their gifts, skills, heart, and walk with God.

### Discipling

We most often use the word "discipling" in the context of learning more about Jesus Christ from one of His followers. The process begins when a woman places her faith in Jesus Christ and may continue throughout life. Formal discipling may be done in the context of a small group that covenants for a period of time to be accountable to the leader and the group members or in a one-on-one relationship.

### Small Groups

Many women's ministries offer a variety of small group studies ranging from "seeker" studies for nonbelievers to in-depth inductive studies for the serious Bible student. Many small group studies are biblically based but begin with a felt need, such as improving relational skills within the family, child-rearing techniques, emotional issues, weight control, addictive behaviors, learning to share one's faith. A quick browse through a Christian bookstore will make you aware of the variety of study aids available.[3]

### One-on-One Relationship

Many believe that disciple-making is most effective in the context of a one-on-one relationship. One person allows another to walk "with her," pointing out how the Scriptures and Jesus Christ permeate all of life. The goal is to produce a spiritually mature person.

A discipling group or one-on-one relationship attempts to instill the essential spiritual disciplines for growth: a daily time in the Word, in-depth Bible study skills, an active and effective prayer life, evangelism skills, Bible memory, and spiritual leadership skills. Accountability is a key factor which can monitor the application of truth to life.

### Equipping

When a woman has encountered adequate models, been encouraged by them, been taught the Scriptures, experienced the impact of a mentor on her life, and been discipled in her faith walk, she is probably well on her way to being equipped to teach others. She may need to understand the process to reproduce it in another. An effective women's ministry will incorporate ongoing training for leaders as well as for women who desire to develop skill in transferring their Christian walk into the lives of others.

## CONCLUSION

Susan Hunt (1992) restates the words of the eighteenth-century poet and historian Matthew Arnold in this way: "If ever the world sees a time when Christian women shall come together purely and simply to encourage and equip other women to live for God's glory, it will be a power such as the world has never seen" (p. 18). The church can play a vital role in impacting families, our culture, and ultimately, the world, with this power by strategically bringing women together in nurturing relationships. Love will produce love; self-control will produce self-control; purity will produce purity, which will result in families with mothers, grandmothers, sisters, and aunts who reflect the beauty of Jesus Christ in the home and in the community. Then "no one will malign the Word of God."

**Notes**
1. Getz, Gene A. (1977) provides a full treatment of each of these life issues in *The measure of a woman*. Ventura, CA: Regal Books.

2. For a detailed treatment of the teaching ministry, the reader should consider Gangel, K.O., and Hendricks, H.G. (Eds.), (1988). *The Christian educator's handbook on teaching*. Wheaton: Victor Books.

3. Ortlund, Anne (1978) provides an excellent training manual for small group leaders with sample studies for women in *Discipling one another*. Waco, TX: Word.

**For Further Reading**
Brestin, D. (1988). *The friendships of women*. Wheaton: Victor Books. This book combines lessons from biblical friendships and contemporary relationships. Its easy-read style creates a refreshing challenge to a woman-to-woman ministry.

Briscoe, J. (1980). *Thank you for being a friend.* Grand Rapids: Zondervan Publishing House. This book can be used to raise the awareness of women in regard to their impact on others.

Curry, A. (1993). Mentoring and discipleship. In K.O. Gangel and J.C. Wilhoit (Eds.), *The Christian educator's handbook on adult education* (pp. 310–320). Wheaton, IL: Victor Books. A helpful delineation of discipling and mentoring that includes ideas for incorporating mentoring principles into traditional discipleship programs.

Gangel, K. (1993). Biblical foundations for adult education. In K.O. Gangel and J.C. Wilhoit (Eds.), *The Christian educator's handbook on adult education* (pp. 13–30). Wheaton, IL: Victor Books. A biblical study of adult education with a helpful look at Titus 2.

Gray, J. (1992). *Men are from Mars, women are from Venus.* New York: Harper Collins.

Hunt, S. (1992). *Spiritual mothering.* Wheaton, IL: Crossway Books. Susan Hunt approaches Titus 2 with years of implementation of the principles behind her. While imparting vision she also gives practical recommendations.

Kraft, V. (1992). *The influential woman.* Dallas: Word Publishing. Kraft challenges women to be involved in mentoring relationships and examines the curriculum as established in Titus 2.

Kraft, V. (1992). *Women mentoring women.* Chicago: Moody Press. This is an outline of the "Heart-to-Heart" program designed to establish and develop older women/younger women relationships.

Porter, C., & Hamel, M. (Eds.). (1992). *Women's ministry handbook.* Wheaton, IL: Victor Books. This book is the most thorough work at this time on developing, organizing, and administrating an effective women's ministry.

Schroeder, I. (1987). The source of male/female differences and their implications for Christian nurture. *Christian Education Journal, 8,* 73–84. This article describes and reports studies in brain research and learning styles.

Stonehouse, C. (1993). Learning from gender differences. In K.O. Gangel & J.C. Wilhoit (Eds.), *The Christian educator's handbook on adult edu-*

*cation* (pp. 104–120). Wheaton, IL: Victor Books. This chapter reviews the findings of three studies focusing on the unique developmental processes of women. Included is a helpful discussion of their implications to the local church context.

Willis, W. (1985). How to enlist volunteers. In the *Christian Education Profile*. Wheaton: Scripture Press. A succinct paper with ample help to the layperson desiring to develop an effective recruiting technique.

# SEVEN

# TEACHING COUPLES TO COMMUNICATE: THE PROBLEM OF RUTS
*Dennis Rainey*

My bookshelves are full of books about communication in marriage. Within minutes I can find a file full of clipped magazine articles with titles such as, "How to Talk to the One You Love," and, "Do Men and Women Speak the Same Language?"

Looking through these books and articles, I find that most teach the same basic principles, over and over. I imagine if you looked through your books and files, you'd find these same principles in one form or another. For example:

"Be brief."
"Be specific."
"Avoid absolutes."
"Disregard negative statements."
"Don't be afraid to say you're sorry."
"Find points of agreement."
"Use *I* statements rather than *you* statements."
"Choose your words carefully."
"Ask questions."
"Listen."
"Select an appropriate time to communicate."
"Don't push your own agenda."
"Be quick to acknowledge your own failures."
"Don't exaggerate, distort, or stretch the truth."
"Avoid generalities."

All these are great principles. I teach many of them myself at our marriage conferences. I cannot shake a few nagging questions, however: *How many couples already know many of these principles? How many couples would admit they once communicated much better than they do now? What causes the change? And how can we best help couples learn and apply these principles?*

To me, teaching couples to communicate requires more than a few, basic how-to's. You've got to deal with a more basic issue— *the problem of ruts.*

## CREATURES OF HABIT

Have you ever watched what happens when you begin pouring water onto sand? At first it trickles off in several different paths. Then currents come together into one, thicker stream. This flow carves through the sand, forming a rut that runs deeper and deeper. And as you continue pouring water, it will flow through this small riverbed.

People fall into ruts as well. We are creatures of habit. We like ruts . . . especially comfortable ones. Predictable and familiar, ruts offer us security.

Like a numbing narcotic, however, ruts also cause us to waste a lot of our lives. We would do well to apply to our lives the advice printed on a sign at the beginning of the rugged Alaskan Highway, a dirt and gravel road more than 1,000 miles long:

## CHOOSE YOUR RUT CAREFULLY . . .
## YOU'LL BE IN IT FOR THE NEXT 200 MILES

It's hard to avoid ruts in marriage. It's an old, familiar story: a couple begins marriage with a rush of excitement and intimacy. They vow to share everything—their thoughts, their fears, their dreams.

Then, as months and years pass, their choices and actions begin to follow a predictable pattern. They fail to deal with conflict . . . they erect barriers to protect themselves emotionally . . . they fail to insulate their marriage from unhealthy influences in the culture . . . they allow themselves to become so busy that they find little time with each other. Can you see how the rut begins to form?

Without realizing it, many couples allow their marriages to drift into a state of isolation. They feel a lack of closeness and intimacy. They share a bed, eat at the same dinner table, watch the same TV, share the same checking account, and parent the same children—but both husband and wife feel alone. They have sex, but they don't have love; they live together, but they don't share life with one another.

In survey after survey, couples state that poor communication is the major problem in their marriages. I disagree. Poor communication is a symptom of a deeper problem—isolation. Unfortunately, by the time many couples become aware of isolation in their marriage, they have entangled themselves in such a web that they have no idea how to break free from it. The marriage is crippled by boredom and apathy, and it dies from emotional malnutrition and neglect.

*The best thing you can do to help couples learn to communicate is to help them deal with isolation. And one of the most important ways to accomplish this is help them break free from their ruts.* Rather than focusing merely on the mechanics of interpersonal communication, you need to put them into a new environment in which they can learn and practice these principles.

Many accomplish this in counseling sessions and numerous others in marriage conferences. But I'm a firm believer that one of the best settings for couples to learn about communication already exists in your church—the *small group.*

## BENEFITS OF SMALL GROUP ENVIRONMENT

When you put couples into a small group, it gives them the opportunity to see Jesus Christ work in their relationship in a fresh way. Here's why:

- The mere act of pulling couples away from their homes breaks their normal routine. There's nothing to distract them—no television, no work. They have no choice but to focus on their relationship.
- It gives them a chance to hear others talk freely about personal things. This can give them courage to open up, and it encourages them as they build their marriages and families.
- It provides an atmosphere of encouragement—they can look

on their problems in a positive light and hear how other couples have worked through similar struggles.

- They even have the opportunity to help other couples. Christians become excited when they see God use them.
- It helps them begin looking at the Scripture together and applying the Word to their lives. Most couples don't do this in an organized way.
- It allows them to interact with each other on a regular basis about significant issues in their marriages.
- Finally, it creates an atmosphere of accountability that couples need to help them walk in obedience to God.

I also should mention two important benefits of a small group for church leaders:

- It allows you to reach more couples. Many counseling issues can be resolved in these groups, freeing you from many individual sessions.
- It gives you the opportunity to train lay leaders for ministry. I often meet couples so committed to helping families grow in Christ that they've made small groups the focus of their ministry. In effect, they are helping shoulder the burden of ministry rather than giving it all to their pastors. Isn't that how ministry should work?

## ESTABLISHING AN ATMOSPHERE FOR COMMUNICATION

Let me first say that I favor home Bible studies for this type of small group. They're friendlier and more casual, and you have more flexibility in arranging the couples so they can sit comfortably to see and hear each other. At the same time, I realize many churches prefer to use their already-established Sunday schools for small-group interaction, and that's great. I would, however, like to suggest a few guidelines if you're serious about using small groups to help couples communicate:

### Participation
*Couples need to participate in the learning process.* Many small groups—whether in the home or in Sunday School, use a *lec-*

*ture* format rather than a *participatory* format. In other words, class members learn biblical content from a speaker and have little interaction with each other.

To help couples communicate—to break them free from their ruts—they need more than head knowledge. They need to begin talking—about marriage, about *their* marriages. Group members need to learn truth by discussing Scripture among themselves and by sharing personal experiences.

Your group leaders must be committed to this type of small-group dynamic. They need to adopt the title "facilitator"—a directive guide who encourages people to think, to discover what Scripture says, and to interact with others in the group. They are not lecturers, but guides.

This does not mean that they allow group members to ramble aimlessly and pool their ignorance. And it doesn't mean the group should be allowed to misuse Scripture. Group leaders must be reasonably skilled in handling the Word of God.

Finding group leaders willing to take on that role may not be easy. But couples need to do more than sit and listen. The very act of participating in group discussion will encourage them and improve their marriage communication.

Your choice of topics for this type of participatory small group study is another important factor. I recommend focusing on topics directly related to marriage and communication. Yes, this means less emphasis on the Scriptures than you would find when studying, say, the Gospel of Mark, but remember your goal—to help couples improve their marriages and grow in their relationship with God. To accomplish that they need to focus on key topics.

### Safety

*Couples need to feel safe in the group.* The size of the group is important. In some Sunday School classes, this may mean splitting the group into smaller segments. Four to seven couples, including the lead couple, is the optimal group size. Fewer than four may put too much pressure on some individuals, stifling their freedom to grow. More than seven will not allow solid relationships to grow among all the couples involved.

A feeling of safety also requires a commitment to *acceptance.* Your group leaders should set a tone of honesty, admitting their own failures and encouraging other couples to tell how God has helped them work out problems in their marriages. Many couples, stuck so deep in their ruts that they can hardly see out, forget that other couples experience the same types of struggles.

Often you'll find that some people—husbands, most often—come reluctantly to these small groups. Perhaps they are there just because their mates or other couples nagged them to come. Some may be suspicious of a "Bible" study. Others may be fearful of revealing any weaknesses in their marriages. And some may feel they don't need any help in relationships.

You can dispel a great deal of anxiety and resistance at the first session. Simply begin by mentioning that you know there are probably some who came reluctantly. Share a few reasons people may feel that way, and affirm that regardless of why anyone has come, you are pleased each person is there.

Briefly comment on how the concepts in the study have helped you in your marriage and express your confidence that each person will enjoy the study and benefit from it. Also, share with the group that at no time will they be forced to share publicly with the group. What each person shares is his or her choice—no one will be embarrassed.

### Accountability

*Couples need to be held accountable to apply what they've learned.* Accountability is a scriptural principle that tells us to "be subject to one another in the fear of Christ" (Eph. 5:21). This means I choose to submit my life to the scrutiny of another person in order to gain spiritual strength, growth, and balance.

Accountability means giving another person the freedom to make honest observations and evaluations about you. It means you're teachable and approachable. True accountability involves letting another person into the interior of your life.

When people join a small group, they open themselves to at least a small measure of accountability. My experience has shown that many group members make commitments to apply aspects of the studies to their lives, but never follow through on those commitments. A small-group leader can help group members get the most out of the study by establishing an environment of friendly accountability.

Several years ago, when our ministry began creating some small group studies called the HomeBuilders Couples Series, we included a "HomeBuilders Project" in the study format. After each group session, couples schedule a time—preferably on a date—when they work through a series of questions designed to help them apply the principles they've just learned.

Couples who complete these projects see their communication improve much more than those who do not. We have found, however, that many couples fail to complete the projects unless the leader holds them accountable. So we tell the leaders to state publicly during the first session that, next meeting, they will ask each couple to share something they learned from the Home-Builders Project. Then—and this is crucial—at the next session, the leader needs to follow through. If the couples know they will be held accountable, they'll be more motivated to complete the projects. And they'll be glad they did!

However, it's important to make this an environment of *friendly* accountability. Group members need to know the leader is not there to condemn or embarrass anyone, but to help. The more the leader works on establishing a relationship with each couple, the more they will trust him or her.

One way to establish friendly accountability and to help couples know each other better is to pair up the couples in the group and assign them to be prayer partners or accountability partners. Have them call each other at some point between group meetings to exchange prayer requests and to see if they've completed their projects.

Another possibility to consider is making a special effort to hold the men accountable to initiate discussion with their wives. The leader would need to commit himself to calling the men between sessions.

## STEPPING OUT OF THE RUTS

Over and over I've seen couples' lives change when they pull themselves away from the old habits they form in the home environment and begin working on their relationship in a fresh way. One of my favorite stories concerns a woman from Iowa who wrote our ministry several years ago.

"My husband and I were married twenty-nine years and ten months before our divorce," she said. "Our life together had become practically nonexistent. We no longer communicated unless it was to growl at one another. I hardened my heart toward him and he closed his mind toward me."

This heartbroken mother of three grown children moved to Seattle to begin a new life. There, she met Christ through the witness of a fellow nurse, and began attending Overlake Christian Church. She also went to a home fellowship meeting that happened to be using one of the studies in our HomeBuilders Couples Series.

"It knocked my socks off!" she wrote. "I was still so very angry over the way my marriage had ended and with my life in general. But something was beginning to happen inside of me. For the first time in thirty years I was able to understand what was missing from our marriage. We did not have a personal relationship with Jesus Christ."

After she attended the third session, she wrote her former husband to tell what she was learning. To her surprise, he called her immediately after receiving her letter.

"We talked for the first time about what the Lord wants us to do in marriage. Believe me, that in itself was a wonder because we were never able to speak about the Lord in that way."

He decided to fly to Seattle and participate in the remainder of the study. They began communicating for the first time in many years and decided to put their lives in the hands of God. Soon they called each of their children to let them know they were going to remarry and become a family again.

"We are both overwhelmed with God's working in our lives," she wrote. "Our children are ecstatic about our upcoming event, and so are we. We know it won't always be easy, but we both are willing to work hard in fulfilling God's wish in our lives to have the kind of marriage He wants us to have."

This couple dug such deep ruts during thirty years of marriage that they saw no hope of change. Perhaps most of the couples with whom you work will avoid that type of pain. But they may need your help—to pull them out of their own ruts and to encounter Jesus Christ in a fresh way.

### For Further Reading

Allender, D. (1992). *Bold love.* Colorado Springs: NavPress. Provides practical advice on dealing with "difficult relationships. Many people learn to ignore the offenses of a "fool" or an "evil" family member, but Allender shows how to help change that behavior and set limits on that person's ability to control and manipulate.

Kimmel, T. (1993). *Powerful personalities.* Colorado Springs: Focus on the Family. This book shows how to deal with controlling personalities—family members who use fear, rage, shame, bondage, or strength to dominate or manipulate.

Lewis, R., and Hendricks, W. (1991). *Rocking the roles.* Colorado Springs: NavPress. Examines the societal stereotypes of "headship" and "submission" and provides an insightful look at biblical roles in marriage.

Rosberg, G. (1992). *Choosing to love again.* Colorado Springs: Focus on the Family. The author describes the natural sequence of conflicts and offers proven, step-by-step methods for resolving conflict.

# FAMILY CONFLICT: CAUSES AND CURES
*Samuel L. Canine*

The strains of "Pomp and Circumstance" coming from the radio flooded into Tom's consciousness as he sat dismayed with his head in his hands. Just a year ago excitement and anticipation filled him as he walked the commencement aisle for his degree.

Life held such promise. Peggy stood firmly by his side when they packed up their little apartment for the move to his first pastorate. But now an argument with Peggy the night before revealed such serious disagreement between them he wondered if they could ever rebuild what they had lost in the last year. In addition, Bill and Betty Jones, a key couple on the church's leadership team, had just walked out of his office after announcing their divorce plans.

Why do too many experience divorce as the ultimate relationship failure? How could it happen between two people who were committed to love Jesus first? Tom felt the paralysis of despair along with the unexpected foundational crack in his own marriage. He had found himself unable to help the two sitting before him a few minutes ago. How could he find a way to heal the breach between them?

It would be so simple to point to immorality as the cause for the failure. Then he could label it, counsel it, and file it away under the title, "They should have known better." Instead he saw in both relationships a series of little things—unresolved conflicts, hurts, and sore spots that remained unhealed. Each couple faced significant differences in attitudes and values. It all started small but then grew to unmanageable proportions. As a pastor who cared deeply for his wife and those in his church, he should have a better understanding of the ways to deal with these conflicts. But he didn't, and now he faced frightening consequences.

How can a church help struggling families like these? What role does a congregation play in assisting a family in conflict management?

## THE CONFLICT PROBLEM

The church cannot continue to pretend family conflict does not exist. Unfortunately, hurting families frequently scream for help to an increasingly deaf church. We confuse work with wellness when we assume that any active, ministering family in a church is healthy. But a church ministers effectively when it recognizes, responds, and redirects the hurting family to wholeness in the home.

### What Conflict Is Not

*Abnormal*

As long as sin permeates the human experience, conflict must exist. Only the removal of sin will remove conflict. Therefore, plans for constructive management should occupy our thinking.

*Personality Problems*

We sometimes use this as an easy way to excuse our responsibility for the fight. "We just cannot get along!" Statements like this would be better rendered, "We choose not to get along!" Was divorce the only alternative for Bill and Betty? Were they that incompatible? Or did they make a conscious choice to break up their home and take the consequences of such behavior? When and where did they arrive at the decision to split rather than stay in the marriage union? Tom pondered if he and Peggy could escape the traps and snares that seem to have caught Bill and Betty. This couple faced far more than personality problems; their world was caving in around them.

*Mere Disagreements*

The struggles and fights that families experience foment deeper than casual disagreements. A disagreement may be the threshold of conflict, but we wage the family battles inside the war zone called home. Disagreements were nothing new to Tom and Peggy, but previously they managed to struggle toward an acceptable solution. Tom was not so sure this time.

## What Conflict Is

Let's consider five elements that will help us understand the nature of conflict: (1) Interdependency; (2) Interactive struggle; (3) Incompatible goals; (4) Interference; and (5) Interface of opposition and cooperation. Each element contributes to our understanding of conflict. In the following paragraphs we will associate a childhood game with each of the five conflict components to help visualize the struggles.

### Interdependency—Teeter-totter

Conflict requires two parties. Just as the teeter-totter requires two children to make it work, so conflict features an interdependency among those participating. You cannot fight without an adversary. If one member of the family breaks the relationship by no longer identifying with the family, he or she severs interdependency. While pain and a sense of loss may persist, conflict *per se* no longer exists within this immediate family.

### Interactive Struggle—Tug of War

The pull of one person affects the position of the other. One individual's progress becomes the other's regress. For one to win, the other must lose. A well-watered mud pit makes the contest more exciting and improves the picture of this conflict dimension. Conflict seeks to pull the other person through the mud to bring him or her to your side. Tension becomes a major part of this pulling process. When Peggy saw the long hours Tom put into pastoring, she felt sacrificed for the church. She knew Tom loved her, yet she could not understand why church needs found a higher priority with Tom. Her jealousy created such guilt that Peggy suffered from tension headaches. The struggle baffled her, but she knew it was real.

### Incompatible Goals—Kick the Can

This version of hide-and-seek features a tin can that someone kicks while everyone else runs and hides. The person designated "It" retrieves the can, places it in an obvious location, and begins to search for those in hiding. If "It" sees you, the race begins to the

109

tin can. Should "It" touch the can and call your name, you are caught. However, if a hiding player outruns "It" and kicks the can, she goes free along with all who have been previously caught.

Conflict originates when we both want the same thing but cannot have it. Parents can fight over a child being athletic or musical. A husband may go to war with a wife over her career vs. his career. Frequently, the conflict surfaces between primary vs. secondary, good vs. better, or better vs. best. A limitation of money, time, people, space, or energy accompanies incompatible goals.

### Interference—King of the Hill

Each individual attempts to outdo all other participants and occupy the solitary position at the top of a hill. Only one can be on top. If you are on top, then your opponent must pull you down so he can be on top. Conflict thrives on hindering, harming, and hurting the opposition. Each party senses that the adversary consciously wants to keep him or her from good or progress. "I could be a better son if she were not my sister." "I could be a better wife if he were not my husband." The interference may be real or perceived, but conflict contains this element.

### Interface of Opposition—Red Rover, Red Rover

One line of players interlocking hands dares an individual from the other line of players to break through the human "wall." If the invited player breaks through, the challengers lose a player to the runner's team. If the line holds, the charging runner must join the resisting line. The game requires both opposition and cooperation. Both opposition and cooperation have their place in family conflict. Cooperation exists while the family relationship continues; but opposition shows up in conflict episodes the family experiences. Opposition and cooperation occur simultaneously, creating frustration or guilt. This dimension often strains unity and stymies growth in family units.


## THE PRESENT CONFLICT PROGRAM

### Too Little, Too Late

Andrew Cornes (1993) reports: "In 1960 there were 393,000 divorces in the USA. This reached a peak of 1,213,000 in 1981" (p. 10).

Today, marriage disintegration has leveled to slightly less than 1.2 million per year (Cornes, p.11). For the past thirty years the church has experienced this tidal wave of societal marriage breakdown.

Helplessly and defensively, Tom reflected on the surprise announcement Bill and Betty made. This young couple with so much promise was about to become another divorce court casualty. No wonder churches scramble to minister to single-parent families, sponsor divorce recovery groups, and practice damage control seeking to correct the psychological fallout of ruined homes. Tom wondered why he found himself so frequently in a reactive stance rather than a proactive posture to strengthen families in the church.

## Too Surface-Oriented

Generally, churches do a better job of monitoring behavior than developing and measuring attitudes and values. Conflict seldom resides just at the behavioral level. When we view conflict looking at the words only, we see only a fraction of the problem. Every message we communicate includes what we say (content level) and instructions about what the receiver should do with the message (relationship level). We constantly send both these messages as we communicate.

The relationship level informs each person of his or her role in the family and provides a fertile field for conflict to germinate, grow, and yield a harvest. Bill and Betty did not take care of the relationship level in their marriage. As Tom reflected, he could remember times when Bill would humorously put Betty down in social settings. At the time it seemed funny, but now it became clear what this poison had done to their relationship.

When we fail to establish a strong relationship level, we also rob the content messages in the communication. We have insufficient time to register the content of a message because we are trying to determine what message we received at the nonverbal, relationship level. Conversely, where the relationship enjoys good health, we can invest maximal time deciphering the content of the communication.

Transformation of the inner person reveals the very heart of what Christianity should accomplish. The home provides a laboratory to test transformation. Does the church today probe at this lower level, or does surface living take priority with most congregations? The severity of destructive conflict will rise when we neglect to move below surface behavior.

### Too Time-Consuming and Costly

Family conflict problems could easily fill most of a pastor's schedule. Working with strained and bruised families requires more time and energy than planning the next fund-raising drive for the church. The hours invested in getting to know the family seem overly costly; it appears a poor investment of pastoral resources to rejoice with those who rejoice and weep with those who weep (Rom. 12:15). We excuse our less than effective ministry by suggesting, "They probably will need professional help anyway so let's just start them out with the paid professional counselor." But most pastors want the best methods to help those committed to their care and wrestle with how this can best be done. How can a church exercise preventive principles and demonstrate a proactive versus reactive posture as we help families manage conflict?

## CONFLICT PREVENTION AND PRINCIPLES

### Teach Realistic Doctrine

Books, marriage seminars, and family conferences have merit only when they closely adhere to the principles delineated in the Bible. When a family faces the storms of conflict, the burden of responsibility to navigate the storm still resides with the individual and the family. The transcultural Scriptures guide families in any age or context, helping them resist peer pressure and move away from the status quo.

The Lord's way for the family may not be as complicated as some have made it. Families can legitimately differ from one another in many areas. We seem to have a fetish for finding a success story, then trying to convince all other families to emulate that model. In truth, families can function quite differently, vary widely in structure, and still enjoy God's approval and blessing.

### Reexamine Family Roles

A family that flexes within relationships creates an atmosphere in which it can manage conflict constructively. A rigid, inflexible family association almost invariably produces a destructive conflict management style. The sad smile on Betty's face and her lack of verbal defense when Bill used her as the butt of his jokes suggested an inflexible one-up, one-down relationship. All those years of suppressing how she really felt helped destroy what both assumed would last forever.

Too often we hold opinions as our convictions without solid biblical support. For example, some quickly preach "submission" to wives on the basis of Paul's correspondence with the Ephesians (5:22). We accurately exegete the original as a military term meaning "to be in rank and file." Wives are then to understand the imperative force and serious obedience required, "as you are to the Lord." But these teachers find it difficult to admit that the preceding verse reveals a mutual submission out of reverence for Christ with the following verses displaying a husband who lays down his life for his wife. Contextually, this mutual submission has clear husband/wife responsibilities in view. An open, honest approach to the Bible produces flexible, mutual, loving family relationships instead of biased, opinionated, rigid war zones we try to call homes.

Clear identification of conflict issues presupposes an open, trusting relationship in which all family members have the freedom to communicate with energy and exactness. A wise church will help the family address conflict issues early, clearly, and lovingly. When we delay identifying the problem(s) creating family strife, we weaken relationships and muddy the communication process. Tom has to learn that an effective church teaches a family to adjust the tension at the earliest stage rather than help them pick up the pieces after the explosion. What course of action might Bill and Betty have taken if he or Peggy had spoken up sooner?

In retrospect, this marriage could have been rescued. If Bill and Betty had developed an open climate, including emotional times when even tears and anger found acceptance, perhaps the story of their marriage would read differently.

Such openness requires a mutually loving relationship built by God. Conflict will test the strength of this alliance, but any family can pass the exam when God's love permeates the relationship. Bill and Betty lacked the missing dimension of God's love working in their lives. In their individual lives obvious evidence of God's love was present, but it did not exist in their day-to-day relationship.

### Spotlight Good, Practical Examples

When we consider preventative principles, one generation should help another in the management of family conflict. How can we encourage the older generation to assist the younger generation? We would all agree that members of the body of Christ share an interdependency (Eph. 4:16). Why not put feet to this by engaging older godly couples to share in the premarital counseling ministry of the church? Where this has been implemented dynamic results have occurred.

### Shepherd the Flock Conscientiously

Any shepherd will do a better job when sheep are known individually. The mechanics of ministry include far more than mastery and communication of a well-preached biblical text on Sunday morning. When a pastor chooses to be invisible during the week, he will usually be incomprehensible on Sunday morning. Personal pastoring plus powerful preaching produce positive, persistent products.

How can a church leader plan and orchestrate a ministry in the local church without investing time with God's people? Only the shepherd who knows where the sheep feed can plan the direction of the flock. A good leader serving as coach helps establish a strategy or plan that people execute to move the cause of Christ forward. The people as team players (Eph. 4:11-16) use their abilities as the Lord gifts them. A good leader also stands on the sidelines, as a cheerleader, giving enthusiastic applause for the accomplishments of others as they faithfully and fruitfully serve our Lord. This appreciation helps establish a positive environment where serious conflict cannot flourish easily.

### Clearly Communicate Roles, Relationships, and Priorities

We can improve conflict management with clear communication of family roles. Questions like "who is responsible to whom? for what? and when?" carefully answered reduce some of the stress that disturbs many families. A good church will help build relationships among family members.

When we cannot agree about expectations, we cannot agree on results, a perfect setup for encouraging conflict. When a family seriously discusses issues, roles, values, and attitudes, it takes giant steps in reducing ugly conflict situations. What's considered important to the family and why? Will the family follow a participatory style of leadership in which each member has input? To what extent do children enter into any sense of participatory family management? When we answer questions like these, we progress toward positive management of conflict.

## THE CONFLICT MANAGEMENT POTENTIAL

When a church helps a family manage conflict productively, five clear benefits emerge:

(1) Constructive conflict management builds stronger relationships. Like the physical body, a relationship needs resistance to develop muscle. Weaker relationships are characterized by avoidance or denial of conflict experiences. The risk comes if the conflict turns ugly and threatens to destroy the parties involved. Instead, family members teach the principles of fair play. What's fair? Each individual has the opportunity to express his or her thoughts clearly and completely while we protect each from personal injury or causing personal injury to any other family member. When the smoke clears we may see scars, but we'll also see a strengthened communication muscle beginning to form.

(2) In a world overflowing with bruised and broken family relationships, God's children should shine as a bright light in this dark world. How desperately we look for relief from the family fighting that literally destroys people and family ties. For example, a man who comes home irritated from work, yells at the kids, and complains to and about his wife displays a negative picture of the Fatherhood of God. But when God's grace moves in and through the same man, he gains the power over an irritable spirit. Now he has the freedom to appreciate family members and demonstrate godly qualities to them despite daily crises and irritations.

(3) Positive conflict management affects the next generation living in the home. When children see conflict as a part of the human experience and learn from their parents fair ways to fight, it starts them down a realistic road to godliness. Pretensions, hypocrisy, and denial repel a child from the so-called values parents claim.

(4) When families positively manage conflict on their own, it frees the church to develop other ministries. Families broken over

115

conflict gobble an inordinate amount of leadership energy and time. Other programs and projects frequently suffer since time remains a fixed commodity or scarce resource in church life. With preventative conflict management, innovation and creativity can flourish in the corporate life of a church.

(5) Constructive conflict management helps to indicate quality growth. We can measure quantitative growth easily since numbers, buildings, and budgets have obvious size. But we struggle to ascertain if quality occurs. Healthy families managing conflict productively produce gains in character development, an indication of quality growth.

Tom realized that Bill and Betty's relationship had moved beyond repair. In time, the divorce process was followed and finalized. As Tom and Peggy together grieved for the Joneses, they became convinced that preventive measures, not corrective approaches, should characterize their own relationship and ministry.

As a couple, they began a fresh, inductive search of Scripture to personalize marriage relationship principles. They contacted mature couples in the church who could serve as good role models for them and other young couples. To help family tensions among the flock, Peggy suggested they open their home for hospitality at least twice a month. Tom loved the idea. They planned to work toward crystallizing individual roles and responsibilities, knowing these might be unique to them. At present, they know areas where they still disagree, but they possess the desire to work toward a mutual solution. Once established, they agreed to review these statements every six months.

Tom and Peggy now know conflict situations will never disappear from their relationship, but they have committed themselves to a fresh approach. They face the future with a confidence that no conflict is stronger than the God who cemented their relationship from the beginning.


**For Further Reading**
Dobson, E., Leas, S., and Shelley, M. (1992). *Mastering conflict and controversy.* Portland, OR: Multnomah Press and Christianity Today, Inc. A very practical book answering many questions you have thought about but never asked. Multiple authorship gives you good exposure to three leaders in the conflict field.

Gangel, K., and Canine, S. (1992). *Communication and conflict management in churches and Christian organizations.* Nashville: Broadman Press. While written with organizations in mind, this book provides valuable insight into such topics as negotiation and bargaining, nonverbal communication, and constructive vs. destructive management of conflict.

Sande, K. (1991). *The peacemaker.* Grand Rapids: Baker Book House. A biblically based book focused on management of conflict which leads to peace. The author deals with both sides of a conflict and has a practical peacemaker's checklist which is invaluable.

# NURTURING CHILDREN AT HOME
*V. Gilbert Beers*

Everything but God seems to change, sometimes as dramatically as an erupting volcano, and sometimes as quietly and imperceptibly as the most remote star. But of all change, there is one more remarkable than any other—growth through nurture. It is quiet change, but nonetheless powerful, dynamic, with lasting consequences.

Flowers burst into radiant beauty, but may fade within a day. A tree grows, and may continue to grow for several hundred years, nurtured by the earth, sunlight, and rain. But a child grows and leaves a heritage on earth for generations to come, with eternal consequence for each generation.

Growing things require nurture, a feeding of sorts, to accomplish the growth toward maturity that God planned for them. Growing plants and animals require relatively simple nurture, but growing people require multifaceted nurture—physical, emotional, psychological, mental, and even spiritual. Nothing else in creation requires such a complex process to mature. And nothing else in creation produces such long-lasting fruits from its nurture.

Unlike plants and animals or anything else in creation, people grow, or at least should grow, toward a special affinity with the Creator Himself, a personal relationship that no other living thing can enjoy. That is because only people have that unique quality called personhood—a mysterious gift from God that reminds us of God Himself, though a dim and flawed reflection, falling far short of His Personhood.

In this chapter we will reflect on the nurture of the growing person through the childhood years, especially what should be provided at home through parents. We will also reflect on the ways in which the church can help parents with this nurturing process.

## THE ROLE OF THE PERSON
## IN DEVELOPING SPIRITUAL MATURITY

Every human being is fully a person at birth, though immature. Before the newborn lies a long road of maturation, a road that never ends during life on earth. Every day on this long road finds a complete person, growing through nurture into that maturity God expects.

This is part of the mystery of growth, that while personhood is there all along, it is not fully finished. The child has just begun the maturing process in which multifaceted change takes place every moment of every day.

Agents of change—parents, teachers, and all significant others— are shepherds of that maturing process. Shepherds guide the process, but the Lord Himself produces the change. This remarkable role of change agent provides parents and other shepherding figures with the unique, high, and holy privilege of partnering with the Creator in advancing the task of creation. Shepherding at its best begins with this assumption.

For the growing child, the nurturing process forms a delicate integration of numerous sources of strength—physical, sociological, emotional, mental, and spiritual. Each source of strength is vital in developing a mature person, for to be truly mature, one must not only develop in each of these areas, but in all of them in harmony with the others. Maturing does not mean growing in five unique ways simultaneously but independently; it means growing in five unique ways that are interrelated and interdependent.

Christian education is especially concerned with spiritual nurture because it forms the cohesive force for all nurture. At the very core of spiritual nurture is its source, the Bible.

## THE ROLE OF THE SCRIPTURES IN NURTURING CHILDREN

God has chosen to reveal Himself and His truth through His Word, the Bible. His truth is more than static teaching; it is life-changing and life-giving. How we respond to that truth determines how we mature in the way God expects, for His life-changing truth helps us mature in mind (belief), heart and soul (character), and expression (conduct).

## Learning Biblical Truth

Throughout the pages of His Word, God has provided a wide range of life-changing truths—about God the Father, Christ, the Holy Spirit, sin, salvation, and so on. He also provides truths about us, to show the kind of persons God wants us to become. Then He helps us, through the learning process, to connect the truths about Himself with the truths about ourselves.

At each age level, a child is capable of understanding and assimilating certain doctrines or truths, as long as they are presented in an age-appropriate and interesting manner. It is vital that the maturing child not only understand but internalize these truths in order to cultivate the kind of relationship with God that He wants. Understanding truth takes place when truth is clearly communicated. But appropriating truth takes place when a person desires that truth as his or her own and accepts it as such.

For example, think about the following basic doctrines concerning God: God loves you, God takes care of you, and God is with you everywhere. These appear in the preschool scope and sequence of almost every Sunday School curriculum.

To understand and appropriate the truth that God loves me challenges me to love God. Thus I respond to the truth that God loves me by accepting His love and also loving Him. To recognize that God takes care of me is important, but not enough. I should also thank Him for His care and, because of His care for me, I should also care for others.

To know that God is with me everywhere encourages me to trust Him when I feel lonely or alone. To know the presence of the Lord is to cultivate the practice of His presence and that enriches our walk with Him.

## Responding to Biblical Truth

To nurture life, Bible truth about God or other key doctrines cannot remain passive. Each truth encourages a personal response and a personal application. Truth requires me to change as a person, and then requires me to do something about that change. Through

God's truth, I become a different person, one who matures God's way. In part this change comes as my beliefs change, and as a result I change. Exposure to Scripture over time has a greater effect than simply learning information about God. Reading the Bible can be a way of spending time with God, and contact with Him through His Word strengthens our relationship with Him.

Life-changing truth appropriated into one's belief system is the stuff that forms a Christian worldview. That belief system incarnated, or appropriated into one's personhood, matures character. That character expressed becomes conduct.

A child is capable of understanding and accepting some rather mature truths if they are presented in an interesting, age-appropriate manner, at the maturity level of the learner. Likewise, the joy and delight of the presenter is a key factor also. Even age-appropriate truths presented in an abstract way and a disinterested fashion may not be easily accepted.

### Appropriating Biblical Truth

Values are discussed widely in the media but are often misunderstood. To the unbeliever, values may seem to be moral attributes—such as goodness, faithfulness, loyalty, truthfulness, honesty, and patience. But this view is too limiting and too naturalistic.

The vital role of the caregiver, at home or at church and Sunday School—the shepherds of growth through nurture, is to present the life-changing truths of the Word in an interesting, joyful, and delightful manner, in harmony with the ability of the age level of the learner to appropriate those truths. When presented in that way, the child will find God's truth winsome and will desire it as his own. She will believe and form a biblical value system, which then will be internalized as character and lived out as conduct.

Life-changing truths (doctrines, teachings) become *beliefs*, which become *character traits*, which become *conduct*. For example, the Bible teaches us that God is always with us, taking care of us. That is a truth, doctrine, or teaching. When a person truly believes this, he or she weaves this truth into a biblical, or Christian, world view. Appropriation simply means that "truth" is true also for me. It becomes an integral part of my worldview. If I firmly believe this truth, I will respond with trust in an ever-present God who takes care of me. That trust is a moral or spiritual value, in other words, a character trait.

## THE ROLE OF THE PARENT AND HOME
## IN NURTURING CHILDREN

In His great wisdom, God established caregiving roles to impact the maturing child. Each role is important—parent, grandparent, extended family member, neighbor, friend, teacher, pastor, and others. Each of these can and should be a significant other in the child's life. But of all of these roles, that of the parent is central.

Parents have the privilege of spending the most time with a child. They live in a close environment with the child, an environment which more than any other can and should be a nurturing context. The parent has the opportunity to be shepherd, guide, counselor, teacher, friend, companion, disciplinarian, and role model. The parent can provide for the child a refuge from life's storms and equip the child to weather storms away from the refuge.

Parenting is at times a formidable challenge. Most parents are busy with other things, and it is tempting to let the parenting process take second place to lesser things, to put in a video or let TV take over the significant other role. Those who dedicate themselves to the parenting process do so from a deep commitment. They pay a high price in time and energy.

Parenting is training, the inculcation of precepts. It is teaching and helping children learn. It is sharing the teachings of Scripture so the child understands what God expects. Parenting is bonding, that special process that welds family members together for a lifetime. Parenting is discipline and delight interwoven. Parenting is role modeling, since the way we live teaches much more than what we say.

Parents need a source of strength and encouragement, and the church often becomes that nurturing environment for them. Parents need other role models in the parenting process, and the church may well provide those parental role models as well. Parents need a source of wisdom and understanding, a listening ear, a recognition that their most frustrating moments are not unique, and the church can provide those also.

One other significant role the parent can play is that of fellow pilgrim, helping children see that they face struggles also and that they seek to resolve their struggles in God's strength and wisdom. Part of parental role modeling is demonstrating a Christian response to everyday problems. To pretend that parents never have problems is not helpful to children. They need to learn how to respond to problems that come to us all. Significant others in the wider family, or in the church, can also model this to both parent and child.

## THE ROLE OF THE EXTENDED FAMILY
## AND SIGNIFICANT OTHERS IN THE CHURCH

Every child needs a father figure, a mother figure, grandparent figures, aunt and uncle figures, cousin figures, and friend figures. But father figures do not always appear as fathers or uncle figures as uncles.

One of the significant roles the church can play in the nurture of children is to provide *alternative figures* where they are absent in a child's life. In today's fractured family life, vital family roles are often missing, and what better place to find alternative models for those family roles than in the church? A man across town cannot completely step in and fill the role of father to a child who has none, but he can do something. A caring person can become "aunt" or "uncle" to a child who needs a good one. And older people who feel they are no longer needed can discover that they are enormously useful as they become wonderful grandparent figures to children who have no grandparents, or at least none nearby (see chapter 13).

The church context is one which provides *nurture* to the parental nurturer, provides parental role models to inquiring parents, provides formal or informal learning about the parental process, and provides a sense of reality for those who think other parents are perfect. The congregation is a wonderful resource of "just friends" for parents who are hungry for friends in carrying out this difficult role.

The church also exemplifies the spirit of *bonding* which should prevail in the parenting process. As the parent should provide experiences that bond parent and child, so the church should provide experiences that bond parent to parent, teacher to parent, pastor to parent, and older counselors to parents.

The church can also be a nurturing center for parents, a feeding station of sorts. This feeding may be in the Scriptures, a resource for successful living. It may be a nurturing in the everyday experience of living out the parental role. When parents, who nurture others, need nurture, they should find it in the church.

Perhaps as significant as any role, the church should become a *safe haven* for the parent, a refuge from the difficulties of parenting and earning a living. In today's violent society, the role of safe haven becomes even more vital to a young parent, particularly a young single parent who faces the difficult parenting process alone.

The church may also be a *place of healing* for the wounded parent. Of all places, the church should provide an understanding ear to those who have suffered from divorce or family strife, or for those whose children have gone astray. In this sense, the church nurtures the parents who must nurture their children, counsels the parents who must counsel their children, shepherds the parents who must shepherd their children, and provides role models for parents who must be role models for their children.

If the church does not provide these services to young parents, who will do it? If lonely parents do not find these roles filled, how will they cope?

Without Christian nurture children lose perspective. It is no wonder we find children giving birth to children and children killing children. The society and family that should have provided the nurture they needed failed to do so.

### The Lasting Effects of Christian Nurture

To nurture a child God's way is more than building that one life, even for a lifetime. The immediate family is heir to this nurture, for that family will be enriched by a child who walks with God. Following generations benefit, for the child becomes in time a parent, perhaps a grandparent, or even a great-grandparent. Generations may be the benefactors of faithful parents and faithful churches that give full attention to nurturing their children. The church that has provided a nurturing environment becomes the benefactor too, for the children grow to assume leadership roles in the church. This, in turn, nurtures the church everywhere.

The highest privilege on earth, for parents, extended family, and church is the nurture of our children toward maturity. The children of today are the leaders of tomorrow—leaders of homes, churches, communities, nations, and the world. How we apply ourselves to this high and holy privilege will determine the future of all these entities. Church and home must work in concert in this task, not independently. When we apply ourselves with joy and delight and commitment, the fruits of our work will be beyond belief.

## For Further Reading

Barna, G. (1991). *What Americans believe.* Ventura, CA: Regal Books. A survey of the beliefs and attitudes of Americans. Reflects the vital importance of building belief systems early.

Gangel, K. and Wilhoit, J. (1994). *The Christian educator's handbook on spiritual formation.* Wheaton, IL: Victor Books. A handbook on spiritual formation, with several chapters that apply to the spiritual formation of children.

Kilpatrick, W. (1992). *Why Johnny can't tell right from wrong.* New York: Simon & Schuster. Where America has gone wrong in parenting and the need to pass on a moral heritage to our children.

Louv, R. (1990). *Childhood's future.* Boston: Houghton Mifflin. A newspaper reporter's three-year journey across America, interviewing parents and children. Reveals the failures and needs in childhood nurture.

# SINGLE PARENTING IN THE CHRISTIAN COMMUNITY
*David R. Miller*

The United States is one of the most religious nations in the world and one of the most divorce-prone as well. Most Americans say they believe in heaven and hell, attend religious services regularly, and belong to religious organizations. However, based on the rising divorce rate in the Christian community, American Christians apparently do not believe in the permanence of the marriage bond (Popenoe, 1988, p. 284). Surveys of church leadership conducted by the National Association of Evangelicals and others illustrate that the world has effectively invaded the church family when it comes to divorce. Pastors consistently report escalating concern with both the frequency and severity of problems that cause families to come to them for help and feel frustrated when so many "churched" marriages end in divorce (Stellway, 1990, p. 34).

## SINGLE PARENTING IS HERE!

Divorce and single parenting have arrived. Approximately 75 percent of divorces involve minor children (*Business Week,* 29 June 1992, p. 29). Victims and survivors of divorce fill our pews. Children of divorce populate our Sunday School classes and children's activities. Pastors are searching for trained female counselors to join the church staff because of the growing number of divorced women asking for counseling. Single and stepparent seminars and workshops proliferate. The scarcity of "once-married persons" for deacon and elder boards is causing some churches to reconsider requirements for those offices.

## The Need

There can be no rational objection why the Christian community should not respond to the needs of single-parent families. While the American family in general experiences many types of transitions, the trauma of any change is magnified when only one parent tries to meet family needs. Families of all types are being "de-institutionalized" as they lose or surrender important functions such as child-rearing to non-family providers (Popenoe, 1988, p. 98). Day care and other services have stepped into the void created by the rise of the one-parent family.

Single mothers usually find they need to work outside the home after a divorce, thus limiting already stretched parenting energy (Eggebeen, 1988, p. 59). Parents in general are not the strong spiritual or values-teaching force they once were. As families of all types lose the battle to civilize and socialize children, non-family forces eagerly step into the void created by divorce and other family disruptions.

The same demons that confronted the traditional American family face the single-parent family in legions. Everything negative is magnified and everything positive, diminished. Virginia Satir, an acknowledged and respected family therapist, described divorce and single-parenting in these words:

> Divorce is a metaphorical surgery which affects all areas of life of the individual. For many people, divorce is a broken experience, and before they can go on with their lives, they need to be able to pick up the pieces. This period often includes deep emotional feelings of despair, disappointment, retaliation, hopelessness and helplessness (Fisher, 1981, p. 1).

Church leaders and the Christian community have a mandate to find ways to serve the needs of single-parent families. If we do not meet the challenge, others will step in.

## Picking Up the Pieces

Single parents need recognition, support, and acceptance from the church. Comments from single parents unhappy with a church experience can be summed up in the words of one single mother:

> I don't feel like I belong anywhere. I am no longer married, so I don't fit the marrieds' Sunday School class. There is a singles' Sunday School class but they talk about dating and finding the right mate when I'm looking for help with my children and getting over a bad marriage. Anyway, I'm not ready to date again. I don't know where to sit in church. It seems that married women are uncomfortable around me. I just don't feel like I belong here.

Helping a stressed single parent takes many forms, not the least of which is sound instruction. The church can be extremely helpful in providing Bible-based information and practical encouragement. Those attempting to help single parents and their children must be careful to recognize that the Bible has very little to say of a specific nature on the subject of single parenting. We rely on principles of Christian living such as honesty, morality, love, and Holy Spirit leadership rather than spending time and effort stretching passages to fit situations they were never intended to address. The Bible has much to say on the subject of good parenting and sound instruction. Discipline, appropriate love, avoiding dependency, and acknowledging God's ownership with parent stewardship of children must be as crucial for the single parent as for any parent.

## QUESTIONS SINGLE PARENTS ASK

A church seeking to develop or enhance a single-parent ministry will need to address the following questions from single parents:
1. How do I parent alone?
2. Is it acceptable to feel as lonely as I do?
3. What can I do to better cope with my situation?
4. How can I better manage my finances?
5. Is there really life after divorce for a Christian?
6. Can I raise my children in a way that will please God?
7. Am I strong enough to trust God to meet our needs?
8. What can I learn from Bible characters? Am I wrong to ex-

pect specific lessons on single parenting from the Bible?

9. Will I ever be "really" accepted by the people in the church?

10. What resources does the church have that can help me as a single parent?

These are the questions the church-attending single parent often raises. They reflect the pain and disruption caused by the divorce and new parenting demands. The next sections will look at ways the church can address these issues. The questions themselves illustrate the challenges of ministry to single parents—the questions are real and reflect the struggle just to get through the day, but they are also self-oriented and lack a significant spiritual thrust.

## DEVELOPING A MINISTRY TO SINGLE PARENTS

### Step One

Once the single-parent segment of the church community is recognized as being large enough to warrant special help within this church, one approach is to bring in a *credentialed and trained* workshop/seminar leader to conduct weekend sessions for single parents. The emphasis on credentials and training stems from frequent disasters wrought by well-intentioned but naive people who do not recognize the fragile spiritual and psychological status of many single parents.

With a trained workshop leader, the first step should accomplish several goals:

1. Workshop sessions will provide a sense of recognition for single parents in the church. The workshops will tell the participants, many of whom will be from the unchurched or "other churched" community, that *this* church not only cares but stands ready to help in practical and realistic ways.

2. The workshop sessions will build an initial sense of "groupness" that, with proper nurturing, can grow into a viable Sunday School class, thereby providing more fellowship opportunities and outreach into the community.

3. The third goal is perhaps the most important. Participants will receive help! The workshops should, if properly handled, provide practical and spiritual help with the very real concerns of living as a single person and raising children.

**Step Two**

Once single-parent identity has been established through the workshops and initial help has been offered, the church then assumes care of single parents and begins to minister through the Sunday School class and normal ministry arms of the church. During this second step, church leaders appoint an appropriate person to serve as teacher of the Sunday School class. This person may also hold the title "Pastor to Single Parents."

## THE RIGHT LEADER

Just a word on the selection of the right person to lead a single parent ministry. Because more than 90 percent of custody decisions grant primary or complete care of children to their mothers, church leaders should be careful to select a single-parent pastor/Sunday School teacher who not only demonstrates a compassionate heart and sound Bible training, but who demonstrates a solid personal marriage.

Single mothers are often in a vulnerable and emotionally needy state as they enter or reenter the church community. They are experiencing stress over finances, child care, unmet social, spiritual, and sexual needs, and need both support and reassurance. Single mothers often feel rejected and undesirable and may be vulnerable to showing inappropriate expressions of affection to the single-parent pastor (Miller, 1994, p. 1). (I emphasize female membership and male leadership because single fathers with custody probably make up no more than 3 to 5 percent of all single parents. A typical single-parent Sunday School class of fifty will include one or two fathers with custody, and while the desire to minister applies to single fathers as well, they often do not present themselves to the church as needing the same services as single mothers.)

Based on this reality, the one selected to lead ministry to single parents must be securely married to a spouse who is, in every sense, a partner in ministry. A male pastor must be willing to counsel, disciple, and otherwise minister to divorced women in the Sunday School class only with his wife or another person present. He must be willing to avoid all appearances of evil by responding to crises and other emergencies with the same care with which he conducts counseling sessions. If he must respond to an emergency

131

phone call late at night from a class member, he will help by telephone only unless his wife or a church staff member can accompany him to the home.

Spiritually, the single-parent minister must be mature, well-grounded in spiritual matters, and holding an excellent and unblemished record of ministry, either professional or lay. There must be no question of moral character. A compassion and heart for ministry must be matched by a record of Bible study and intercessory prayer. He or she must be willing to put feet to concern and become an advocate for those in the Sunday School class. If the person selected to lead the ministry to single parents is a woman, the same spiritual requirements apply, as does the need for ministering with another person in emergencies or on home visits. In today's world one's moral judgments are always under scrutiny and preventative caution is basic. The Sunday School teacher/ministry leader, whether male or female, must work hard to avoid any appearance of impropriety.

## HELPING THE SINGLE-PARENT FAMILY REALIGN ITSELF

We can summarize answers to the ten questions single parents ask as we visualize the single-parent family going through the process of realigning itself to a new reality. I believe we can synthesize four major areas of concern based on expressions of need by single parents in the Christian community.

### Economic Concerns

In the great majority of single-parent families, standard of living declines substantially, especially in the first year or two following the divorce (Bane, 1976, pp. 103–117). The Christian community and the church can be most helpful by providing specific financial advice and services for single parents. This could take the form of periodic financial seminars offered at no cost to single parents. Many single mothers come from a marriage in which the husband controlled the finances. They have had no experience paying bills or budgeting and could benefit from information on the basics of financial management.

Economically stressed single parents are unlikely to give generously. Yet the importance of giving is not reduced by one's circumstances. I would suggest that stewardship be included in lessons on financial management offered to Christian single parents. The Christian single parent, perhaps more than some others, may need to learn or relearn to trust God in the area of resource management.

Single parents may need help from the Christian community in finding employment. Some churches have instituted a "job seekers" self-help group in which church members looking for work are helped with resume preparation and interview skills. This is precisely the kind of specific and practical information single parents benefit from most.

## Parenting Concerns

Having total or near-total responsibility for the care of children at the same time they need to find a job can create tremendous stress on single mothers. We know that actual contact with both parents declines following divorce and that this reduction has a negative impact on children. The church and Christian community can help by:

1. Offering parenting seminars to single parents (usually mothers) including topics such as creative discipline, sibling rivalry, helping children understand divorce and visitation, showing authority when she doesn't feel very strong, and maintaining a Christian testimony in front of the children.
2. Offering spiritual and personal growth opportunities for the parent. As the custodial parent feels better about herself, is less lonely and rejected, and feels more competent as a Christian parent, she will be better able to meet the children's needs.
3. Providing specific instruction on dealing with a former spouse in a manner that will help the children most. So many divorced people seem willing to sacrifice the children to their own pride that many continue to battle after the war has been declared over. Helping single parents understand their children's needs in this regard should help them control this potentially problematic area.

## Social Life

Single parents often feel lonely, rejected, scarred, incompetent, and hopeless. The church and Christian community can help in the following ways:

1. Establish a single-parent Sunday School class. Even if the class

starts small, this one action will draw single parents to the church by providing them a much-needed sense of identity. Specific lessons on single-parent living can be provided in this environment. The class should provide social activities and special supportive activities for members and visitors as well.

2. Make a special effort to invite single parents to family-oriented church and social activities. Single parents do not want to be mentioned from the pulpit or in announcements, but they do want to be recognized and acknowledged by being included in activities.

3. Approximately 80 percent of divorced people remarry (Westoff, 1975, pp. 10–13). Thoughtful church leaders will recognize the need for help with appropriate mate selection. Divorced people in the church can benefit from social activities which bring them into contact with other divorced, widowed, or never-married people their own age. Generally divorced singles will be ten years older on average than never-married singles. Age identification is an important element in feeling included again.

## Spiritual Life

"Why would God let this happen to me and my children"?

Helpers should be careful to acknowledge (but avoid trying to answer) questions that may be beyond human understanding. The question stated above demonstrates the spiritual situation felt by most, if not all, divorced Christian single parents. Single parents who are believers tend very much to feel:

1. as if they are being punished for some real or imagined past or present sin;
2. that they are permanently marked because of the divorce. Many divorced Christian parents actually feel as if others can tell they are divorced just by looking;
3. as if they are second-class citizens of the Christian community;
4. that they cannot be trusted to control their sexuality;
5. that they must have failed to learn important lessons from God regarding mate selection, otherwise the divorce would not have happened;
6. that their children are now predetermined to repeat their parents' problems in marriage;
7. that they can never again attain a place of leadership in the church.

Pastors and congregations have a delicate job to do when reorienting single parents into the church community. They must emphasize forgiveness, focusing not only on God's unlimited forgiveness for past behavior that may have contributed to the divorce, but forgiveness also for the former spouse who may have been verbally or physically abusive. Reorientation will also include welcoming the divorced parent into full Christian fellowship with all the opportunities for ministry, fellowship, and service available to others.

## CONCLUSION

The challenge is apparent! As the family experiences a period of decline in all areas, the church must step in to fill the void before the world takes over. With 79 percent of divorced men and 75 percent of divorced women remarrying, the need for remarriage counseling confronts us (Wallerstein & Kelly, 1975, pp. 600-616). The need will not be reduced! The challenge will be met by someone, and if the Christian community fails to respond we may never regain the lost opportunities.

Those ministering to and counseling single parents must manifest good will and compassion. They must show empathy and a sense of presence as people share life stories and problems. They must demonstrate Christian love and concern while allowing recovering single parents to find their own way. To properly serve single parents, pastors, counselors, and Sunday School adult class leaders must be available who are ethical and moral, resistant to temptation and flattery, and soundly and permanently married. Divorced class leaders must have dealt with their own concerns, standing ready to serve as both a sounding board and an example of overcoming. Single parents more than any other group in the Christian community should be able to identify with the following words of encouragement.

"Joshua said to them, 'Do not be afraid; do not be discouraged. Be strong and courageous. This is what the Lord will do to all the enemies you are going to fight' " (Josh. 10:25).

In the broadest sense, the Christian community is the light that illuminates the path to recovery and reconciliation. If we do not show the way, they may not be able to find it.

135

## For Further Reading

Hodges, W. (1986). *Interventions for children of divorce: Custody, access, and psychotherapy.* New York: John Wiley & Sons. An excellent compilation of research and application by one of the leaders in the field. Used as a resource manual and textbook by counselors.

Miller, D. (1994). *Counseling families after divorce.* Waco, TX: Word. One of the most current and comprehensive books on the subject of the impact of divorce and remarriage on all members of the family. Written from a Christian perspective, the book follows the Craig family through the trauma of divorce, single parenting, and remarriage. Specific remedies are offered throughout.

Popenoe, D. (1988). *Disturbing the nest: Family change and decline in modern societies.* New York: Aldine De Gruyter. Popenoe compares family changes in the United States and Sweden and suggests that the eventual outcome of our social and political changes may be more dramatic than is generally discussed. The author develops an interesting and concise history of the American family and points out developments that have encouraged family decline.

Stellway, R. (1990). *Christiantown.* New York: The Haworth Press. An intensive demographic and attitudinal examination of "Christiantown" (Wheaton, Illinois) finds that Christians are not as different from others when it comes to family values, marital satisfaction, economic concerns, and many others. A prime value of the book is that it is one of the very few research-based discussions of the Christian family in America.

Visher, E.B. and Visher, J.S. (1988). *Old loyalties, new ties: Therapeutic strategies with stepfamilies.* New York: Brunner/Mazel. Husband and wife authors exhaustively explore the ramifications of remarriage, the reasons for hope, and the causes of failure. Chapters are filled with useful and practical information for the helper, all of which is presented in a professional and research-based format.

PART THREE
# THE CHURCH'S EDUCATIONAL MINISTRY TO FAMILIES

# ELEVEN

# DIVORCE—HOW THE CONGREGATION RESPONDS
*Brian and Deborah Newman*

When was the last time Susie or Ken made an appointment to see you? You know Susie and Ken, the sweet couple with the two school-age children. They joined your church about three years ago. You've seen them around the church. You thought they were well plugged into church activities. Today you can only guess why Susie wants to talk to you. Where else would she go when she realizes her marriage is falling apart? Here she comes, wearing that same hopeless face you've seen in other "Susies" before her. She comes to dump the pain and sorrow of a broken marriage at your feet, and looks to you to fix it. How do you feel? A bit overwhelmed, we bet. Sympathetic, sure; but there's another part that cringes at these intrusions. After all, you *are* a Christian leader; you must hate divorce—just like God.

## MINISTRY FOR BROKEN MARRIAGES

In reality, as long as Susies and Kens attend our churches they will come to the pastoral staff first. What can we do to help? How can the church respond?

### Think Through Your Position on Divorce
This involves much more than coming to theological conclusions; that's probably the easy part. Christian leaders are trained to study God's Word. When it comes to divorce, knowledge of the Scriptures and a review of the literature will eventually bring us to

some theological position on the issue of divorce and remarriage.

That's good. We all need a solid theological position. But all Christian leaders also need a counseling position. Pastors and teachers are not necessarily good counselors, and if they spent all their time doing counseling, other areas of the church would surely suffer. Yet all of us will do initial counseling, often observing the first frantic grasp for direction from parishioners. What is your approach to helping Susie?

Will Susie be helped by a mini sermon on the "Drudgery of Divorce"? Probably not. She needs someone who will offer her hope—hope that no matter what may happen, how out of control her life may seem, God loves her and can heal and sustain her. The church's response to divorce needs to be a resounding message of hope! People struggling with broken marriages need hope that God will guide them in this time of crisis. How do you offer such hope?

We need to think through several practical issues as we counsel people in marriage crisis. For example, counselors quickly learn the importance of *impartiality*. It is all too easy to get caught up in what one deeply hurting spouse has to say. Her hurt is real and she pours it out in your office. Can you be impartial and objective enough to reach out to Ken even after you've heard all Susie has to say?

Should you ever recommend separation? What if Susie tells you about physical violence against her and her children? Would you instruct her to seek a place of safety? Do you know a place to recommend?

Becky came to counseling because she was considering leaving her husband, Paul. She had discovered he was emotionally involved with someone at work. A Christian leader told her she had no biblical grounds for divorce, since he had not been sexually unfaithful. This counsel may be consistent with one popular view of Scripture, but it is insensitive to Becky's situation and fears. Becky needs to understand the truth of God's Word in the context of relationship. As we acknowledge Becky's anger, we pave an avenue for sharing God's love.

Another response could be to tell Becky that you know living with a man who has hurt her so deeply seems impossible: "Why would a God who loves you instruct you to keep your marriage vows even in this context?" Focus on the reality that God loves Becky and wants the best for her life. Put her in touch with His power and nurture her relationship with God. Encourage her to work through her anger and to obey His Word.

These are important issues for a Christian leader to think through. What is your position on counseling those in marriage crisis? What strategies does your church or organization utilize to serve these desperate people?

## Develop Support Resources

It would be helpful to have a few men and women with whom you could put Susie and Ken in touch after they come to your office—after you ask the couple's permission first. You can assign someone mature in the Lord, who also understands the struggle of marriage, to pray for and support the needy spouse(s). This type of encouragement needs to come from several people in the congregation so no one person begins to feel overburdened.

Susie needs encouragement. She desperately wants someone to pray with her and support her, and this desperate need in women like Susie has triggered failure in too many pastors and Christian leaders. When hurting and vulnerable women come for help to a man who feels disrespected and unappreciated at home, it often leads to sinful choices.

Pastoral staff members are not equipped to manage all the Susies and Kens alone. That's why the church body needs to be equipped to help. What kind of person can we trust in this position? We've already mentioned maturity and experience. Other personal qualities require a person who can keep confidences, can be impartial, is committed to God, can say "no," and can offer hope. How does one enlist such people? The best way is to watch their lives and consult with them personally about their willingness to help in this ministry.

Also, every Christian leader needs a referral list for counseling. Often we need to encourage couples and individuals to seek professional help. Always refer someone who has become suicidal or clinically depressed to a professional counselor or a medical doctor unless you are competent to deal with these issues yourself.

## Prepare a Place to Belong

We hope that, through the power of Christ, Susie and Ken would reconcile their marriage. But your church is full of other couples already divorced and in need of special ministry. How does your church reach out to these people?

Beyond offering hope, the church needs to provide a place to belong within its small group ministry. Divorced people go through larger amounts of loneliness than the average person. They must make major adjustments in socializing, caring for the house, balancing the checkbook, and a host of other tasks.

A singles' department that focuses on older vs. younger singles is very helpful. But some, in different stages of divorce, do not want to attend any kind of singles' group. Sometimes, the only other option is a couples' class. Sometimes we can address the needs of divorced and other people in the church by having at least one Sunday School class or small group divided by ungraded gender. Make sure your church is divorce-sensitive. Everyone needs a place to belong.

Single parents need role models for their children as well. Encourage members to help a child whose father lives 600 miles away, to let her know there is a fill-in dad when hers isn't available. Be there to offer free baby-sitting to a single parent who might very much need a break. There are scores of ways to help out a single parent. Consult with these folks and make every effort to serve their special needs.

Many churches offer a recovery group for the divorced, which can also serve as an outreach opportunity. People often undervalue the severity of the trauma divorce causes. Think about Jesus' description of marriage—as two draw together, they become one flesh. Have you ever had flesh pulled apart? It hurts! It creates pain and bleeding. The flesh left behind needs time to heal. Sometimes physical therapy is required.

The same holds true when it comes to divorce. A recovery group should be led by someone who has experienced firsthand the agony of divorce. Only such a veteran can offer guidance and hope to individuals in the group. Several series provide excellent teaching for a recovery group focus. Check with your local Christian bookstore for more information.

### Rebuild the Lives of the Divorced

No other kind of rejection is quite as devastating as divorce. Divorced Christians live in a great deal of mental and emotional pain. Many feel cut off from God and the church because they feel they have failed and there is no hope.

The church needs to beam out God's message of hope. Jesus didn't confront the Samaritan woman with guilt and shame. He simply praised her for admitting the truth about her life and her failures in relationships with men. When people hit bottom, we need to give them hope, not condemnation.

The Samaritan woman would have stayed far away from church. She didn't even want to be around the people of her community; she came for water at a time of day when no one else was around. As if five marriages weren't a bad enough record, she felt guilty living with a man without being married. Jesus found her; He showed her that He knew all about her. Oh, that the church would be a place where people didn't feel they had to hide previous marriages and divorces to be accepted!

The Samaritan woman had the sweet experience that so many long for—complete exposure with complete acceptance. Beyond the acceptance, Jesus offered her hope; that hope lay in relationship with Him. And what a transformation took place! From shame-ridden recluse, the woman became a testimony for God. Relationship with Jesus had transformed her life.

Whether the divorce was his fault or hers, the divorced person needs to be given the truth that God doesn't close the door on the divorced. Rather, He says "Come home; come to Me; I want you; I still want you to belong to Me." Whatever your church's position on divorce and remarriage, rejection of its victims cannot be biblically justified.

Divorced people need hope that Jesus really is enough. Proverbs 14:12 says, "There is a way which seems right to a man, but its end is the way of death." "What seems right" to a divorced person trapped in the pain of rejection often is finding someone to belong to. Many people run to the arms of another so quickly they don't have time to recover from the grief of the broken marriage. They don't move beyond the denial stage of grieving. People find it hard to wait and move through their grief, anger, hurt, financial burdens, and other problems. The church needs to encourage the divorced to commit all relationships to God and wait for His timing and direction about future marriage.

## PREVENTATIVE MEDICINE

We are all familiar with the saying, "An ounce of prevention is worth a pound of cure." But an entire church body can be influenced by our divorce-minded society. Congregations need to respond to divorce by making an effort to prevent it. This can be done in several ways, but only if pastors educate the entire body about divorce with compassion.

### Education with Compassion

Remember the successful ad campaign for a hamburger restaurant in which an elderly lady went to other hamburger places and asked, "Where's the beef?" On any given Sunday the same question could be asked of many of our churches. With divorce such a widespread reality, many pastors tend to stay away from teaching about divorce for fear of offending half the congregation. This type of response only reinforces the confused views of our society. God takes our vows seriously. Since the church is commonly where sacred vows of marital fidelity are made, the church needs to take responsibility for educating people about the importance of these vows.

This is a tough, extremely controversial, and very sensitive teaching. However, it is also very needed in our society today. If we don't hold forth the truth in our churches, how will we fight cultural perversions of truth and morality?

In the Gospels we observe Jesus making strong and straight-forward statements about His position on divorce. In Matthew 19:9, for example, He says, "And I say to you, whoever divorces his wife, except for immorality, and marries another woman commits adultery" (NASB). Jesus is Truth, and He did not hold back Truth when asked about divorce.

We also see how Jesus treated people sinning in these matters. Think about how He responded to the woman caught in the very act of adultery (John 8:3-11). We've noted His treatment of the woman who had been married five times and now lived with a man who was not her husband (John 4:17-18). Teaching on divorce and the truth about divorce is much needed in a society that promotes a divorce mentality.

Sensitivity and caring are crucial when addressing this issue. Christ did not found the church to burden people with blame. That's what the Pharisees tried to do when they dragged a woman from the arms of her lover and threw her before Jesus to be judged and stoned. The Pharisees rarely acted with compassion. We must respond as Jesus did—recognizing there is sin involved, and pointing to the reality of forgiveness. A pastor can sympathize with those whose lives have been devastated by divorce, but he also needs to instruct those people about how to get their lives back in sync with God and His plan for them. Indeed, forgiveness is the only hope for each of us, whether divorced or not.

In every sermon that discusses divorce, the emphasis should not be on condemnation. The attitude toward the already divorced needs to be one of support and restoration. At the same time we must teach the devastation of divorce and the importance of keeping marital promises.

### Premarital Counseling

A second area for preventative medicine is *premarital counseling*. Many pastors have begun to take a stronger look at whom they marry. They require that each partner make a personal commitment to Christ, be committed to sexual purity, receive premarital counseling, and take special premarital testing. Some larger churches make special classes a prerequisite for marriage.

In our society, we must study and pass a test to be able to receive a driver's license. Learners are required to practice with adult supervision. Even if our government doesn't require more than a blood test for marriage licenses, the church can and needs to add its own biblical guidelines.

The church needs to teach people how to be married. As C. S. Lewis said, "One of the ends for which sex was created was to symbolize to us the hidden things of God. One of the functions of human marriage is to express the nature of the union between Christ and the church" (1948, p. 32).

### Strong Families

Third, the church needs to *emphasize strong families*. Central to Jesus' case against divorce in Matthew 19:4-6 is His reference to creation. God's design for human relationships rests upon a monogamous, committed relationship between a man and a woman. From this union, families, churches, and societies are formed. Strong marriages result in healthy families, churches, and societies. The church needs to help couples "hang with it" through the stages of marriage. We wrote *Passages of Marriage* to enlighten couples to the realities we see every day in the counseling office. Many people abandon marriage over normal and necessary difficulties that each couple must face.

The church can also help build strong marriages and families through mentoring couples. Older mentoring couples can be grouped with younger marrieds to provide a role model and caring friends to call and discuss difficulties with. Providing marriage enrichment opportunities through special weekend get-a-ways and teaching times is also helpful.

## CONCLUSION

To review, the plan for ministering to the church body regarding divorce should be twofold. First, remember the importance of prevention. The entire church body is served by firm, but loving teaching on divorce, strong premarital counseling requirements, and opportunities to build strong marriage and family relationships. Second, there needs to be ministry to divorced people themselves. Divorced people need support and recovery groups, a church body sensitive to the challenge of single parenting, and other needs of the divorced, and encouragement to grow in dependence on God, not marriage.

After Susie turned to her pastor for help, Ken insisted on a trial period of separation. Their church was there for them. People didn't ignore either Susie or Ken. Susie found tremendous support from her new friend, Annette, the woman the pastor enlisted to support Susie. Together they prayed and discussed responses to Ken's hurtful behavior. With Susie's permission, Annette informed her children's Sunday School teachers about the sensitive family situation. Both teachers made extra efforts to support them. The pastor and Annette's husband, Tom, kept in contact with Ken. Finally, Ken agreed to see a Christian marriage counselor. Today, the family is still together. After several years, Susie and Ken have become two of the pastor's best referral contacts when other troubled couples come into his office. Today they both would say, "The church helped save our marriage."

### For Further Reading

Burns, B., and Whiteman, T. (1992). *Fresh start divorce recovery workbook.* Nashville: Oliver-Nelson Books. A workbook that guides readers through a biblically based approach to healing and recovery.

Duty, G. (1967). *Divorce and remarriage.* Minneapolis: Bethany House Publishers. A compassionately written book for those who have experienced divorce, it gives direction about the biblical teachings on divorce.

Jones, T. (1990). *Single again handbook.* Nashville: Oliver-Nelson Books. This book focuses on how to be single again and addresses how to live alone, friendships, single-parenting, sexuality, etc.

_____. (1990). *Sex and love when you're single again.* Nashville: Oliver-Nelson Books. This book addresses the needs of single adults and teaches appropriate sexual behavior along with instructions about learning what real love is.

Keener, C. (1991). *And marries another.* Peabody, MA: Hendrickson Publishers. A biblical and scholarly treatment of the New Testament teachings on marriage, divorce, and remarriage.

Munroe, M. (1992). *Single, married, separated and life after divorce.* Shippensburg, PA: Destiny Image Publishers. This book focuses on the need to heal and be an emotionally healthy single before a new relationship. It discusses the biblical concepts of marriage, separation, and divorce.

Talley, J. (1987). *Life after divorce.* Colorado Springs: NavPress. A guide to help single mothers through the difficult realities they face after divorce.

Whiteman, T. (1994). *Love gone wrong.* Nashville: Oliver-Nelson Books. This book helps examine what went wrong in the first marriage and gives ideas for healthy relationships in the future.

# MINISTRY TO STEPFAMILIES
*Beth E. Brown*

Family life education should be fundamentally proactive—committed to nurturing healthy families who understand the dynamics of love and life-long commitment. Church leaders must teach and model familial fidelity, integrity, and love as they prepare young people for the realities and responsibilities of Christian marriage and family. Churches must teach toward the ideals of wholeness and health.

But in this broken world the family relationships God created us to enjoy (Gen. 1–2) have been marred by sin's entrance into human experience (Gen. 3). Many people struggle to hold their families together, but they don't always succeed. Some are broken by death, others by divorce.

## GRIM STATISTICS

Today more than half of first marriages in America end in divorce. Second marriages fail at an even higher rate, usually within four years. Marriage and family expert Paul Cullen (1990) predicts that, if current trends persist, before the end of this century the United States will have more single-parent and stepparent families than traditional ones (p.18). At present, 1,300 stepfamilies are being formed every day in America.

Reconstituted families will be a reality of the next century. So while churches continue to promote spiritual, emotional, moral, and economic health in first-marriage families, they should also be committed to the success of these blended families.

## NEGATIVE STEREOTYPES

Stepfamilies fill the pews of American churches Sunday after Sunday, yet we often overlook their unique needs and circumstances. Perhaps this is because of the church's general discomfort with the entire matter of divorce. While churches rightly teach the biblical ideals of partnership, fidelity, love, and permanence, they sometimes struggle to be authentically compassionate toward the divorced (see chapter 11). Regardless of a particular church's view of divorce and remarriage, it would seem reasonable that every church support the success (certainly not the failure!) of second marriages. Churches should provide help so that reconstituted families can find the stability and joy they have not known before.

Perhaps because the stereotypes surrounding the role of stepparents are so horrific, some Christians opt to avoid the topic altogether. Childhood tales of *Cinderella, Snow White,* and *Hansel and Gretel* teach us that stepmothers are ugly and cruel. Many have grown up learning to associate the word "wicked" with the word "stepmother." Worse yet are stereotypes surrounding the word "stepchild," often used to describe the marginalized and victimized of society.

One young woman finally reconciled her role as a stepmother, personally overcoming the negative stereotype, when she recalled that Jesus was raised by a "stepfather." It seemed unlikely to her that God would have sent His only Son to be raised in a "dysfunctional" family! Rather, God saw Joseph's role as important to the nurture of baby Jesus as he grew to manhood. Likewise, the church must value the role of stepparents (Brown, 1991, p. 21).

The church must labor to replace destructive stereotypes with visions of health, celebrating the courage of families trying to start over. How can we support reconstituted families? By acknowledging the existence, complexities, and realities of stepfamily life, offering practical advice for dealing with family stresses, and encouraging families to participate in support groups where they can talk about their shared experiences.

## ACKNOWLEDGING BLENDED FAMILIES IN THE CHURCH

Church leaders can do a great deal for stepfamilies by simply offering public recognition of their existence. This can be done in a variety of ways. The pastor could periodically include stepfamilies in public prayer or occasionally use sermon illustrations extracted from the experiences of a blended family.

On Mother's Day, as we rightly acknowledge and encourage biological mothers, we should also recognize a multitude of other women: adoptive mothers, those who wish to be mothers but are unable to have children for a variety of reasons, women who are gifted as singles, and stepmothers working to build healthy relationships with their stepchildren. The same care can be used to include stepfathers among the men honored on Father's Day.

As the church announces elective courses and support groups for those seeking to better understand the needs, challenges, and rewards of blended families, these families will feel legitimized. Being made to feel that their reality is accepted and supported by the local church can encourage both the children and the parents in blended families.

## PRACTICAL TOPICS FOR STEPFAMILY LIFE EDUCATION

### Loss

All stepfamilies are born of loss. The term "step" derives from an old English word meaning "bereaved." In colonial America, most stepfamilies were formed after loss through death. Many women died giving birth, and numerous parents lost their lives to unchecked diseases and the hard work demanded by the times. Today, for every stepfamily formed after the death of a biological parent, six are formed through divorce.

This beginning through loss makes the dynamic of a stepfamily radically different from first-marriage families. Death shakes the family's foundation—either the physical death of a parent or the death of a marriage. And a death must be grieved.

This means that churches need to encourage broken families to grieve. They must give all family members the gift of time to face and move through their grieving. Perhaps a father finished his grief work and remarried quickly, without understanding that his children

151

were still in the midst of their own grief. The children may react with confusion, and even anger, to a second marriage that began before they were ready. They may feel that loving (or even liking) a new stepparent at this early stage betrays the missing parent.

Teaching about loss will help stepfamilies face the painful reality of the preceding death or divorce, and will also help shatter the myth of instant happiness that soon brings disillusionment and disappointment into the experience of stepfamilies. All too often the new couple feels that since the home now has two parents again, things will be fine; this is rarely the case.

## Time

Stepfamilies do not come to a clear understanding of their identities and roles quickly. Ralph Ranieri (1987) warns against the "as if" tendency: "A blended family cannot be expected to operate as if it were a nuclear family. This is an unrealistic expectation which denies the unique strengths and ignores the inherent problems of the blended family" (p. 23).

Educator Patricia Papernow (1984) made an enormous contribution to our understanding of stepfamily life when she observed and described some rather predictable stages in a stepfamily's development (pp. 355–363):

1. *Fantasy.* The stepparent fantasizes about how his or her love will compensate for the family's previous loss. The children fantasize about how family life used to be.
2. *Assimilation.* The family members try to live out their fantasies but are disappointed and confused. Sometimes they experience jealousy, hostility, resentment, and rejection.
3. *Awareness.* Family members admit to their disappointment in each other and in their family life. This is the stage at which the family is likely to seek help.
4. *Mobilization.* Honest feelings are shared and conflicts are common. Very often family members polarize over issues.
5. *Action.* The parents actively work to define their roles and relationships. They evaluate past traditions and current ways of living together. The stepparent begins to develop a relationship with the children independent of the biological parent.
6. *Contact.* The marriage grows stronger now that family members honestly communicate their feelings and the couple begins to work at intimacy. Finally, the stepparent clearly de-

fines his or her role in the family.

7. *Resolution.* In this final stage of development, the stepfamily is stable and strong. A new family history has begun and the children feel free to develop their own identities.

During the chaotic and painful early stages of development, churches need to offer support, helping both children and parents see the normalcy of their struggles and nourishing perseverance and faith. Most second marriages end during the first few years of marriage when dreams shatter and relationships are insecure. Yet, Papernow (1984) discovered that four years are required for "fast" families to move through these stages; seven years for "average" families; and even more time for others. The church ministers by reminding stepfamilies of the need for time and by standing with them as they work through the difficult transitions that will eventuate in family stability.

## Strong Marriages

Not only do husband and wife experience the usual adjustments a man and woman face in a new marriage; but they often face additional stresses, such as adjustment to the children's needs and personalities, added financial pressures in cases of divorce, legal entanglements left over from a first marriage, and often a load of guilt over the failure of the first marriage. Clearly, the church can be a place to help these marriages.

Preventively, churches can offer divorce recovery workshops for divorced people and their children. Paul Cullen (1990) warns that "guilt, anger, and decimated self-esteem resulting from divorce or death of the first spouse also contribute to the major struggles in second marriages" (p. 18). People must work through their emotions and roles in a previous relationship before beginning another.

Marriage retreats, typically designed to strengthen all marriages in the church body, can include issues unique to couples in a stepfamily. Perhaps those in blended families can have time together to share their common struggles and to suggest discovered solutions.

Second marriages have some unique strengths as well. Couples may be more realistic about the work required to enjoy a healthy marriage and be more willing to expend the effort. They may have more maturity as they make decisions about their relationship, having gained some wisdom from previous mistakes. Very often,

153

the couples are more established in their careers, which can alleviate some of the pressure on their relationship and in their family life. Churches would do well to help these couples see their strengths and build on them.

Couples experiencing happy second marriages describe relationships characterized by good communication, minimal conflict, and shared decision-making (Keshet, 1988, pp. 30–31). Knowing this, churches could enrich marriages by offering seminars in communication skills, conflict management, and shared decision-making, along with a core curriculum of Christian discipleship.

Clearly, the church's central role is to nurture the faith of its membership, helping everyone to enjoy a personal relationship with God through Jesus Christ and to grow in relationships with others. As couples in second marriages come to understand God's love for them, they will be empowered to love each other more completely. They can then learn to live out Ephesians 4:32 in their marriages: "Be kind to one another, tenderhearted, forgiving one another, as God in Christ has forgiven you."

### Additional Issues

While the three topics above are primary to the long-term survival of reconstituted families, there are several other areas of typical concern. These include where to live, how to handle money, and the best approach to family discipline. All these areas could be topics for family life education in the local church.

## SUPPORT GROUPS FOR STEPFAMILIES

One of the most effective ways for stepfamilies to feel encouraged by their local church is for the church to establish support groups in which they can share their experiences with each other. The seminar-only approach tends to intimidate participants, who hear what the experience of a healthy stepfamily should be, compare this to their own reality, and leave feeling inadequate. These families need experiences in which their own struggles can be normalized; they must realize that all stepfamilies go through painful adjustments.

They also must find hope for healing. Hope becomes the key gift of the church as congregations contextualize the Gospel into stepfamily life. Stepfamilies must believe that God can work in their homes as He can in any home. While these families share their struggles, they can also share how God's grace is at work, bringing them through difficult relationships, losses, and adjustments, and providing healing, hope, and even joy. Often, the solutions and advice families share with each other can have greater effect than advice from the experts, because they learn to discover for themselves God's presence and guidance in their own family life.

Small churches with only one or two reconstituted families can cooperate with other congregations in the community. Several churches could promote a community-wide support group for stepfamilies, which could help church families as well as reach out to the unchurched. John and Emily Visher started The Stepfamily Association of America with chapters throughout the country. These groups can address many practical questions and could be helpful in conjunction with the church's support groups.

## THE MINISTRY OF STEPPARENTING

All too often, the church sees congregants with special needs as problems to be addressed. However, it would be far more productive to see stepfamilies as homes with great potential for healing and growth. Stepparents should make a commitment at the marriage altar to serve each other and their children. This ceremony initiates a powerful opportunity for ministry.

Having acknowledged that stepfamilies are born of loss, the church can also acknowledge that godly stepparents can be God's agents of healing, helping children deal with their loss and bringing a restored sense of family into their lives. Knowing that this restoration takes time and work, the role of the church is to value this process and to support the ministry of its stepparents.

The twenty-first century church must have a vision for the healing of family life, through proactive teaching, through the modeling of godly family relationships, through ministry to the broken, and through support of the reconstituted family. While knowing that in this world there will tribulation in our families, the church can herald the good news that, through Christ, families can overcome loss and live with hope.

## For Further Reading

Brown, B. (1991). *When you're mom no. 2: A word of hope for step-mothers.* Ann Arbor, Michigan: Servant Publications. A practical guide written to give stepmothers realistic vision for their new lives, practical help in establishing new relationships, trouble-shooting tips, and spiritual encouragement that will guide them in building a strong and healthy family life.

Einstein, E., and Albert, L. (1986). *Strengthening your stepfamily.* Circle Pines, MN: American Guidance Service. A good overview of the topic.

Juroe, D.J., and Bonnie, B. (1983). *Successful stepparenting.* Old Tappan, NJ: Fleming H. Revell Company. Centers on the psychological reactions and defenses of stepchildren toward blended family situations with suggestions on how to deal with the problems.

Lewis-Steere, C. (1981). *Stepping lightly.* Minneapolis: CompCare Publications. A humorous book written to give the positive side of stepparenting.

Visher, E.B., and Visher, J.S. (1988). *Old loyalties, new ties.* New York: Brunner/Mazel Publishers. The Vishers, after forming a stepfamily together and researching the dynamics of stepfamily life, saw a need for stepparents to support one another. They formed the Stepfamily Association of America, headquartered in Baltimore, Maryland. They write in the language of researchers, but their material is excellent.

# PARENTING PROGRAMS IN THE CHURCH
*David M. Carder*

"... 'Til death do us part." A familiar phrase, universally associated with marriage, but rarely if ever applied to the role of the parent. Yet parenthood is the longest social relationship on earth. It is the most common—everyone has parents—and one of the easiest to enter. Some would say this relationship is the most emotionally draining, requires the most sacrifice, demands huge amounts of money, causes most of life's frustrations, and at times even ruins the marital relationship that established it. Good parenting requires one to parent differently across the life cycle of the child. And about the time you get it all figured out, they leave home!

This brief chapter will address five questions:

1. What is our target, or goal—i.e., what does a healthy family look like?
2. Why should the church get involved in parent training?
3. What exactly is parenting?
4. How can the church assist its parents in their task?
5. Where can the church and its parents turn for help?

## OUR GOAL: WHAT DOES A HEALTHY FAMILY LOOK LIKE?

In designing and executing a parent-training program in the church, we need to have in mind our target or goal: that of fostering better parenting skills and ultimately more healthy families in general. If we do not keep this goal keenly focused and ever before us, we will end up expending a lot of energy in programming and "busyness" without necessarily achieving our purposes.

What does a healthy family look like? Family researchers have studied this rather elusive question and have collected some findings that will help us in our task. The following two models have proven helpful and will be reassuring to parents as they apply them to individual situations.

**Parenting Activity**

University of Minnesota researchers were interested in what kinds of parenting patterns best fostered the following four qualities in children:

1. *Self-respect*—a strong sense of self-worth in the child;
2. *Conventionalization*—an appropriate sense of conformity to authority figures;
3. *Religiosity*—the degree to which the child has accepted his/her parents' religious values and practices;
4. *Counterculture*—the degree to which the child chooses behaviors contrary to his/her parents' values.

Further research led them to identify four types of parenting patterns along two common axes: control and support. *Control* was defined as "the ability of parents to manage a child's behavior" and *support* was defined as "the ability to make the child feel loved."

The following chart shows us how *control* and *support* axes interact to produce four distinct patterns. Those parents who scored low in support and low in control researchers called *neglectful*; those low in support but high in control they called *au-*

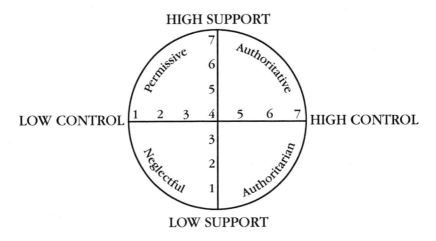

*thoritarian*. Those high in control and high in support they called *authoritative;* those high in support but low in control they called *permissive.*[1]

The following table demonstrates the results of this research. On the left side are the kinds of adolescent behavior under study. On the right side are the parenting patterns, which appear in order of how often each surfaced within that category of adolescent behavior (e.g., the negligent and authoritarian parenting patterns produced the most counterculture adolescents; e.g., the authoritarian and permissive parenting patterns produced the most adolescents who followed their parents' religious values, etc.).

## Study Results

| Adolescent Behavior | Parenting Patterns |
|---|---|
| Identification with counterculture | 1. authoritarian and neglectful |
| | 2. permissive |
| | 3. authoritative |
| Religiosity | 1. authoritative |
| | 2. permissive |
| | 3. neglectful |
| | 4. authoritarian |
| Self-worth | 1. authoritative |
| | 2. permissive |
| | 3. authoritarian |
| | 4. neglectful |
| Conformity to Authority | 1. authoritative |
| | 2. permissive |
| | 3. neglectful |
| | 4. authoritarian |

It is fairly obvious that high control and high amounts of support are significant predictors that children will follow in their parents' footsteps and family values. Parents can evaluate their own (and their spouse's) behaviors along each of these axes. In time, they can also ask their older children for their opinions.

### Family Atmosphere

In another study, two qualities surfaced as being of major importance in helping family atmosphere: a quality of support called *cohesion* on the horizontal axis and a quality of control called *adaptability* on the vertical axis. This form of evaluation has ten specific questions, in two classes of five questions each. Family members can rate their families on the basis of their own perceptions and place them somewhere on this circumplex chart. Remember, perceptions will be somewhat different from family member to family member.

*Family Cohesion:*
Circle the number that you feel best describes your family.

1. How *close* do you feel to other family members?
   1) not very close 2) generally close 3) very close 4) extremely close
2. How often does your family spend free time together?
   1) seldom 2) sometimes 3) often 4) very often
3. How does your family balance separateness and togetherness?
   1) mainly separateness 2) more separateness than togetherness
   3) more togetherness than separateness 4) mainly togetherness
4. How *independent* or *dependent* are family members?
   1) very independent 2) more independent than dependent
   3) more dependent than independent 4) very dependent
5. Answer either part A or part B:
   A. For married couples: How *close* are the husband and wife?
      1) seldom close 2) somewhat close 3) very close 4) extremely close
   B. For single-parent families: How *close* is the parent to another adult?
      1) seldom close 2) somewhat close 3) very close 4) extremely close

Add your responses to the five questions to get a **Total Cohesion Score:** _____

*Family Flexibility:*
Circle the number that you feel best describes your family.

1. What kind of leadership is there in your family?
   1) one person usually leads 2) leadership is sometimes shared
   3) leadership is shared 4) no clear leader
2. How often do individual family members end up *doing the*

*same kinds of things* (roles) around the house?
1) always 2) often 3) sometimes 4) seldom
3. What are the *rules* (written or unwritten) like in your family?
1) rules very clear and very stable 2) rule clear and stable 3) rules clear and flexible 4) rules seldom clear and change often
4. How is *discipline of children* handled?
1) very strict 2) somewhat democratic 3) democratic 4) very lenient
5. How open is your family to making *changes* when they appear necessary?
1) seldom open 2) somewhat open 3) generally open 4) very open

Add your responses to the five questions to get a **Total Flexibility Score:** _____

Now, using your point total for each scale, locate your perception of your family pattern on the following chart.[2]

# Family Map

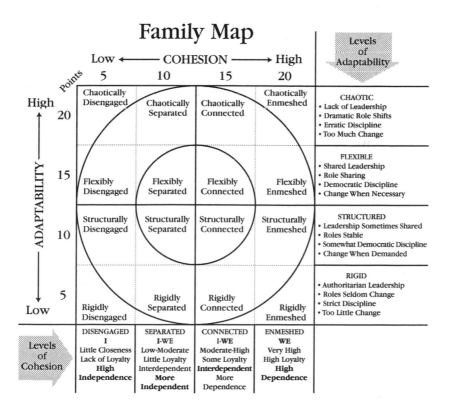

The more "centered" the family is, the better it usually functions across the family life cycle. If scores within a family cluster are in a certain area, members can then begin to talk about how they would like to move in another direction. What would it take to effect change? How they would do it? What kind of new interactions would that involve? Using each other's scores on the same ten questions, they can identify specific directions and behaviors they want to implement in their family.

## WHY SHOULD THE CHURCH GET INVOLVED?

Approximately half of America's children will grow up in homes in which one of their biological parents is missing. Within that group, many will grow up in a single-parent home. Other children will develop in blended families that take three to five years to bond after the remarriage of the adults. Besides those missing a biological parent, other children will grow up in abusive homes filled with substance use, physical beatings, sexual molestation, and angry emotional reactions. Since most of us parent as we have been parented, it is no wonder that this less-than-ideal cycle repeats itself. To break that pattern, the church must take an active role in helping its young couples both prior to and during their parenting task.

Any church plan for a parent-training program should provide some recovery resources for the adult children of alcoholic and dysfunctional families. Sometimes such help is beyond the ability of a small congregation. However, community resources and other churches can help meet this need. Most parents will tell you that they have done or said the very things to their children that they promised themselves they would *never* do. Painful childhoods often etch painful parenting practices deep in one's subconscious mind. We repeat them automatically without much thinking later on. Pain-free parenting requires healing from the painful parenting one might have received.

Many couples, after an adolescent and young adult absence from the church, begin to return to the pews upon the news of a pregnancy or after a recent birth. In this generation, extended families are often not available for support, so the young couple is bewildered and in need of both peer support and information.

They are about to begin a lifelong task for which they have had little if any preparation. Of all the transitions in life, new parenting might be the most teachable moment.

Two additional influences will impact both the content and style of any church's parent-training program. Though highly influential, these concepts are difficult to identify. Awareness is at least a start, and both at the planning stage of the program and within each marriage, a discussion is necessary about two key ideas. I've dubbed these two concepts "the God-parent" (God as father/parent) and "the pastor-parent" (the pastor as parenting role model):

1. What is the church's perception of *God as a parent?*
2. What kind of parenting pattern does the *pastor-parent* himself portray in his own family living and in his teachings from the pulpit as he "parents" the congregation?

## WHAT EXACTLY IS PARENTING?

Good parenting contains some of the following practices:

- It is a relationship with the child that exercises appropriate parenting skills.
- It is a practice that meets age-appropriate needs.
- It is a process, not a product.
- It is an environment, not just a list of "dos" and "don'ts."

Four concepts appear to be significant factors in healthy family patterns:

1. The parents' *aptitude* for flexibility.
2. The parents' *attitude* toward their parenting task.
3. The parents' *ability* to bond emotionally with each child at various stages of the life cycle.
4. The parents' *appropriate* use of control.

### Parental Flexibility

Within each family system the influence of age abounds. The first child often experiences a very different family than the last child. Research indicates that a five-year gap between births starts the birth order influence over. Career paths of parents—even the task of caring for aging grandparents—all require immense flexibility. Family systems that are always "doing more of the same" (i.e., parenting dysfunctionally, as they were parented) in their

163

well-intentioned but misguided search for consistency, appear to injure, not help, their children.

Flexibility is required on the part of the parents as they themselves age in their parenting process. You can't parent the same in your mid-forties as you did in your mid-twenties. Just the diminished strength with increased responsibilities requires flexibility.

The child himself is in an active developmental process and needs flexible parenting patterns during the years he is in the home. A parent-training program must stay focused on this truth. The child needs different kinds of parenting at different stages in her life.

Flexible parents must adapt to the different personality patterns of each child within their family. Parents, further along in the process, support the notion that one of the "tricks" to good parenting is to be able to identify your child's personality pattern early on in the process.

Finally, flexibility is required to cope with the culture we live in, where change is the only constant. *This is not your father's Oldsmobile,* as the car ad slogan goes.

### Parental Attitude

Spousal differences in attitude toward parenting purpose and tasks are important to identify. All partners in a marriage come with their own perceptions toward the parent role. Some want to enjoy their children; others feel the need to control and reshape what they consider a rebellious bent in their child. Still others want to re-experience their own lost childhood. Unfortunately, few parents develop original attitudes toward the parenting process but instead bring with them the patterns from their families of origin.

Each spouse should be aware of felt responsibility levels. The key question here is, "How responsible do you feel for how this child turns out?" Not only might the spouses disagree between themselves, but this level of felt responsibility changes over the course of several births in the family. First-time parents invariably rate themselves at a nine or ten (one is low, ten is high). Third-time parents are definitely inclined toward the low end of the scale. They have come to realize that many other influences besides their parenting skills impact their child's development. They are not as much in control of the outcome of this process as they once thought. Identification of these attitudes is very important to young parents.

## Ability to Bond Emotionally

Many factors influence the bonding that takes place between parents and their newborn child. Some, such as the child's health, the mother's postpartum health, the couple's financial and medical resources, and the support of extended family systems, are beyond most churches' capacity to influence. But a parent-training program can include specific ways for the caregivers to bond with this infant, such as gentle holding, verbal and visual stimulation, and pleasant tone of voice. This attachment will help the child meet developmental tasks critical at each stage in his young life. Consistent nurturing given by consistent caregivers generates basic trust—which is foundational to healthy development.

## Appropriate Use of Control Measures

At least three factors come into play in the area of control/discipline that should be built into any parent-training program that the church wants to offer:

1. Tolerance of the child's individuality—that is, not all children need the same thing.
2. Awareness of the child's varying needs and developmental tasks across the family life cycle.
3. Anger management skills for the parents. This includes managing their own anger at the child's behavior and also specific ways to manage the child's anger. Children are not miniature adults. They have no experience with life. If adults themselves have difficulty with control issues, it is easy to understand why children do too.

## HOW CAN THE CHURCH ASSIST ITS PARENTS IN THEIR TASK?

Churches that incorporate parent-training programs into their ministry may use any of a number of models discussed here.

## General Information[3]

This appears to be the most common model, especially in small or rapidly growing churches that haven't yet stabilized their parent-training programs. The program is generalized and takes advantage of whatever specialist or speaker happens to be in the area. It has little organized or structured curriculum and no cyclical training for parents. Parent-training programs are offered through a variety of departments (i.e., the preschool program, the children's department, the youth department) and no one individual holds responsibility for the parent-training program. This is not to say that it is not effective; every little bit helps Here, though, parenting is often seen as a series of right techniques as opposed to a consistent pattern, finely-tuned for a specific age.

## Formal Skill Training[4]

In this model a church chooses a curriculum and repeats it on a cyclical basis throughout the calendar year. This approach has many advantages, such as a consistent teaching base to which can be added a number of additional concepts and adjunct programs. Predictable scheduling is helpful for parents' long-range plans. Teacher recruitment is easier, and a shared knowledge base makes for better interaction between parents. Weaknesses include a tendency to see only one "right way," that it requires too much conformity, and that it makes the instructor the "specialist"—a role in which he or she might not feel comfortable.

## Targeted Need[5]

No formal cyclical curriculum exists in this model. Many parents' needs are identified through regular surveys. Because it is niche-marketed and need-driven, response is good. It is an excellent model to use where *target concerns* are identified. However, as a model for parent training, it can be crisis-oriented—not the best approach from an overall perspective. Other downsides include the fact that it does not develop a consistent base of knowledge; it is overly dependent on technique; and it is highly dependent upon the skills and knowledge base of the presenter.

## Age Specific[6]

These are five- to seven-week presentations focused on specific needs of a certain age group of children. It combines available specialists with a specific course outline. The actual training is less formal than in the formal skill training model. The advantage is that it requires parents to step out of their own adult fellowship for a shorter period of time, and requires less intense commitment, (five to seven weeks as compared to twelve to fifteen weeks for the formal skill training model.) It also allows more time in the parent-training track to incorporate other *target concerns* if any arises. Some problems are that the internal consistency of each course offering is not high due to the change of instructors; the lack of written curriculum; and the impact for change of parenting patterns in the home might be rather limited because of the short time frame in which the class is offered.

### Target Concerns Curriculum

These are brief courses (five to ten weeks) that can be built into any church's training program either through an elective curriculum, weekend seminar, video presentation, or week-night program. Courses like these help alleviate the ever-growing counseling ministry demanded of the pastoral staff. They foster networking among parents facing similar issues in their parenting process and encourage confidence in the church as a place that understands and attempts to meet families' daily needs.

### Parental Anger[7]

New converts have often come out of painfully abusive and angry homes. Even though they have found Christ in their personal lives, their parenting tasks will often provoke some of that old anger and hurt. This model attempts to address those needs.

### Sibling Issues[8]

Here birth order concepts, ways to manage interaction among siblings, and helps for developing individual talents will be the emphasis. Identification of normal sibling interactions will help many parents relax. The resulting lowered tensions will keep parents from using shameful messages. Finally, sorting out family rules and roles will bolster the child's budding sense of self-esteem.

### Faith Development[9]

A child's ability to trust in God has a developmental process just as does his or her verbal ability, physical skills, and mental cognition. Most Christian parents sense this, but they are uncertain how to foster it. They want to know more about how to nurture faith and to normalize its involvement in the child's daily life; the church has many answers for them. As the parents foster and model an atmosphere in the home where prayer, Bible reading, and Christian living are valued, they will find their children better equipped to face life. Parents should not overemphasize these practices slavishly or legalistically; rather, they should focus on natural discussions with their children of those instances where faith intersects daily life. Thus they will foster the understanding that *faith fits every moment of every day,* and avoid the aberrant notion of faith-for-Sundays-only (a concept which, though believers would rarely if ever consciously endorse, is nonetheless widely held).

### Childhood Temperament/Personality Patterns[10]

Though sometimes parents are tempted to think otherwise, one of the great truths of Christianity is that no child is an accident. Each one is individually woven together in his mother's womb by the hand of Jehovah. Learning to go with the child's "bent" and attempting to understand his or her personality goes a long way toward good interaction in the parenting process.

### Molestation Prevention[11]

Unfortunately it is a sign of our times that child molestation occurs with frightening frequency in the church. The increasingly stringent standards placed on schools and scouting organizations, make them less of a safe haven for pedophiles, who are migrating to the church. We must train our children to recognize inappropriate behavior and how to say no. Sometimes our most fundamental Christian teachings to kids—e.g., respect of authority, that adults are good and that they care for you—predispose children to abusive experiences. We in the church need to recognize the threat within our gates.

### Divorce Recovery for Children[12]

Five- to ten-week courses help children better understand and express their feelings over their parents' divorce. The program needs separate tracks for elementary and early adolescent ages. Smaller churches can participate in a community-wide program. Though current research indicates that divorce is almost always damaging to children, some symptom alleviation is achieved by being able to talk about it, being able to mix with other children who are going through it, and by learning to not blame oneself as the primary cause of the split.

# WHERE CAN THE CHURCH
# AND ITS PARENTS TURN FOR HELP?

## Available Resources

Although a church might not be able to offer a complete curriculum of parent training, it can provide numerous resources to improve its parent training in whatever form it exists.

1. *Small group parenting fellowship.* These social connections, built around a shared spot in the family life cycle, encourage parents to share their stresses and to draw support from each other. In groups like these, specific target concerns can be shared and resources disseminated. For parents, the sense of "fit" comes from the shared age of the children in the group, not the age of the parents. A new small group may need to be formed when most couples in the current group have had their first conception (about every five years or so).

2. *Church-wide resources.* Most churches can provide some sort of check-out library that includes books, tapes, video series, etc. It is helpful if bibliographies are annotated. Parents should be kept abreast of recent acquisitions for the library. Leaders can also circulate brochures of local conferences, speakers, and seminars that would be supportive to their congregants.

3. *Media resources.* Radio and TV often have helpful programming in this area. Some of it will be more biblically sound than others, but advance notification of forthcoming specials will be helpful to parents and will demonstrate their church's concern for their parenting task.

4. *Community resources.* Educational institutions, social services, and hospitals all offer various parent training and support groups. In smaller churches especially, it is important to identify what the community offers parents. Some secular parenting curricula have been available for years and provide many good skills for parents.

5. *Professional referral list for parents.* Every family could benefit from some individualized and focused help when in transition and crisis. Each church can provide a list of professionals in the area. Some Christian organizations such as Focus on the Family,[13] The American Association of Christian Counselors,[14] and Christian Association of Psychological

169

Studies[15] may provide referrals to members of their organizations; check with them.

6. *Surrogate extended family systems.* Some larger churches are able to offer surrogate grandparenting support and other kinds of intergenerational opportunities. Older individuals separated geographically from their own grandchildren often welcome the opportunity to be surrogate grandparents. We should establish appropriate boundaries and guidelines to make it safe for both parties. In smaller churches this can be encouraged on an informal and individual basis.

## Necessary Ingredients

Six ingredients surfaced in a recent survey of churches which offered parenting programs. They are not necessarily listed in order of importance, nor do all ingredients need to be incorporated as a group in the design stage of the parent-training program.

1. *Relief for moms.* The primary caregiver needs relief. Options could be a Dad's Day/Mother's Day Out[16] or Mothers of Preschoolers (M.O.P.S.),[17] a program allowing moms to get away and take care of other household needs and themselves, while child care is provided for a half or full day.

2. *Parent training curricula* need to include specific educational/informational and behavioral content. Parents' training time is too limited to focus on the motivational aspect alone. It needs some go-home-and-try-this stuff.

3. *Child care* must be provided for any parent-training program. Several respondents to the survey said that this is the one ingredient that, if neglected, will sabotage the attendance and benefit received.

4. Parent training will be most effective if done within *"normal" or "usual" training times* (Sunday mornings, evenings, or Wednesday evenings) at church, as opposed to unusual or additional weekday times. This minimizes any embarrassing stigma (e.g., "I must be a bad parent if I have to attend parenting classes") and boosts attendance.

5. *Resources must also be available on an as-needed basis,* not only when the church is open. An example would be by phone, during evening hours when dads are home, and during relief periods mentioned in item 1 above (e.g., M.O.P.S.).

6. *Self-care.* A physically exhausted and emotionally deprived

parent is not much good to anyone. Permission to care for one's self, encouragement, and instruction need to be provided to parents during this difficult period of time.

Families want and need help, the church can help, and resources are available to help. In the next decade there will be major efforts on the part of local churches to train their congregant parents in practical, biblical parenting patterns and skills.

## Notes

1. For more information, see Eisenman, T. (1985), *Big people, little people:A course for parents of young children.* Elgin, IL: David C. Cook.

2. Family Circumplex Scales developed by David H. Olson, Ph.D., Professor, Family Social Sciences, Univ. of Minnesota and President of PREPARE/ENRICH, PO Box 190, Minneapolis, MN 55440-0190. © 1992 PREPARE/ENRICH Life Innovations, Inc.

3. For additional information and sample curriculum on the general information model, contact The Vineyard, 5340 E. La Palma Ave., Anaheim, CA 92807.

4. For additional information and sample curriculum on the formal skill training model, contact Saddleback Community Church, 23456 Madero, Ste. 100, Mission Viejo, CA 92691.

5. For additional information and sample curriculum on the targeted need model, contact Willow Creek Community Church, 67 E. Algonquin Rd., South Barrington, IL 60010.

6. For additional information and sample curriculum on the age-specific model, contact Family Ministries Director, First Evangelical Free Church of Fullerton, 2801 N. Brea Blvd., Fullerton, CA 92645.

7. For additional information and sample of curriculum on anger resolution, contact Kathy Miller, PO Box 1058, Placentia, CA 92670. Kathy's book, *The angry heart,* may be ordered from the author.

8. For more information, see Kevin Lehman (1985), *The birth order book: Why you are the way you are.* Old Tappan, NJ: Fleming H. Revell.

171

9. For more information, see James W. Fowler, et al. (eds.) (1991), *Stages of faith & religious development: Implications for church, education & society.* New York: Crossroad.

10. For more information, see J. Brauner, with D. Jaenicke (1991), *Connections: Using personality types to draw parents and kids closer.* Chicago: Moody Press.

11. For more information, see William Katz (1984), *Protecting your children from sexual assault* with Lyn Heitritter, *Little ones activity workbook.* Young America, MN: n.p.

12. For more information, see Suzy Yehl Marta, *Rainbows for all God's children.* (Schaumburg, IL: Rainbows, Bumblebees & Me Publishers).

13. For further information, contact Focus on the Family, 420 N. Cascade, Colorado Springs, CO 80903.

14. For further information, contact the A.A.C.C. (American Association of Christian Counselors), 242 W. Pratt, Ste. 1398, Chicago, IL 60645.

15. For further information, contact C.A.P.S. (Christian Association for Psychological Studies), PO Box 310400, New Braunfels, TX 78131-0400.

16. For further information on Mother's Day Out, contact First Evangelical Free Church, Children's Ministry Director, 2801 N. Brea Blvd., Fullerton, CA 92635-2799.

17. For further information on M.O.P.S., contact Mothers Of Pre-Schoolers International, 1311 S. Clarkson, Denver, CO 80210.

## For Further Reading

Cataoldo, C. (1987). *Parent education for early childhood.* R. Honeycutt (Ed.) New York: Teachers' College Press. Published posthumously by an internationally recognized early childhood authority, this work is designed for the student in training and professional practitioner in early childhood education. Besides a good review of early childhood development, several chapters are devoted to working with parent education to maximize this rapid growth period of the child's life.

Dangel, R., and Polster, R. (Eds.). (1984). *Parent training: Foundational research and practice.* New York: Guilford Press. A review of fourteen major parenting programs ranging from normal situations to specialized applications for abusive parents, autistic, non-compliant and children with disabilities.

Ganahl, A. (1994) *Parenting: Does research support biblical principles? A review of the literature.* Psy. D., Rosemead School of Psychology. People setting out to structure a parent-education program for their church would do well to reflect on the four parenting concepts surveyed in this brief review of literature. Ganahl combs sixteen empirical studies (within four areas of nurturance, discipline, individual differences of siblings, and parental modeling) and finds helpful patterns applicable to the establishment of church-based programs.

Honeycutt, R., and Culpepper, A. (Eds.). (1983). *Review and expositor, 80*(2). This entire volume is devoted to the religious development of children. Though somewhat dated, a number of excellent contributions are still worth reading for the professional interested in establishing parenting programs in the church.

Oeffling, S. (1988). *The influence of church parent training on the self-esteem of preadolescent children.* D. Min., Biola. A well-thought-out, practical, and statistically supported parent-training program focusing on self-esteem improvement for a broad-age range of children. Includes a course outline broken down by class session, evaluation forms, and suggested readings for parents. In short, everything a local church would need to get started in at least one area of parent education.

Sell, C. (1991). *Transitions through adult life.* Grand Rapids: Zondervan Publishing House. A good review of adult development written in lay terms and designed for general reading and education. Draws widely from the field, has a good bibliography, but does not explore much new ground on adult education. A wealth of necessary information for those who work with adults and their children.

# REACHING FAMILIES THROUGH THEIR CHILDREN
*Jody Capehart*

As Christian educators and leaders, our endeavor is to reach families for the kingdom. This chapter will look at one of the most effective ways of reaching families, through ministering to their children.

## THE IMPORTANCE OF THE FAMILY UNIT

The importance of families cannot be overestimated. Yet many families today are not the safe havens we once thought they could be. Survey after survey indicates that Americans say families stand at the top of their priority list. So why do statistics reflect a different picture? "The first portrait of marriage and family in the church that emerges reveals that nearly three in four (73 percent) of our kids live with both mother and father; about one in four (23 percent) are the children of divorced parents. Thirteen percent of our kids live in single-parent homes and 1 percent live with both a stepfather and a stepmother" (McDowell, 1987, p. 282).

## A LOOK AT THE FAMILY TODAY

We do not have to look far to see what is happening to children and families today: the message bombards us from every direction. Pick up any newspaper or magazine and you will see the results of the stress-induced society in which we live. Dr. David Elkind addresses this issue in his book, *The Hurried Child* (1981): "Today's child has become the unwilling, unintended victim of overwhelming stress" (p. 3). For too many children, the time of innocence is short-lived. The indications of this reality loom all around us:

- Nine-year-old Susan is very withdrawn. She does not participate with other children as she used to. Further investigation shows that her father sexually abuses her on a regular basis.
- A newborn baby in the church nursery suffers from the effects of her mother's alcohol abuse.
- Security policies for all paid and unpaid workers in the church are becoming the norm not the exception, because of the increase in abuse to children.

This paradigm shift in stress crosses all educational and economic lines; it does not just affect the poor and uneducated. Stress may come from a different cause, but its manifestations are very similar.

Seven-year-old Caroline lives in a home of parents who seem to pour their lives and funds into helping her be the best she can. She is enrolled in ballet on Monday, gymnastics on Tuesday, attends church programs on Wednesday, piano on Thursday, and French classes on Friday. Saturdays are consumed with games and other competitive events related to these many programs. Caroline is having trouble sleeping at night. She seems irritable and cries easily. Her parents wonder, "Why?" They work so hard to provide every advantage for their child.

In many homes children learn more from television than from their parents. As Robert De Moss states, "The latest research shows that 98 percent of the homes in America have television and 96 percent of the homes have indoor bathrooms—which goes to show that there is more garbage going in than going out" (a speech given in Sacramento, California for CLASS on October 14, 1994).

## THE MEDIA'S PORTRAYAL OF THE FAMILY

The media present a view of life often antithetical to the Christian worldview. The barrier lines between secular views and those held by Christians once tended to be distinct; yet today those distinctions are becoming blurred. For example, 80 percent of all

4th- through 6th-grade private school children surveyed indicated they had watched the sexually explicit *Porky* films and/or the *Nightmare on Elm Street* type horror films. All the movies in these series are rated R. Children raised on death will be less sympathetic to death issues such as abortion or euthanasia. Why should they be compassionate when they enjoy seeing people getting killed? (De Moss, 1992).

What is the impact of media on our children today? How can we counteract such a powerful medium of communication? How can we be instruments to help children discern right from wrong? How can we be more effective in reaching children and, in so doing, try to reach their families as well?

## MAKING CHILDREN THE FOCUS OF OUR MINISTRY

James Dobson and Gary Bauer write in *Children at Risk* (1990, p. 46) that there is a "civil war of values" raging today for the hearts, minds, and souls of our children. If children are the target for the enemy, then we the church should aim for the same target. The Great Commission crosses all denominational barriers. The mandate is clear: "Go into all the world and preach the gospel to all creation" (Mark 16:15).

If we place the child at the center of the target, we can begin to move out in concentric circles to embrace the family. First, let's see what we can do to reach families *within* our churches.

177

## REACHING FAMILIES WITHIN THE CHURCH

### Providing Programs with Excellence

Excellence begins by providing godly role models who teach in children's programs. Do your programs meet the following criteria based upon Deuteronomy 6:4 12?

1. A love for God that permeates all life experiences.
2. Meaningful activities for children to learn spiritual truth.
3. A supportive atmosphere that helps the child learn and practice acceptable behavior.
4. A purpose to grow into spiritual maturity.
5. Training in developing and living a godly worldview in all that we say and do.

### Programming to Meet a Variety of Needs

A variety of programs may be needed within the church to reach the differing needs in our congregations. Most churches provide Sunday School and children's church programs. Perhaps we need to consider providing a program for children with special learning needs as well. Or consider providing an intergenerational program to include the whole family in Bible study. The options are as many as the special needs of each congregation.

As part of the goal of outreach, many churches provide such programs as AWANA or Pioneer Clubs on a weekly basis. As we reach children of parents outside the church, we seek to find ways to reach their parents as well. One effective tool is to provide parent classes or support groups while the child attends a club program.

We must be careful not to assume that church members are born again and living the Christian life. Many who have trusted Christ and now walk with God still face struggles and problems. Let's reach out to those needs first. What are some of the needs we find in the church today?

Many Christians choose to believe that the grim statistics describing our society in general and the family in particular will not impact the church. We were led to believe there was a safe distance between our Christian worldview (and subsequent lifestyle), and that of the world. But the "frog in the kettle" paradigm shift has desensitized us to a degree in facing the stark reality of today's statistics.

## Family Values in the Nineties

A *Newsweek* magazine story responded to the "family values" debate in the 1992 U.S. presidential election with a fold-out cover that trumpeted: "*Whose* values? *Whose* family? *Who* makes the choices?" *Newsweek's* questions echo Stephen L. Carter's dilemma: where are the "settled rules by which to determine ... truth" in the areas of marriage and family? (McDowell, 1994, p. 187) Josh McDowell's comprehensive study of youth from evangelical homes shows that an amazing 57 percent cannot affirm that an objective standard for right and wrong even exists (1994, p. 193). His program *Right from Wrong* offers no quick fix, but does meet the needs head on. It is simply a thorough, biblical, and practical blueprint for understanding moral absolutes and passing on core values to the next generation.

## The Effect of Divorce

The statistics on families affected by divorce continue to cause concern in the Christian community as well. "The divorce rate has climbed from 9.2 (per 1,000 married women) in 1960 to 20.9 in 1991, a 120 percent jump. Within that same period, the percentage of children who live with single mothers has rocketed from 8 percent to 22 percent (an increase of 175 percent) while births to unwed mothers have increased from 5.3 percent (of total births) in 1960 to 28 percent in 1990 (a leap of 400 percent)" (Cromartie, 1993, p. 32). Churches must deal with this reality. What can we do to reach out to the single parent, the blended family, and the child from a broken home? One of the most effective ways we can minister to these people is to provide support groups. Groups that begin within the church for single parents or blended families quickly attract the needy and hurting from outside the church community.

## REACHING BOTH WITHIN AND OUTSIDE THE CHURCH

By addressing a specific need—such as the resulting pain of divorce—we can help. The exciting aspect of this ministry is that as we seek to equip those *within* the church and give them tools to strengthen their walk with the Lord, we begin to reach those *outside* the church.

### The Strength of Support Groups

Aggressive churches utilize a number of support groups to reach those within the congregation as well as those outside:

1. Children with Attention Deficit Disorder
2. Mothers of Preschoolers (MOPS)
3. Blended families
4. Children of alcoholics
5. Homeschooling families
6. Parents without partners
7. Parenting before and after work

Through support groups we have crossed the barrier of the second concentric circle, which represents those on the periphery of a church family. They may come for a support group or a special event, but are not a part of the active, believing congregation.

In addition to groups, how else can we minister to them through their children? Three kinds of programs fall into this category:

1. Annual events such as Vacation Bible School.
2. Events held on a regular basis such as Bible clubs, latch key kids ministry, bus ministry, Awana, and Pioneer Clubs.
3. On-going programs such as elementary schools, child care, or Mother's Day Out.

These programs can become a way for children to break out of the bondage of their world and begin to bond to people who can lead them to Jesus Christ. Satan desires that the family remain in a state of bondage. Church leaders must find ways to help people break free of these ties.

### Annual Events

Historically, Vacation Bible School has its roots in teaching the Bible and sharing the Gospel with children on the streets. It was clearly established as an evangelistic outreach program. "The program lasted for two hours each day and included worship, music, Bible stories drawing, Bible memorization, nature study, marching games, and exercises, salutes to the flag, and handwork, even cooking and sewing for the girls. For seven years Mrs. Hawes conducted her program for unchurched children" (Daniel, 1984, p. 10). If we keep the same clear focus, VBS can continue to be that kind of tool.

In my ministry experience, I noticed that the majority of children attending Vacation Bible School programs were coming from *within* some church. In fact, many children attended several Bible

School programs at different churches. While this provides a wonderful opportunity to reach children with the Gospel and disciple those who know the Lord, it does not fulfill the original purpose of VBS to the degree that it could.

## Taking VBS into the Neighborhoods

Churches can be more effective if we make a concerted effort to go into neighborhoods where there are unchurched families and extend invitations to VBS. We may need to provide transportation to bring these children to the church. Since some families have a parent who could come to VBS, we may want to provide a class on parenting or a "neutral" subject such as crafts. Many may need this level of entry into the church structure. A Bible study may be more than they can handle at the initial phase and would be better received later.

In our search to find the most effective way to provide a VBS program that truly reached more children for the kingdom, we explored alternatives to the traditional VBS program. We looked at where the real need existed, and we found it in the inner city as well as apartment complexes all around the metroplex. As we researched this further, we saw that many churches had targeted the inner city, but few were addressing the need in the apartment complexes. We began with those within one mile of our church and then we continued outward. The needs in our own neighborhood staggered us. We found hundreds of children left alone all day to care for themselves while their parents worked. One of the most frightening aspects of this truth is what agent was being left to baby-sit these children: television.

A 1991 survey revealed that only 2 percent of respondents think that television should have the greatest influence on children's values, but 56 percent believe that it *does* have the greatest influence—more than parents, teachers, and religious leaders combined (seminar notes, Robert De Moss).

## Developing Ministry Focus

Our ministry began to take on a focus—the apartments—and a clear target—the children. In most of the complexes we found children with little or no parental supervision. After much prayer, we decided to take the VBS program to the children. We began by doing a Five-Day Club with curriculum provided by Child Evangelism Fellowship. Most of the apartment managers were very guarded about letting us come in and would only allow the club to meet in a parking lot. But the children came and the clubs grew. We had varied responses at the different complexes. In one complex adults came to listen as well. Parents and children trusted the Lord and began to attend our church.

At a complex which had a much more challenging group of children, we didn't see the fruit that week. With them, we began a Homework Club that continued one day a week after school in the club house all year. We gradually began incorporating some of the children into our Wednesday Night Club Programs. With another, we began a CEF Good News Club that continued all year. We had varying degrees of success, but the common denominator in each was that children accepted the Lord. We targeted the children, and in some cases discovered families who came to our church as a result.

### Cross-cultural Challenges

An interesting dilemma began as a result of our new ministry: the cross-cultural differences between the children who regularly attended our church and those whom we were inviting. Their worlds were so far apart. While our junior girls discussed lip gloss, the girls we bused in talked about who was drunk last night and who slept with whom.

Now we had a new area of ministry to address. We had to find common denominators and help them learn to love one another in Christ. We prayed that our own church children would learn how to be more accepting and tolerant of cultural differences. We prayed that God would use this training to equip them to be more effective in reaching those from outside their comfort zone for Jesus Christ. In order to reach the families, we first had to learn how to build bridges with the children. What an excellent training ground this became to provide first-hand missionary experience for our children!

### Holiday Events as Outreach

The fall provides a splendid time for churches to reach out into the community with such events as fall festivals and craft fairs. While the primary focus of these events is usually more social and practical, there are ways to use them as outreach tools as well. Some churches distribute tracts or church brochures listing other programs. As people find out about your ministry programs, especially those that address specific issues such as single parenting, they may return. Many people who are not comfortable coming to church for a service will come to an event. This can be a way of opening the door to reach them through other avenues.

## A Gift for the Community

At our church we have also added a December program called "The Joy of Sharing Christmas." We invite schools to come during the day, and the evenings are open to everyone. We start with caroling, then give a walking tour through four scenes from the Christmas story. At each the Gospel is woven in through live drama. It is very effective to hear the shepherds talking around the fire beside real sheep. Or to hear the wise men discussing the Messiah outside under the stars.

At the end the children go into one room to decorate cookies and play games while the adults are ushered into a room beautifully decorated with lovely homemade Christmas goodies. They can stay and visit with those in the church family as long as they want. For many, this is an avenue into church which they find easier to use.

As they begin to feel cared for and develop relationships, families will be more likely to attend on a Sunday morning. The point is that we provide many different doors into the church to reach people. Often people will come to a special event such as a fall carnival, a holiday bazaar, or a live Christmas presentation because they think their children would enjoy it. Often the children get the parents to the event.

## Summer Programs

Summer programs also provide avenues to reach children effectively:
1. Day camps
2. Choir camps
3. Resident camps.

Parents may need child care and see a camp as a positive solution. A church committed to providing an excellent program for children in all respects can begin to draw in families. When parents see their children happy, well cared for, and challenged to grow, they have a secure feeling about the church that provided the program. What a wonderful avenue to help reach the family as a whole.

## Ongoing Outreach Programs for Children

Many churches use specially written programs, such as Awana and Pioneer Clubs, to meet this need. These programs are designed to encourage outsiders to come. Child Evangelism Fellowship has designed Good News Clubs that can be taught at the church or in local neighborhoods.

To see which programs fit best in your church, look to where the needs are. It has been said that the secret of success is to find a need and meet it with excellence. Here's an example of a need.

The statistics on latchkey kids are alarming. In *Children's Ministry That Works* (1993, p. 203), Jolene L. Roehlkepartain writes: "The National Education Association reports that 2.1 million kids go home to an empty house after school. When child development researcher Hyman Rodman surveyed 709 kids, he found many are alone after school. The percentage of kids who go home to an empty house:

50% of 9 year olds
70% of 10 year olds
82% of 11 year olds
76 % of 12 year olds."

## Providing Child Care

Your church can provide care for children who would otherwise be home alone. But successful day care programs require essential planning:

1. Determine if there is a need.
2. State the purpose.
3. See if your facility can handle it.
4. Determine a budget.
5. Find personnel.
6. Find people to attend.
7. Determine the program, schedule, supplies, and transportation.

Examine the needs in your church and community to see which kind of program to provide. You can do this with a formal questionnaire or survey to assess the needs and/or by having a meeting with interested people in your congregation. "In a survey of more than 1,500 churches having day-care centers, researchers learned the percentage of these churches that offer the following programs:

| | |
|---|---|
| Preschool program | 96 percent |
| Care of handicapped | 64 percent |
| Toddler program | 45 percent |
| Before/after school | 29 percent |
| Infant program | 29 percent |
| Mothers' program | 28 percent" |

(Roehlkepartain, 1993, p. 200).

## Ongoing Programs for Children

Many churches have found it effective to provide a Mother's Day Out program, child care, a preschool, or elementary school to serve their own congregation as well as the community at large. These provide another excellent way to bring families into the church. Again, as parents trust you with their children, they begin to trust you as an organization. As you gain their trust, you can build upon that foundation. For example, a Mother's Day Out program may provide classes for mothers on different parenting issues. You may also want to provide a package for all new parents that includes a parenting book written from a Christian perspective. As they learn about the practical aspects of parenting, they learn about the Lord as well.

Often the best Gospel we can present is the testimony of our lifestyle. Parents are often too busy trying to survive while holding down a job and trying to maintain a home for their children. They appreciate whatever support we can provide. We can be a real help to them as their children journey down the precarious paths of childhood.

In *Children at Risk* (1990) James Dobson and Gary Bauer ask who will guide children as they walk the ever-increasing challenges of the "corridors of childhood"? Let the church be there for the children and for their families. Let us provide loving people to guide the children, trained teachers to teach them, nurturing and skillful caretakers to care for them, and programs to equip their parents.

The opening sentence of Allan Bloom's book *The Closing of the American Mind* (1987) states, "There is one thing a professor can be absolutely certain of: almost every student entering the university believes, or says he believes, that truth is relative" (p. 25). The worlds of education, media, and music often conflict with the very basics of our Christian faith. Yet our children are being raised in this frightening arena of moral chaos.

There are no "quick fix" answers to the challenges that loom for our society in general and children in particular. The statistics alarm us and serve as a catalyst to motivate us to action. We must look at the root causes for what is happening to our culture today. The polarity of values creates a cross-cultural war, and children are the victims.

The church can be the bridge to build back a society based upon Judeo-Christian values. Yes, the task is great, but we have an even greater God. "Let us hold unswervingly to the hope we profess for He who promised is faithful" (Heb. 10:23). The hope is Jesus Christ. The church is the body to communicate that hope. The children of today are the leaders of tomorrow, and our investment in their lives will reap rich dividends for eternity.


## For Further Reading

Barna, G. (1991). *User friendly churches.* Ventura, CA: Regal Books. This book shows churches how to be more in touch with the needs of those they want to serve. It provides principles that will help you to better develop your own church's strategies for reaching people through your unique ministry.

Choun, R., and Lawson, M. (1993). *The complete handbook of children's ministry.* Nashville: Thomas Nelson Publishers. This is a comprehensive handbook that covers all areas of children's ministry. It provides practical information as well as "how to" helps for developing children's programs.

Dobson, J., and Bauer, G. (1990). *Children at risk.* Dallas: Word Publishing. This book motivates the church to action as we view the children of today and what is happening as a result of the "civil war" raging for the hearts, minds, and souls of our children.

McDowell, J., and Hostetler, R. (1994). *Right from wrong.* Dallas: Word Publishing. This book presents the statistics of what is happening to our young people today as they face a crisis in understanding truth. It provides a biblical and practical blueprint for understanding moral absolutes and passing on core values to the next generation.

Roehlkepartain, J. (Ed.). (1993). *Children's ministry that works.* Loveland, CO: Group Books. This book provides innovative ideas on how to develop successful children's programs that provide outreach opportunities.

St. Clair, B. (1994). *The magnet effect: Designing outreach events that draw kids to Christ.* Wheaton, IL: Victor Books. This book gives practical ideas on creating events designed to draw unchurched kids to Christ. An outreach event planner that walks you through the entire process.

# FIFTEEN

# CHRISTIAN EDUCATION FOR SPECIAL CHILDREN
*Jane Schimmer*

The fact that Christian education should provide for the needs of all children sounds like a foregone conclusion. However, this is not always the case. Many evangelical churches foster Christian schools, serving the family of believers, so it should be logical that these schools serve the needs of Christian families for all children who qualify to attend. By this we mean that these schools, as well as the Christian education programs in churches, to the greatest extent possible, should have programs for all children, including those we would term *exceptional*. The word refers to students whose needs are not satisfied in the regular classroom, either because they have learning deficits and are struggling to meet the norms of the classroom system, or because their capabilities remain unchallenged within the system.

The Gospel reminds us that every individual is of great value to the Heavenly Father. This principle should guide Christian educators as they choose programs and curricula to meet the needs of all students.

## THE EDUCATIONAL MANDATE

Public schools have a mandate which actually fulfills this principle. Public Law 94-142 ensures help for handicapped students within the school system. Further, the Individuals with Disabilities Education Act (IDEA) and Section 504 of the Rehabilitation Act of

1973 provide for appropriate education for children with attention deficit disorders. Among other things, the law spells out the need for classroom modification and the need for access to a resource person.

## THE BIBLICAL MANDATE

The family of believers has an even greater mandate: an expression of the law of love found in Galatians 6:2 and 6:10:

Carry each other's burdens, and in this way you will fulfill the law of Christ. . . . Therefore, as we have opportunity, let us do good to all people, especially to those who belong to the family of believers.

Paul gives us a beautiful picture of the body of Christ and how it should fit together, "just as He wanted them to be. . . . those parts of the body that seem to be weaker are indispensable. . . . If one part suffers, every part suffers with it . . ." (1 Cor. 12:18-26). The idea here indicates coming alongside and helping others bear up under a burden with which they are struggling. In the word *suffer* the root *fer* means to "bear, carry, or bring," and the prefix *sub* or *suf* means "under." We can be God's instruments—His hands to show Himself faithful to their needs. As Christian educators, we should help every child in our care toward maturity and success, giving them "training in righteousness" (2 Tim. 3:16). Then they can be all that God wants them to be, fulfilling His plan for them and His church. We are to be making disciples "thoroughly equipped for every good work." (2 Tim. 3:17) In this positive light and sense of responsibility, accountability, and joy, we approach the task.

## WHO ARE THESE EXCEPTIONAL CHILDREN?

### High Achievers
On one end of this spectrum would be those children who have met no obstacles in their academic life, whose abilities allow them to enjoy the highest achievement in the classroom. These

children need more stimulation and challenge. They must not be frustrated or held back from their goals. Usually these children are called gifted. However, in terms of classroom performance, it might be preferable to refer to them as high achievers. Very often the *learning differenced* child, whom we will discuss, is also gifted, yet not always in ways rewarded in the traditional classrooms of our schools and churches.

## Severely Handicapped

At the other end of the spectrum are children who generally could not function in the traditional classroom. We would call these children severely handicapped. They are the children with emotional disorders or severe physical handicaps and the educable, trainable, or severely mentally retarded. Both the high achievers and the severely handicapped are part of God's family. Children encompassing a wide variety of needs will be found in every local family of believers. Progressive Christian educators must determine what is possible in terms of serving these children in churches and Christian schools.

We can more easily provide for the high achiever than the severely handicapped child. However, expertise in teaching and accelerated curricula and programs would be required to adequately serve these children. At present, most Christian high schools respond to this need by offering advanced placement courses, but the options are considerably more narrow in local churches.

The severely handicapped, however, require a much higher degree of specialization in teacher training, programs, and facilities. Most Christian schools and churches are unable to provide such services because of the cost. This leaves a void in the lives of Christian families to whom God has entrusted the care of one such child and who desire Christian nurture for all their children. There are, however, some fine Christian residential facilities of note, each with its own inspiring story: the Melmark Home in Berwyn, Pennsylvania; the Hidden Treasures Christian School in Greenville, South Carolina; Faith Mission Home in Free Union, Virginia; and the Shepherds College of Special Education, Union Grove, Wisconsin.

## Learning Differences

By far the largest group of children requiring special academic help are those with adequate to high intelligence who find them-

191

selves struggling in the classroom. These children are physically and emotionally healthy, their senses are unimpaired, and they generally do not suffer from being economically or socially disadvantaged. School testing usually ensures that the children accepted will have an I.Q. equal to probable classroom success. A distinguishing factor in the children of this group is that their classroom performance does not parallel their I.Q. As they pursue academic work, identifying signs or "red flags" of trouble begin to surface.

Some leaders in the field of special education feel that as many as 20 percent of children in any given classroom, Sunday School, or Christian school, are likely to experience difficulty learning by conventional classroom methods despite the intelligence to do so (Cox, 1980, p. 76). These children will have to learn in an alternative or different way. Thus the phrase *learning differenced* has replaced *learning disabled* to describe them. This more gracious and probably more accurate assessment of their dilemma acknowledges that, for various reasons, children do learn in different ways. It allows for some responsibility on the part of educational leaders to provide for different methods of learning. The most common category within the learning difference designation we refer to as *dyslexia.* Processing language—reading and using words—is at the heart of the problem. This creates havoc because of its centrality to the academic learning process. The terms *specific language disability or language learning difference* may also be used.

Children with attention deficit disorder (ADD) and attention deficit hyperactivity disorders (ADHD) are also included in this group of those who need to learn differently. Such children have trouble paying attention, focusing on a given task, assimilating and organizing information for retention and usage. They will generally miss enough in the classroom that remediation and modification are as necessary for them as for other children who have a learning difference specific to their language area. Often a child will be diagnosed with both disorders.

### A Positive Approach

Most educators know that a significant number of these children are "gifted" in areas other than written language.

Many educators view below-grade-level achievement as a prerequisite to a diagnosis of a learning disability. Thus, an extremely bright student who is struggling to stay on grade level may slip through the cracks.... Recent advances in both fields have alerted professionals to the possibility that both sets of behavior can exist simultaneously (Baum & Owen, 1988; Fox, Brody, & Tobin, 1983; Whitmore & Maker, 1985).

Children who are both gifted and learning disabled exhibit remarkable talents or strengths in some areas and disabling weaknesses in others. ... Because these students are bright and sensitive, they are acutely aware of their difficulty in learning: they tend to generalize their feelings of academic failure to an overall sense of inadequacy.... Research has shown that this group of students is often rated by teachers as most disruptive at school ... frequently found to be off task ... complain of (physical symptoms) ... easily frustrated and use their creative abilities to avoid tasks (Baum and Owen, 1988, Whitmore, 1980).

The fact is that learning differenced children will often excel academically if we adjust the learning environment to their learning styles and modify the tasks of reading and written language to fit the way the children process information best.

## A PROFILE: AT FIRST GLANCE

A profile of the learning differenced child is easily recognizable to a teacher in any classroom. Most of the time they present a quick study in many areas, and their bright demeanor belies the fact that they cannot read well, memorize accurately, get directions straight, or always understand exactly what the teacher means. Often they stand out because they cannot sit still, keep their hands to themselves, finish their papers, or pay attention.

### Classic Symptoms

Each child is different. However, in language learning there are a few classic symptoms that teachers should be aware of:
1. Difficulty in "word finding": recalling names of objects or the appropriate word needed.
2. Difficulty in following a multi-part direction.

3. Difficulty in copying words correctly.
4. Difficulty, for kindergarten and first grade children, in recognizing and reproducing alphabet letters. (They often appear backward or upside down.)
5. Difficulty in spelling: retaining the memory of letter arrangement in words and/or putting them on paper.
6. Difficulty in reading: blending letters together into sounds in a word. Words can be read inside out (*melon* for *lemon*) or backward (*was* for *saw*).
7. Difficulty in organizing their thoughts and reproducing them on paper.

One can easily see why the classroom is not their comfort zone. It is also understandable that these children do not want to read Scripture aloud or memorize and recite it. Many children struggling with learning differences view their situations as greatly handicapped, although it is often hard for them to express how they feel. One child drew a grasshopper with a broken antenna to express his dilemma. Today, he is a commercial artist. This ability to graphically represent a feeling illustrates the giftedness found in many learning differenced children. This was his creative writing, his "expressive" difference.

**Famous Achievers**

These well-known men, all of whom struggled with academic difficulties, provide encouragement to many learning differenced children. They provide ample proof that giftedness and disability do coexist:

Hans Christian Andersen (writer)
Woodrow Wilson (President of the USA)
Nelson Rockefeller (Vice President of the USA)
Harvey Cushing (brain surgeon)
George Patton (General of the Army)
Paul Ehrlich (bacteriologist)
Albert Einstein (scientist)
Thomas Edison (inventor)
August Rodin (sculptor)
Bruce Jenner (athlete)

Expertise and help was generally not available to them, but caring people were. Today, with accessible knowledge and training, remediation can provide such students equal footing with classmates. It can be better for these students; there are ways. As Jesus reminds us, "To whom much is given, much is required" (Luke 12:48). A well-known television advertisement said it best: A mind is a terrible thing to waste. As Christian educators, we cannot let that happen!

## MEETING NEEDS THROUGH EFFECTIVE TEACHING

As we understand students, we can better provide for their success in both classroom and Sunday School. In either case, the desire is to make disciples, to create a love of learning of God's Word and ultimately to know the Father Himself. Many Christian educators across the country practice the fine art of teaching and meeting needs in exemplary fashion, and church educational staffs can follow that example.

### Multisensory Involvement

It is well documented that much anger can result from classroom failure. In order to prevent this in the classroom and meet children's learning needs, we must teach them the way they learn best. The learning of basic language skills needs to be taught as a complete multisensory language program involving reading, spelling, handwriting, verbal and written expression. This multisensory approach, presenting information to the eye, the ear, and the muscle simultaneously, allows more reinforcement of the information being presented and provides for these language-learning differences. Awareness of the most effective methods will make optimum use of the time we are given with these children. In addition, many excellent strategies can accommodate learning differences in the classroom.

Although Sunday School lessons do not teach language skills, traditionally they do rely heavily on language skills. Bible memorization verses, books of the Bible, sequencing a story orally, oral Bible reading (with all the non-phonetic words), and the age-old Bible drill can be traumatic for a child with a language learning difference. A few simple changes in how to present and how to have the child "process through" and give you back the information can make all the difference in "disciple making." The message can get through unimpeded by embarrassed failure.

195

**Classroom Variety**

The following are some examples for Sunday School or Christian school classrooms.

1. Tell a Bible story with film and/or visual aids.
2. Have the children put the story in sequence with pictures on blocks or cards.
3. Act it out afterward; rehearse it verbally by discussion.

*Verbal reinforcement and review* are always important after any activity-based experience so that the student truly "gets the lesson" and is not just carried away with the fun of the medium.

The object is to use anything and everything to excite and maintain interest and make a strong impression. In appealing to as many senses as possible, information actually becomes alive and real. It can teach both mind and heart. Consider these possibilities:

1. Action—skits and plays
2. Visuals—films, posters, pictures, artifacts
3. Manipulatives:
   a. dioramas
   b. puppet shows
   c. flannelgraph
   d. blocks or cards with words and/or pictures to sequence
      1) books of the Bible
      2) stories
      3) lines of a Bible verse
   e. draw their own idea
4. Charts and time lines
5. Music—a great "hook" for memory

**Important Do's and Don'ts**

1. Don't ask learning differenced students to read aloud.
2. Always give clear instructions. Tell it, show it, rehearse it together.
3. Have students paraphrase or give feedback, then "walk" them through rephrasing.
4. Explain vocabulary! Often these children are very literal.
5. Minimize spelling and speed drills requiring reading.
6. Encourage lots of communication; pay close attention to the child's needs.
7. Help students to be structured in their verbalization.
8. Get them involved in "hands-on" projects.

9. Visit the children's homes and spend time with them outside class.

These suggestions are meant to stimulate and encourage the seeking of creative alternatives.

## SPECIAL EDUCATION PROGRAMS—
## YOU DON'T HAVE TO START BIG

Many existing programs are of excellent quality both in caring and expertise and must be applauded for the effort and sacrifice involved. The creativity, commitment, and wisdom on the part of these schools would place them in an elite category of excellence—serving the whole body of Christ. However, many of our Christian schools and churches have only begun to provide special education programs to our needy children.

In a 1991 survey of randomly selected schools across the nation belonging to the American Association of Christian Schools (AACS), 6 percent were found to have special education programs. Schools participating in this study were selected from the 1989 directory with a membership of 1,030 schools. (Everett, Sutton, & Sutton, 1993, pp. 67-72). The 1994 directory for the Association of Christian Schools International (ACSI) lists 370 of its 2,831 schools as having special education programs, or 7.65 percent (ACSI Directory, 1994).

The questions that beg at the doors of our Christian schools are: Do you want our child? Do you have a program for him or her? Must we send our child with learning differences to a school where God's Word is not central?

Churches and schools have their own questions to answer: What is our purpose? Are we prepared? Where do we go to get prepared? Who can help us? Educators must be diligent to find the expertise available. Inservice and conferences on the subject of exceptionality and learning differences are a must to raise the awareness of Christian school teachers as well as Sunday School teachers. However, first the Christian school board and the Christian education staff in the church must be challenged and excited.

In Christian schools across our country, principals, teachers, and sometimes parents, in an aiding and supporting role, have caught the vision and worked to provide support and success for these children. Even where no funding or expertise is available, teachers, touched by a child's special need, spend after-school hours or other personal time helping struggling children in their classes. These teachers have reported success with impressive innovative methods. Meeting just one of these dedicated Christian teachers renews one's flagging vision There are many unsung heroes in Christian education. Probably much more special help is being given than formal program statistics show.

Most communities have access to centers, either on the university campus or in private enterprise, where educational diagnostic testing is done and remedial help is available. In addition, Christian schools have had the availability of qualified personnel through the forum of teacher and administrator conventions, inservice, and special workshops. Resources are available when the school board and administration begin to set up a program. This is no small job, and budget is a chief concern in the process. Several important components must be considered in setting up this program:

1. Admissions policy
2. Space for remedial work
3. Hiring or engaging remedial specialists
4. Classroom teacher awareness and inservices
5. Screening procedures
6. Formal testing resources
7. Coordinating "release time" from class for remediation
8. Coordinating modifications in the classroom
9. An ability grading policy.

School programs today are varied ranging from the use of outside therapists, itinerate remedial specialists, to a full program with several staff persons and a support program school-wide. Sometimes a remediation specialist will serve several schools until the caseload of children needing help is sufficient to support a full-time staff person. Most programs, of necessity, begin small and grow.

It is imperative that we do our job well and meet the needs of the children God has committed to our families (Gal. 6:10). Let's teach these minds in the ways best suited to them with all the expertise we have so it will break through their intellects to their hearts and motivate them to love and serve. These bright, creative minds are needed to fill the ranks of the body of Christ. Perhaps there is a future Missionary Aviation Fellowship pilot in class, or maybe a mechanic who will keep the planes running. One student might possibly be an excellent radio technician or a builder, another a songwriter creating in a dimension that lifts the spirit. Perhaps one of these "three dimensional" thinkers will use her scientific expertise or art to further magnify the God of creation. We cannot miss one child; we teach for eternity.

Dr. Joe Sutton said it best: "In sum, whether our roles are teacher educators, administrators, or classroom teachers, we must all accept greater responsibility in learning more about mildly disabled students. To deny their existence in our classrooms is to admit as Christian educators that we hold a narrow and myopic view of the differences in students' abilities and how they learn" (1991, p. 4).

## For Further Reading

Armstrong, T. (1994). *Multiple intelligences in the classroom.* Alexandria, VA: Association for Supervision and Curriculum Development. This translation of Howard Gardner's theory of multiple intelligences into practical and accessible ideas for the classroom teacher includes concrete examples across the curriculum and food for thought in the area of special education.

Capehart, J., and Warren, P. (1995). *You and your ADD child.* Nashville: Thomas Nelson. This book by behavioral pediatrician Dr. Paul Warren and educator Jody Capehart, is a very comprehensive and practical guide for anyone working with ADD children. It includes necessary medical information as well as lots of practical tips for teaching these children in the school, home, and church.

Cox, A. (1990). *Structure and techniques.* Cambridge, MA: Educator's Publishing Service.

Silver, L. (1984). *The misunderstood child: A guide for parents of learning disabled children.* New York: McGraw. This has been classic reading in the field of learning disabilities. It is a great help to parents who often struggle, along with their children, as these children try to overcome and succeed.

Sutton, J. (1993). *Special education, a biblical approach.* Greenville, SC: Hidden Treasures Ministries. This book is a resource for those involved in Christian education concerning children with special needs and disabilities. Philosophy, basic concepts, and legal requirements as well as descriptions of the educational needs of these children are presented.

Vail, P. (1987). *Smart kids with school problems: Things to know and ways to help.* New York: Dutton. A good resource, this book is a presentation of various learning disabilities and often related giftedness. Practical programs and case studies are also included.

# HELPING PARENTS WITH AT-RISK CHILDREN
*Marlene LeFever*

James is inattentive, disorganized, dangerously impulsive, and for-getful. Detention is a way of life for him. His teachers agree—class goes smoother when he's not there. His parents have tried every-thing—positive reinforcement, grounding, working with the school on a day-to-day basis. Nothing works. Tests show he's smart, but he's so easily sidetracked he can't get anything done. He has no tolerance for frustration. "How's he ever going to make it in life if he continues this pattern?" his father asks, "Can't anyone help me?"[1] In many cases, for children like James, the answer is yes.

There are about one hundred billion neurons, or nerve cells, in the brain, and in a single human brain the number of possible in-terconnections between these cells is greater than the number of atoms in the universe (Ornstein & Thompson, 1984, p. 21). Some-times things go wrong. As God allows us to discover more about the brain, we educators take on more responsibility to apply that knowledge to people in our own ministries.

Children like James are often negatively labeled by Christian ed-ucators and parents alike: "Kid with an attitude." "Kid who doesn't live up to his potential." "Kid who throws his opportunities away."

Others in the congregation pray, "Thanks, Lord, that James is not my son, because I wouldn't have the strength to deal with him."

Unfortunately, today many young people like James are written off. Twenty years ago their symptoms had not been clustered and identified. Ten years ago we would have said these children had minimal brain damage. Then came the label—minimal brain dysfunction. Nobody really knew what the label meant. It was just a tag for children who couldn't function normally. Labels still categorize problem kids we don't know how to deal with. Since one chapter cannot deal with all types of at-risk behavior, we will focus on one as a model for the rest—Attention Deficit Disorder (ADD).

## THESIS

This chapter's thesis is easily stated: When a child has severe, on-going learning or discipline problems, he or she may be dealing with a physical disorder. Help is available for many of these children. It is unconscionable for Christian leaders not to aid parents in finding and applying it. Attention Deficit Disorder is just one problem Christian leaders need to be aware of. As we examine this disorder, use it as an example of all at-risk students. Don't make assumptions. Investigate symptoms.

The possibility of finding help for ADD children and children with other physical malfunctions should caution us against labeling children as bad, uncooperative, or unchristian (Sargent, 1993, pp. 43–48). These children may have a dysfunction for which there is—with searching—help that can save their futures and allow them to be contributing members of Christ's family.[2]

## ADD—ILLUSTRATION OF A DYSFUNCTION

Research on ADD, along with other recently named disorders (Sargent, 1993, pp. 43–48),[3] makes us more accountable than ever before. Now Christian educators and parents, with professional guidance, can often name what's wrong and take steps to help.

In almost any Christian education program that includes twenty-five children, at least one child will have Attention Deficit Disorder. That child is eight times more likely to be a boy than a girl. One counselor estimates that 50 to 60 percent of the children referred to him for behavioral problems have ADD (Wiegand, 1991, interview). Another source claims that 80 percent of adopted children have an ADD problem (Horn, 1993, pp. 9–11).

Briefly, Attention Deficit Disorder is characterized by serious and persistent difficulties in attention span, impulse control, and sometimes, though not always, hyperactivity. "The child must display multiple and severe symptoms of inattention and impulsivity across a variety of settings. Symptoms must be evident for at least six months," states Wade F. Horn, National Executive Director of Children and Adults with ADD (1993, p. 26).

In learning situations, these children will have trouble finishing assignments and following directions. They are fidgety, talkative, disruptive. They operate totally in the immediate. This short attention span causes them to fall further and further behind. As they fail, their self-esteem worsens. Finally, they give up, and then the behavior problems intensify (Mitchell, 1991, p. 14).[4]

## NEUROBIOLOGICAL DISORDER

ADD is a disturbance in the brain neurochemistry, a neurobiological disorder. The link between brain chemistry and behavior seems certain (Elmer-Dewitt, 1990, p. 59). Because of the cycle mentioned above, many ADD children develop secondary emotional problems, but most experts agree that ADD is a biological disorder, and not primarily an emotional one.

Another theory on the causes is forwarded by John K. Rosemond and Jane Healy. They speculate that television may provide an answer to the question, "Why is there an epidemic of ADD now?" A preschool child who watches twenty hours of television a week—well below the national average—will have spent 4,000-plus hours staring at the tube by the time he or she enters first grade. During the first seven years of life—known as the formative years—the environment imprints enduring patterns into the central nervous system. A disproportionate amount of formative time spent staring at a fixed and flickering electronic field may well interfere with the establishment of critical neural skills, including a long attention span (Rosemond, 1994, p. 113).

## TREATMENT

When ADD children are diagnosed early enough and the symptoms are mild enough, the situation can sometimes be managed through parent counseling, behavior modification, and education that involves tactile/kinesthetic learning.

Unfortunately, many are not caught young enough because they are able to cope with elementary school. They begin to really suffer for the first time in middle school/junior high because of the increased independent work load and the need for more sustained attention to detail.

Treatment usually requires the use of some medication. Most frequently used are Ritalin, Cylert, and Dexedrine (Wallis, 1994, pp. 41–50). Most people think these amphetamines slow children down. Wrong. They actually have the opposite effect. They "stimulate the central nervous system, putting it back in tune, allowing the child to pay attention and complete assignments" (Rosemond, 1989, p. 38).

A mother explained the transformation in her son while receiving medication.

Paul's teacher was ready to throw the book at him. He wrote to us, "Paul refused to complete his lab work, has not had necessary materials at least three days this week, and his interaction with the other students is often inappropriate: pushing and shoving, harassing, and pulling clothing, and interrupting."

We explained that Paul had just started taking medicine, but the teacher wasn't ready to buy this new label. "He's just got a bad attitude. He's a bad kid."

We curbed our first reaction to lash out at the teacher for not knowing about our special problem and we began to educate him. The teacher was not convinced, but he agreed to take Paul back long enough to give the medicine a chance to work.

It worked. On his next report card he want from an F to a D-. The teacher wrote, "Behavior continues to be variable, but much improved." Then he moved to a C+. The third marking period was a B and now he is within an A range. Paul's a different person. He's more relational. He's less angry. He's less irritable. He will sit and talk with us at the dinner table.

Move Paul's situation to the church.

I felt tremendous pain for my son. He would come to Sunday School because I forced him. But during the social time, he would grab his juice and donut and go sit in the car because, "No one in there likes me anyway." He was not all wrong in his assessment. My son, my ADD child, is not easy to love.

Without help, ADD children begin a downward spiral: failure > poor self-esteem > failure > poor self-esteem > failure. This spiral can lead to poor social adjustment, behavioral problems, school failure, dropping out, and delinquency and drug abuse.

## THE SIN PROBLEM[5]

The story of James, introduced at the beginning of this chapter, continues in the words of his father:

My child is restless, he can't sit still. He's so easily sidetracked that he can't get anything done. He's a good football player and yet he can't manage to get to practice. Then when the coach says he can't play, he blows.

Can we assume that if James would "get right with the Lord," his misbehavior would improve, and he could move ahead, maturing in his Christian life? Or are some aberrant human behaviors not directly caused by personal sin?

In other words, are there genuine physical and psychological problems not immediately generated by sin? If so, can we find biblical cases to support this opinion (Townsend, sermon, 1991)?

The Bible recognizes more departments to life than just the spiritual and acknowledges other causes for human problems than immediate personal sin. According to Luke 2:52, "Jesus grew in wisdom and stature, and in favor with God and men." Luke divides the one perfect life into four categories:

- Epistemological or knowledge growth ("in wisdom")
- Physical growth ("stature")
- Spiritual growth ("with God")
- Social growth ("with men")

If all of life were purely spiritual, why would the writer bother to mention wisdom and social growth as categories apart from spiritual growth? Why not just say, "Jesus was pleasing God—and that's all that matters"?

Thus God sanctions treating certain areas of life as other-than-spiritual. Trying to reduce all of life simply to the spiritual sphere doesn't have biblical sanction. We are not infallible judges of what is sin and what isn't. It would be irrational for someone to look at James' brain, see that it isn't working correctly, and still persist in calling his physical problem and its behavioral manifestations personal sin. Consider Jesus' reply to His disciples when they wondered if a man's blindness stemmed from sin They asked, "Rabbi, who sinned, this man or his parents, that he was born blind?" To this, Jesus replied, "Neither this man nor his parents sinned, but this happened so the work of God might be displayed in his life" (John 9:3). Jesus gives a profound example that while human suffering entered the world through sin, it is not wise to attribute every specific incident of suffering, disobedience, or confusion to willful sin.

Many Christians have an erroneous idea of what constitutes sin. They mistake explosive anger for sin, just as someone might mistake James' behavior in school as sinful laziness. For example, if the story in Matthew 23 of Jesus haranguing, lambasting, and raking the Jewish leaders over the coals were read without mentioning names, some listeners might pronounce the angry person to be a sinner. He was right, they might agree, to explain to the local leaders that they were hypocrites, but He shouldn't have gotten angry doing it (Townsend, interview, 1991)!

People in our day might be just as wrong if they looked at James' misuse of his potential and called it sin. In ultimate terms, without Christ he is a sinner. But James has no more control of certain reactions than he would if someone suddenly stuck a pin under his skin. This explanation, however, does not relieve James of responsibility for those actions he *can* control.

James also has to take moral responsibility for his actions. Yes, some behavior is produced by a physical disorder. But James is responsible to learn ways to cope. He needs to learn to make amends and take the consequences for his behavior.

When James chooses to behave inappropriately, he is sinning.

## HELP PARENTS PARENT THE ADD CHILD

The ADD child, and children who have other brain dysfunctions, will not thrive in our Christian homes or in our Christian education programs without the right kind of help.
 • *Pray extra hard*—for the child, the parents, and the child's

teachers. The ADD child is usually very smart and fully aware that his or her brain is not doing what is expected of it. Anger and frustration can lead to behavioral problems.

• *Talk—carefully—to parents* if you suspect the child may have a problem. ADD families are at-risk families. ADD is a genetic disorder passed around within families. Many ADD children grow up in single-parent or blended families because adults who have ADD tend to have stormy relationships. A mother shared:

> My 17-year-old son has ADD and so does his father. His father denies that either one has problems, and, as a result, they continually have terrible arguments and don't speak for months at a time. I can't make my ex-husband understand that the reason they fight so often is because they are so alike.

Open the conversation with, "I think your child may have some concentration problems," rather than, "Your child is disruptive." Parents probably hear this same message from other sources. The fact that someone from the church says the same thing may carry extra weight—if the church is supportive, loving, helpful and hopeful.

• *Let the parents know that you don't think they are bad parents.* The child's brain doesn't work normally. Nothing parents do will fully correct this problem. "Bring up your children in the ways of the Lord," parents are told, "and they will not stray from them when they are old." Parents aim for this ideal by modeling Christianity for at-risk children and taking steps to get the medical and counseling help they need.

Some parents may have difficulty accepting that their child should be tested for a physical problem. Help parents view this situation as they would if John or Sharon had a sore throat, a broken toe, or diabetes. Parents would take the child to a doctor and follow his or her advice. This is no different (Wender, 1987, p. 56).

• *Help parents train their child to discriminate* between feelings and behavior.

> For example, the parents of an ADD child should allow him to express his jealous feelings toward his newborn sister, but he should not be allowed to hit her. Feeling jealous and hitting because of jealousy should be recognized as being as different as night and day (Wender, 1987, p. 83).

• *Know that you can't be sure.* ADD is hard to diagnose.[6] Read and ask your doctor if he or she knows anyone in the area who can provide treatment. Make books available to the parents in your church. Admit you're not an authority.

• *Suggest some survival skills* to parents and call the parents frequently enough to check progress so they know you are involved with them in the difficult assignment of rescuing an ADD child.

—Accept the idea that your child will always find sustained concentration difficult. Recognize your own frustration threshold.

—Help your child focus on his or her strengths so self-esteem is bolstered.

—Hold your child accountable for behavior and decisions. Help the child realize when choices are being made.

—Maintain consistent schedules (homework, chores, TV, dinner, devotions).

—Break work situations into short time periods. Some parents use charts, graphs, and lists to help structure work situations and to give the child immediate feedback.

—Give directions one step at a time. Most children talk themselves silently through new tasks as they initially encounter them. They quickly move beyond these subvocal means of regulating their behavior as their responses become more automatic. Children with ADD do not automatically generate these strategies. "Comparing the child to a radio," says John K. Rosemond, "it's as if the child's 'tuner' isn't working properly. Instead of being able to lock into one station and stay there indefinitely, the child drifts randomly and involuntarily from station to station" (1994, p. 109).

—Provide a quiet, non-distracting area where your child can do homework.

• *Facilitate a parent support group at your church.* You may not have enough families at your church to build a group. Combine with other churches and the community your churches serve.

• *Share the flip side with parents.* If ADD children get help, they can channel all that energy they waste into doing worthwhile things, and they can become successful (Winkler, 1991, p. 6).[7]

• *Train Sunday School teachers and youth leaders* who understand ADD and are able to teach the ADD child. This child cannot separate the teacher from the content. If the Sunday School teacher is boring, God is boring. The ADD child needs a teacher who allows students to be responders and thinkers, not passive receptacles of information (Weber, 1994, p. 123).

ADD children need student-centered activities. Lots of changes, lots of variety, and lots of opportunities to move will hold their interest. The effective teacher will provide structure while using a variety of methods that require interaction and high movement.

> Discussions, debates, and story-telling activities force students to hold bits of information in their minds that they can use to respond to others when their turn comes up. Cooperative learning activities oblige students to attend to others as well as their own contributions. . . . And metacognitive discussions about attention compel students to confront their own thought process (Sylwester & Cho, 1993, p. 75).

• *Find creative ways to let the child know that he or she is loved* by you and the church. Let the parents know that the church leadership will make a concerted effort to show this love.

ADD children should feel hugged, even if you don't touch them. Many ADD children don't like being cuddled or touched, but they respond to good eye contact, a warm smile, a friendly joke.

• *Work with parents to build a network of bridges with the school.* Go with parents to talk with teachers and provide resource materials. Don't be surprised if the teacher is skeptical. One teacher told a parent, "ADD is just a fancy label that over-achieving parents dreamed up to explain why their children aren't as successful as they think they should be."

Teachers should be told what medications the child is taking and why. Some medications can cause appetite loss, sleep difficulties, or lethargy. These symptoms can be controlled, but it helps when the teacher knows what's going on.

God calls Christian leaders to love and serve even when that task is hard and even when those to whom we give the most do not show appreciation. We respond with a spiritual eye to the future.

We don't know who our ADD children can become if they learn to live for Jesus with their disability. Perhaps an ADD child will be the genius who finds an energy solution, the missionary who revolutionizes our concept of missions, or the martyr Christ uses to point thousands to Him. We dare not allow parental or congregational attitudes and actions contribute to the throwing away of a child's potential.

## WHERE TO FIND HELP

Association for Children and Adults with Learning Disabilities
4156 Library Rd.
Pittsburgh, PA 15234

Attention Deficit Disorder Association
8091 South Ireland Wy.
Aurora, CO 80016

Challenge, Inc.—A Newsletter of the Attention Deficit Disorder Association
PO Box 488
West Newbury, MA 01985

Children with Attention Deficit Disorders
499 NW 70th Ave., Ste. 308
Plantation, FL 33317

CompuServe Information Services, ADD Forum—Subscribers enter GO ADD

It's Just Attention Disorder: A Video Guide for Kids
Sam and Michael Goldstein, Neurology, Learning & Behavior Center
230 S. 500 East, Suite 100
Salt Lake City, UT 84102

## Notes
1. Case studies cited in this chapter are true and used with permission of the parents involved.

2. According to Laurie Winslow Sargent, "Learning Differences," *Christian Parenting Today* (1991, March/April, pp. 43–48), 300,000 children are born to alcohol-abusing and drug-abusing mothers. These children, like ADD children, often experience significant learning problems and other

developmental delays. According to Dr. Edward Ogata in "Cocaine Babies" (*Chicago Tribune Magazine*, 1993, November 28) one in ten at-risk newborns shows signs of drug withdrawal or responds slower than normal to stimuli. We either learn how to guide these children toward maturing faith, or we admit that the church doesn't care about their future.

3. Names proliferate: Attention Deficit Hyperactivity Disorder (ADHD), Specific Learning Disability (SLD) such as dyslexia and dysgraphia. "According to the U.S. Department of Education, nearly 2 million children in public schools last year received special education for learning disabilities. Many more children remain undiagnosed and untreated. One estimate is that up to 15 percent of all public-school children are learning disabled."

4. "I spent the first twenty-three years of my life unaware that I had a learning disability. School made me feel stupid. By the time math tests came around, my memory went blank. When I did remember, I'd make dumb mistakes on simple addition. Teachers didn't understand. They said I was lazy. After a while, I stopped trying. I thought I was stupid, and no one told me differently. One day I heard Bruce Jenner, the Olympic athlete, describe his learning disability. He told of many of the same problems I'd been struggling with all my life. After taking a series of tests at a learning-disability center, I finally understood my problem and got help. For the first time I realized I wasn't dumb." Andrew Mitchell, from "When 6 x 7 = 47" in *Parents of Teenagers* (1991, February/March, p. 14).

5. Portions of this section were printed in "Attention Deficit Disorder: Calling a Dysfunction 'Sin'" by Marlene LeFever, *Youthworker Journal*, Winter 1992, pp. 91-93.

6. Check local hospitals for ADD and ADHD screening. For example, Kingswood Hospital, Michigan City, IN, placed an ad in the local newspaper: "ADHD—Attention Deficit Hyperactivity Disorder—a big problem for little people. If your child lacks self-control, can't sit still, does not listen, fights constantly he or she may suffer from ADHD. Free ADHD Screening sponsored by the children's unit." Communicating information like this to parents can be an invaluable service.

7. Tom Cruise has ADD. So does Mark Spitz. Henry Winkler of "Happy Days" fame is interested in kids who are challenged. He wrote about his own undiagnosed learning disability as he was growing up: "I was in the bottom 3 percent in the country in math. I was considered a class clown, not living up to my potential, lazy, and I had a very, very poor self-

image, which was somewhere down around my ankles. Now I think it's up to my sternum" (*Chicago Tribune*, 1991 April 14, p. 6).

## For Further Reading

Garber, S. (1990). *If your child is hyperactive, inattentive, impulsive, distractible—helping the ADD child.* New York: Villard Books. Helping children with ADD adjust, cope, and produce.

Hallowell, E., and Ratey, J. (1994). *Driven to distraction.* New York: Pantheon Books. Characteristics of Attention Deficit Disorder and dealing with the child who has it.

Kelly, K., and Ramundo, P. (1993). *You mean I'm not lazy, stupid, or crazy?!* Cincinnati: Tyrell and Jerem Press. Help the person with Attention Deficit Disorder identify characteristics and encourage them.

Moss, R. (1990). *Why can't Johnny concentrate?* New York: Bantam Books. Coping with Attention Deficit Disorder, tips for helping children understand ADD.

Phelan, T. (1993). *All about attention deficit disorder.* Glen Ellyn, IL: Child Management. Characteristics of children with deficit disorder. Excellent facts and statistics.

Silver, L. (1993). *Advice to parents on attention deficit disorder.* Washington, D.C.: American Psychiatric Press. Dr. Silver's advice to parents on raising children with Attention Deficit Hyperactivity Disorder.

Woodrich, D. (1994). *Attention deficit hyperactivity disorder: What every parent wants to know.* Baltimore: P.H. Brookes. Family relationships with the child who has Attention Deficit Disorder. Common questions are answered by a variety of contributors.

# SEVENTEEN

# DEVELOPING A CURRICULUM FOR FAMILY LIFE EDUCATION
*Clarence W. Wulf*

A controversy exists between teaching subject-centered curriculum in contrast to the life-related approach. Do we teach people, content, or both? What is curriculum and how does it relate to the ongoing issues people face? How does it relate to the Bible? Are there simple and practical procedures in developing a family life curriculum plan? How can the church start or improve a teaching–learning process that addresses the issues of family life education? To some, the suggestion that teaching should be relevant means the Bible can no longer be taught. That is a false assumption. We will explore these questions in the following pages.

## CURRICULUM DEFINED

LeRoy Ford in his text *A Curriculum Design Manual for Theological Education* (1991) succinctly traces curriculum from its origins to current usage. Curriculum in its roots meant "a running or a race course" (pp. 33–34). "Traditionally, the course was considered the body of content that the student covered in his educational progress" (LeBar, 1981, p. 211). This basic meaning has long since expanded to include selected educational procedures (Wyckoff, 1959, p. 130).

The instructor therefore uses an interactive approach, creating a variety of experiences involving the content. Learning is the active process of change in which students expand their horizons. It alters perception and perspective, and that awareness should lead to change. Curriculum encompasses a variety of student experiences and activities that interact with content.

A vital curriculum ingredient, then, is the teacher's effort to relate content to the lives of students. In effect, the teacher does nothing for students they can do for themselves.


## CURRICULUM AND THE FAMILY TARGET AUDIENCE

Curriculum planning for family life education cannot be stereotyped into a neat and simple formula. Today's family structure dictates that curriculum be based on spiritual or human lifestyle needs lest it become a fantasy world of yesteryear's morals and values. Change in family lifestyle has occurred rapidly in the latter part of this century, and every indication suggests that change will accelerate in the coming twenty-first century. Changes in America's morals and family structure specifically affect how the church develops family life curriculum.

### Change in America's Moral Fiber
The founding fathers of America's representative form of government decided this republic would reflect biblical values. Separation of church and state meant government would not interfere with the free exercise of religious faith. No one church denomination or belief system was endorsed by the government, leaving the church free to influence society. The underlying prevailing social structure depended on an acceptance of a moral code based on the Bible.

A variety of social factors and legal decisions have now marginalized the Bible in terms of its influence on the family and society in general. The move away from historic Judeo-Christian values has deepened the void and emptiness that places families in jeopardy.

### Change in Family Structure
Richard P. Olson and Joe H. Leonard, in their book *Ministry with Families in Flux* (1990, pp. 9–10) write of nine notable family changes that have taken place over the past several decades. These changes influence how we develop family life curriculum.

1. The "traditional" family of father, mother, and at least two children reflects 10 percent of all families.
2. Divorced persons are much more common today. Death would separate married adults in an earlier century when life expectancy was shorter. Today, with a longer life span, the percentage of separation is basically the same; however, now the separation is much more likely to be due to divorce than to early death.
3. A growing number of single parents raise children. Earlier generations of single parents frequently placed children in orphanages or foster homes.
4. Divorced partners are more likely to share joint custody of children. This frequently requires former mates meeting regularly to make decisions jointly for their children.
5. The step-family is much more common, with its unique characteristics of "his, her, and our" children. At the very least, families include a complex network of persons.
6. In most families today, both partners are employed outside the home. Frequently, togetherness is affected by shift schedules, resulting in families spending less time together.
7. Marriages involving the mixing of religious beliefs or ethnic backgrounds add still another dimension.
8. Couples delay having children or may choose marriage without children.
9. Singleness is the choice of many.

All these situations form the cultural setting in which the church ministers. Curriculum must address these family life needs.

## CURRICULUM SELECTION PRINCIPLES

Family life curriculum, the "race course" of content and experience, must begin where people live in their unique set of circumstances. Curriculum provides the resources to meet their needs.

The New Testament offers examples of Christ's teaching to meet people's needs. Jesus helped His distressed followers when He calmed the sea. Zaccheus was a changed man after Christ found him in a sycamore tree and ministered to him. At Capernaum, the Son of God taught a lesson on humility by calling a small child to Himself and asking, "Who is the greatest in the kingdom of heaven?" In John 2 Jesus averted a social catastrophe by providing a groom wine for his wedding. The biblical record shows Jesus ministering to people by beginning at their point of need.

We must recognize that needy physical circumstances offer us opportunities to deal with deeper spiritual needs. Christ's ministry illustrates this combination of physical and spiritual levels. He models the way the church can develop curriculum that will reach families at their point of need.

Effective curriculum merges the physical and spiritual factors to meet crucial human needs in the name of Christ. This requires identifying personal and family needs. The following suggestions may help us do that:

1. Read current literature, periodicals, and books, and research studies on family life. General family needs often surface in such investigation. This book is a fine start for your research.
2. Ask questions of your church leaders. What family life issues surface most often? What subjects need to be addressed? What biblical texts deal with these issues and subjects?
3. Prepare a checklist of family life issues and distribute it as widely as possible. Survey the pastoral staff, church board or cabinet, Christian education committee, adult Sunday School classes, elders, deacons, men's ministry leaders, and women's work personnel. This should provide sufficient direction for the early phases of family life curriculum selection.
4. Survey family life subject matter produced by Christian publishing companies. Publishers deal with issues they perceive as current.

Of course, curriculum must be Bible based and related to life needs.

The pragmatic curriculum approach centers on "curriculum in life and pupil experience" (Gangel, 1981, p. 179). Begin with a problem, gather data, suggest a solution, and ultimately relate the issue to a Bible passage. The Herbartian, or more traditional Bible study approach, begins with Bible facts. New material is presented. Then the teacher associates the new material with the old and ultimately it is necessary to relate truth to life (Gangel, p. 180).

Extremes in either direction can be a problem. Often the pragmatic approach lacks sufficient scriptural authority and too much time is devoted to the problem rather than the text. The "study the Bible first" approach can lack sufficient emphasis on application to real life.

In summary, family life curriculum must provide equally sufficient Scripture study *and* application. A variety of topics should be considered over the long term, rather than centering just on "hurting family" issues. Courses of study may be intermingled so that we address both need-based issues and Christian development/growth subjects.

## CURRICULUM PLANNING PROCESS

Because families are in a state of flux, often an outward facade of the family hides the real issues. The church has opportunity to meet these needs through disciple–building ministries.

Four factors should be considered when developing a family life curriculum.

### Step One: Identifying a Family Life Need

The four suggestions mentioned earlier should guide the curriculum planner. Reading, questionnaires, inquiries of church leaders, and publishers' materials provide clues to curriculum possibilities.

One good exercise is to write out the teaching objectives and intended outcomes. For example, a series of lessons on "Hindrances to Spiritual Growth" might include the objective: "That class participants be able to identify and explain the origin of problems and implement an overcomers' attitude change."

### Step Two: Selecting Curriculum Materials

Advance curriculum investigation is an important step in being ready to implement a teaching–learning ministry. It is difficult to lay out a continuing relevant curriculum in a textbook because of constant change. New materials become available and existing curriculum is outdated or removed from the market. So I recommend the principle of research for readiness. Implement the procedure of reviewing materials and establishing a family life curriculum resource center.

Figure 1 offers a sample format for an expandable curriculum guide to family life issues. Make your own similar format using the four divisions as a starting point.

217

## Figure 1:
## A Curriculum Guide to Family Life Issues

Note four broad categories under which study courses may be added. Various publishers may have a similar topic resource. Place all such resources on a similar chart. After the first or second time of teaching a subject, optional resources might be considered.

**FAMILY DEVELOPMENT TOPICS**

| Topic | Curriculum/ Title | Publisher | Format | Synopsis |
|---|---|---|---|---|
| Parents and their children | *Hi, I'm Bob and I'm the Parent of a Teenager* | Gospel Light, Regal Books | Manual for leader | Short seven session course. Covers biblical principles of parenting. Designed to develop peer-led parent support groups. |
| Family roles | *You Can Be the Wife of a Happy Husband* | Victor Books | Leader's guide Text | Gives perspective on a married woman's role and keys to marital success. |

**FAMILY AND SPIRITUAL/MATURITY ISSUES**

| Topic | Curriculum/ Title | Publisher | Format | Synopsis |
|---|---|---|---|---|
| Hindrances to spiritual growth | *Defeating Those Dragons* | Victor Books | Text with eight lessons | Overcoming common hindrances to spiritual growth. |
| | *Healing Hidden Hurts* | Standard Publishing | Designed for Sunday School class or small group study | Considers a variety of common hurts that often remain hidden and hinder spiritual growth. |
| | *Spiritual Zest* | Beacon Hill Press | Student text Leader's guide | Various issues— unconfessed sin, how health affects spiritual life, busyness, etc. |
| Stewardship | *Partners with God* | Southern Baptist, Broadman Publishing | Leader's guide Five sessions Worksheets Workbook | Biblical teaching on stewardship. Helps develop a biblical lifestyle. |
| | *Mastering Money in Your Marriage* | Gospel Light, Regal Books | Group leader's guide/Student personal study guide | Put an end to money management conflicts. Learn how to use money to glorify God. |

## FAMILY/MARRIAGE RELATIONSHIPS

| Topic | Curriculum/ Title | Publisher | Format | Synopsis |
|---|---|---|---|---|
| Building marriage relationships | *Build Your Marriage* | Gospel Light, Regal Books | Group leader's guide/Individual student personal study guide | How couples can get closer together than they ever imagined possible. |
| | *Emotions: Can You Trust Them?* | Gospel Light, Regal Books | Both a leader's guide and student text | Deals with the emotions which have a powerful role in our lives. |
| Self-esteem | *Christian Self-Esteem: Parenting* | Southern Baptist | 13-week course with Leader's notebook, Teacher's aids, Text | Helps parents with personal self-esteem and how to build their children's self-esteem. |
| | *The Me I See* | Beacon Hill Press | 13 sessions Leader's guide | Various contributing authors—designed for interaction and dialogue in small groups, Sunday School, or personal discoveries. |
| | *Building Your Mate's Self-Esteem* | Gospel Light, Regal Books | Group leader's guide/Individual student personal study guide | Theme: Marriage is God's workplace for self-esteem issues. |
| Communication/ intimacy | *Communication and Intimacy* | Southern Baptist | 13-week course Couple's guide Learning activities | Identifies how couples can communicate and develop intimacy. |

## FAMILY DEVELOPMENT TOPICS

| Topic | Curriculum/ Title | Publisher | Format | Synopsis |
|---|---|---|---|---|
| Divorce | Video: *Suddenly Single* | Word Ministry Resources | Two videos Four sessions with study guide | Compassionately deals with feelings associated with divorce, confusion, denial, anger, and grief. |
| Single parenting | *Just Me and the Kids* | David C. Cook | 12-week course/ Director's handbook/ Children's leader handbook/ Single parent group/ Leader's guide (includes video) | Designed for kids and parents—a two-track approach— children's ministry, and parents' small groups on the same night at the same time. |

The approach is simple and practical. Write curriculum publishers and request to be included on their mailing lists. Secure curriculum catalogs from every possible source and check them for family ministry courses. Classify the study subjects according to the four broad categories suggested.

1. *Family developmental topics.* List courses dealing with the preparation for marriage and family life. Helps for family life begin with preparation for marriage. People need communication skills to build good relationships. Parents with positive attitudes are much more likely to convey the same to their children.
2. *Family spiritual life and maturity issues.* Societal trends strip away the conditions that make possible an enriching family experience. Congregations need courses of study and experiences that center on marriage commitment and proper balance between work and home.
3. *Building the family and marriage relationship.* Find courses that deal with specific issues of parenting. All families, whatever the parental mix, must walk through a variety of ever-changing experiences with their children. Children leave one stage of growing only to present parents with a whole new set of challenges.
4. *Changing family lifestyles.* Deal with special issues that make up the family experience—abuse, abandonment, divorce, separation by death of a spouse, children in crisis situations, intergenerational concerns, blended families, age-related issues, and much more.

Make plans to address all stages of family life needs. Maintain constant vigilance by keeping current the chart on Curriculum Guide to Family Life Issues. This enhances your ability to meet a curriculum need quickly.

Under the third heading, the sample chart (figure 1) lists three resources on self-esteem. Three different publishers currently have material on the subject. By ordering all available materials, a church can better meet the needs of its unique situation. Meanwhile, all resources become part of a growing family life resource media center. The second or third time the subject is taught, the instructor may consider using a different approach, perhaps from another publisher.

Another good practice would be to maintain a list of publishers, possibly ten or twelve, with addresses and phone numbers. New publishing sources can be added to the list at any time. Computers make it easy to edit the list or update the most recent curriculum courses and information available. Persons who need to research possible curriculum choices would benefit. People who need further details or course description information could be directed to catalogs or curriculum products currently in the resource center.

The meeting of family life needs may be addressed in structured Sunday School classes, home discussion groups, or informally one-on-one. Having resources available in a media resource center helps us meet needs at the time interest is high.

Resources sometimes may meet more than one need. Use the resource for the intended purpose, then set it aside and at another time use it again. Any leader can plan better when resources are readily available.

### Step Three: Finding the Teacher

An old adage reminds us that more things are caught than taught. The best teachers are practitioners. They live what they speak. Modeling the Christian home and biblical lifestyle are valued factors. The teacher willing to be a good listener will soon have people sharing their personal and family needs. Teachers who build relationships with class participants will have an expanding opportunity of ministry. Look for instructors with apparent spiritual gifts, qualities of life, experience, and unique talents for teaching ministry.

### Step Four: Fitting the Course into the Church Schedule

These logistical matters vary widely from church to church. Study courses do not always follow the twelve- or thirteen-week Sunday School quarter system. When you use shorter courses, you may want to plan alternate scheduling. Either change the time the study is presented, or combine the shorter course with another topic to maintain the quarter system schedule.

### CURRICULUM AT WORK IN THE CHURCH

It is not likely that a multifaceted use of curriculum will occur in the early stages of family life education. So how do church leaders implement family life curriculum? One consideration is to choose the area of greatest need. Begin at that point and then expand curriculum offerings. Be ready to provide curriculum in both formal and informal settings.

Family life curriculum includes Sunday School, adult fellowships, discipleship classes, home small group studies, family Vacation Bible School classes, midweek Bible study, and many more group options. It includes any structured classes in the church.

Scheduling family life subjects each quarter by Sunday School leaders works well in churches which offer many adult classes. However, the small church with only one or two adult classes faces its own unique circumstances. That problem can be addressed in part by restructuring an existing class.

Select the adult class with the most interest in family life education; restructure the class time to include a ten-minute concluding segment dealing specifically with marital and family questions. Each week put family life materials on display and available to check out. Books, audio tapes, and videos take the curriculum into the lives of students outside the structured class. Include brief reports to the class on the reading or viewing of materials. Other class members may be motivated to do likewise.

Good teachers want to stimulate self-learning in students. Good teachers involve students in the learning opportunity. Helping students know each other better also contributes to a good learning environment. The teacher could arrange for individuals or couples to share their stories as a social, get-acquainted activity at the beginning of class.

Often people in the class will note that their needs are similar to others' and may begin to network on their own. At this point, informal learning opportunities emerge.

Informal times for learning are those occasions when people sense a need—a teacher, a parent, a friend recognizes a teachable moment. Preparing for times of informal learning requires having resources available at the time of interest.

Informal curriculum means having many resources available for families to use at home, to take on vacation or to listen to during commuting time. Make sure good materials are available for family study times or the coffee time with a neighbor. Resources include videos, audio tapes, books, booklets and magazines. Make available special topical studies on all family-related subjects. Implementation of informal curriculum requires someone to acquire materials. Your resource center of family life materials makes it all possible.

## CONCLUSION

The church's mission is to disciple people to Jesus Christ. First, people experience the new birth in Christ. Once born into God's family, an ongoing nurturing teaching ministry must take place.

Effective educators know how to use teachable moments of instruction, both formal and informal. Deuteronomy 6:5-9 illustrates a teachable moment:

Love the Lord your God with all your heart and with all your soul and with all your strength. These commandments that I give you today are to be upon your hearts. Impress them on your children. Talk about them when you sit at home and when you walk along the road, when you lie down and when you get up. Tie them as symbols on your hands and bind them on your foreheads. Write them on the door frames of your houses and on your gates.

Curriculum is the "race course" of content worked out through life experiences. Plan well and you can guide participants on their journey of life that they may enjoy an ever-enriching life in the family of God.

### For Further Reading

Ford, L. (1991). *A curriculum design manual for theological education.* Nashville: Broadman & Holman. This volume is for curriculum designers and revisers. It puts in perspective the process of learning the content of materials through a variety of methods and learning situations. Specific educational goals are to be determined. This is a detailed methodical analysis of curriculum design.

Gangel, K. (1981). *Building leaders for church education.* Chicago: Moody Press. Develops ministry concepts for local church Christian education. Explains the roles, responsibilities, and how to equip workers for ministry.

Larson, J. (1986). *A church guide for strengthening families.* Minneapolis: Augsburg Publishing House. The writer strategizes how to do family ministry in the church. The premise is meeting needs of every individual, couple, or family and to further their development and well-being. This can be expedited through marriage and family enrichment and planned programs. The text is filled with practical ideas and reproducible masters for teaching ministries.

LeBar, L. (1995). *Education that is Christian.* Wheaton, IL: Victor Books. A classic text updated by James Plueddemann. Contains many Bible examples of teaching, and develops the teaching–leading process. Structuring curriculum is explained. Spiritual development takes place when there is interaction between the student's life situation and the Scriptures.

Olson, R., and Leonard, J. (1990). *Ministry with families in flux.* Louisville, KY: Westminster/John Knox Press. Presents an excellent perspective on the changing family in a changing society. Discusses how the church can respond with a greater concern for people.

# NURTURING GRANDPARENTS IN THE CHURCH
*Kenneth O. Gangel*

A motto hanging proudly in my study proclaims, "When a child is born a family receives two precious gifts, a grandchild . . . and a grandparent." While Jimmy Carter builds houses and serves the world as Ambassador by Appointment, George Bush is quietly setting an example for America's 19 million grandfathers. Both serve well. Sidey, writing in *Time* magazine, says that former President Bush would like to lead grandfathers "back to the playgrounds, classrooms and fishing holes to dispense concern and love for kids. . . . He would grandfather the entire population if he could" (1994, p. 32).

In 1981, there were about 48 grandparents for every 100 parents, compared with just 14 grandparents per 100 parents at the turn of the century. Cherlin and Furstenberg (1992) remind us that "The Bureau of the Census projects that by the year 2000, for the first time in our nation's history, there will be more persons aged fifty-five and over than children fourteen and under" (p. 28)—a fascinating turn of events in the second half of the twentieth century. Because of smaller families and greater longevity, we may be headed toward too many grandparents chasing too few grandchildren before this decade ends.

All this is complicated by blending of families through divorce and remarriage: "This high level of divorce might mean that many single parents will be turning to their own parents for support . . . the increase in divorce has altered the roles of grandparents once again—returning to some of them the greater functional role that was more widespread a few generations ago" (Cherlin & Furstenberg, 1992, p. 50).

In a very helpful article in *Christianity Today* entitled "How Churches Can Be Truly Pro-Family," Jan Johnson (1995) talks about enriching marriages, assisting families under pressure, mending blended families, and numerous other important topics. But the word "grandparent" does not appear once. She can be forgiven on many counts—space limitation, purpose, focus—but this present chapter must deal with a very important dimension of family life education—grandparenting. How can the church help use and influence this vital segment of the population?

## FOUNDATIONS OF GRANDPARENTING

In its premier issue, *Grandparent Times* (*GT*) offered readers five guiding principles; two are worth repeating here since they speak directly to the process of Christian nurture in a congregation. *GT's* sponsoring organization, Caring Grandparents of America (CGA), notes:

> We live in a time of many stresses on the family. Parents are faced with difficult economic and social choices. CGA is dedicated to helping grandparents support today's parents by combining their knowledge of life experiences with an understanding of the changes occurring in our modern world.
>
> There are some enduring qualities, including love, trust, loyalty, integrity and joy. CGA is dedicated to seeing that these qualities are shared between every grandparent and grandchild, regardless of their age (*Grandparent Times,* n.d., p. 1).

When we talk about foundations, we talk about basic understanding. The church cannot minister to any specific age group or segment of its congregation unless it understands their needs and uniqueness. That is certainly true of grandparents, a group the church has always had around and always taken for granted. Now, new research and changing demographics make it essential to expand our understanding.

## Understanding the Importance of Grandparenting

The very day the first draft of this chapter is being written, my son and daughter-in-law are en route with their two children to a new ministry position in another state. During the process of packing up to move, Beth found a note tucked away in the back of one of seven-year-old Lyndsey's dresser drawers. Neither parent had ever seen it before, but apparently it had been written some time within the previous year. Scratched on a pad, her personal feelings won my heart: "My favorit spot is in Poppy's lap. My 2 favorit spot is in Grandma's lap. My 3 favorit spot is on the chair by the counter at Poppy and Grandma's house." No amount of research could have made the message more clear to me—grandparents are important.

As I have already noted above, the importance of grandparents with respect to church ministry is inseparably linked to the demographics of aging. Years ago, George Barna (1990) reminded us:

> Programs of the church must acknowledge that the senior citizens of tomorrow will be more physically vigorous, more interested in adventure and experiences, and more involved in continuing education. Churches that treat older Americans as people who are simply winding down after an exhausting life, waiting to experience heaven, will find that their population of seniors will diminish steadily. . . . Many churches will have to stop thinking of the elderly as a group to be ministered to and see them as one of our most critical groups of lay ministers. As we turn away from our emphasis on being young—and celebrate old age—leaders in all walks of life will be older than we have been accustomed to accepting (pp. 206–207).

As we shall see in a moment, the Bible is hardly silent on this important subject. Proverbs 13:22 says, "A good man leaves an inheritance for his children's children. . . ." In that same book (17:6) we read, "Children's children [grandchildren] are a crown to the aged, and parents are the pride of their children."

But perhaps the greatest grandmother verse in the Bible appears in Paul's letter to Timothy when he tells the young pastor, "I have been reminded of your sincere faith, which first lived in your grandmother Lois and in your mother Eunice and, I am persuaded, now lives in you also" (2 Tim. 1:5). This entire chapter will make the case for what churches must know about grandparenting. But right up front, batting in the number one slot, is the issue of importance. Without that recognition, we need not go further.

## Understanding the Value of Grandparenting

As closely as value links to importance, there is a difference. We do not consider things or people important unless we value them. So stating that grandparents are "important to the church" or "important to their families" requires a recognition of the value they provide in those contexts. T. Berry Brazelton, commonly acknowledged as heir-apparent to the famous Dr. Spock (the obstetrician, not Star Trek character, for all you Boomers and Xers), advances the cause of grandparenting in his book *Families: Crisis and Curing*. He urges grandparents to embrace and stick up for their very special role. Ilene Springer (1990) quotes Brazelton in a popular article.

> As a grandparent, you may serve many purposes for a child which no parent can fulfill. You can offer comfort, family love, experience, hugs and a sense of strength and stability for each member of the family. Without the last generation as a backup, young families can feel anxious and anchorless.... Grandparents can convey what their family stands for by letting children into their lives and past (p. 16).

In a fascinating article entitled "No Market for Grannies," *Newsweek* describes how Russia's "Babushkas" have lost their traditional roles.

> These squat grannies, bundled in kerchiefs and padded clothes, were once Russia's anchor. Even in the cruelest years of Stalinist oppression, they imparted a blend of peasant wisdom and socialist ideology to their offspring and grandchildren: work hard, respect authority, take care of your own, honor your elders. They were the ones who stood in lines and kept food on the table. Child care was their domain. But Russia's encounter with market values has thrust the Babushkas into a new and seemingly heartless world (Elliott, 1994, p. 37).

The article essentially points out that Russia's new system of capitalism, particularly its runaway inflation, has no more room for a group of people who served it during earlier desperate decades. In short, grannies are of no value. That is an assessment no country or church can afford to make.

## Understanding Biblical Examples of Grandparenting

Tim Stafford (1991) says it best: "There is very little information on how to treat the problem of old age in the Bible, because in the Bible old age is not a problem" (p. 31). Though old age and grandparenting are hardly synonymous, it is certainly more likely that people beyond the age of sixty will be grandparents, will have more grandchildren, and will have more time to give to those grandchildren than grandparents in their forties and fifties.

In Scripture, old age is a blessing. Zechariah writes, "Once again men and women of ripe old age will sit in the streets of Jerusalem, each with a cane in hand because of his age. The city streets will be filled with boys and girls playing there" (Zech. 8:4-5). The image is right out of Norman Rockwell—aging grandparents quietly, delightedly watching grandchildren play. Yet the ancient prophet offers it as a promise of God and an evidence of His blessing.

Certainly the Bible does not offer a theology of grandparenting—there are only thirty-seven references to that relationship in the NIV English text. In line with Stafford's observation, however, the whole tone of both Old and New Testaments emphasizes the blessing that being and having grandparents can be a delight from God. In Deuteronomy 4:25, for example, Moses tells the people their stay in the land will be measured by generations, "After you have had children and grandchildren and have lived in the land a long time. . . ." The context is a warning against idolatry, but the principle stands firm. The first book of the Bible describes the Patriarchs, a name hardly relevant until the status of grandfather was attained—Abraham, Isaac, and Jacob.

Stafford ponders why Americans harbor such a jaundiced view of the elderly and concludes:

It is because people in America have a spiritual disease. The spiritual disease is based on a mistaken view of life. According to it, life is lived on a big bell curve. You go up, up, up to the age of, say, fifty . . . and then you go down, down, down, until you die. . . . The contrast between how we think and how the

Bible presents old age is like emerging from a tunnel in the sunlight: At first you cannot see, because you are used to the darkness. In the pages of the Bible you will find no trace of our spiritual disease ... (1991, pp. 30–31).

## Understanding the Needs of Grandparents

Grandparents partake of all the characteristics of other aging adults in the latter years of what we would call, in adult education, middle adulthood. There is an increased awareness of mortality, bringing with it a mellowing but not much flexibility or change in lifestyle until retirement actually hits. It is a time of anxiety about health, a period of marked personal and professional accomplishment. The key tense is the present, and the word that should be frequently used is "celebration."

Senior adulthood is populated by an experienced, resourceful, and often lonely group of people who have reached the age of sixty-something. In a fascinating survey of 2,503 men and women aged eighteen to seventy-five and considered representative of the nation as a whole, 91 percent said that Americans do not take advantage of age and experience; 87 percent think there are prejudices against the elderly; 74 percent think the government does not do enough to help the elderly; 70 percent say they feel sorry for the elderly; 66 percent say the elderly do not understand today's young people; while 88 percent think young people do not understand the elderly (Clements, 1993, p. 4).

What needs must the church address in its program to serve grandparents?

1. Adjusting to retirement
2. Finding new ways to be useful
3. Relating to grandchildren
4. Understanding the aging process
5. Keeping up personal appearance
6. Finding a new self-identity
7. Keeping morale high

These developmental tasks adapted from *The Adult Learner: The Neglected Species* by Malcolm Knowles (1978) fit well with the misperceptions noted above. Like other older adults, grandparents need affirmation, mental stimulation, a sense of independence, and an educational program that enables them to carry out the functions of grandparenting.

## FUNCTIONS OF GRANDPARENTING

Everything in the biblical record, coupled with the demographics of modern North American society, points to a greater role for grandparents in this and future decades. Yet a detailed report published by the Rockford Institute Center and entitled "The Family in America" claims, "Because of trends in American family life and culture, millions of grandparents do not enjoy a secure place in their grandchildren's lives. Though longevity has increased the possibilities for grandparents to contribute to family life, those possibilities are too seldom realized" (Christensen, 1991, p. 1).

So here we have a conundrum. On the one hand, we acknowledge the importance and value of grandparents; on the other, we have very little idea of what they are supposed to do, and society may even militate against their doing it. What does the church need to teach grandparents about how they should function?

### Stabilizing the Extended Family

In the Rockford Institute study mentioned above, one of the researchers claims, "You will learn more about the American family from ten grandparents than you will from ten family experts." If that's true, evangelical publishers of books, magazines, and curricula have not yet caught on. But the secular literature speaks with a single voice—grandparents serve as living historians and family archivists. Kornhaber (1985) observes, "A grandparent's curriculum is often taught nowhere else" (p. 162). Conroy and Fahey (1985) look to grandparents to help "explain the meaning of the religious heritage" within a family, claiming that grandparents are "living stories" for their grandchildren because they serve as "signs of the tradition and transcendent" (p. 200).

In today's fragmented society, when being lonely in a crowd is the daily experience of millions, the church has everything to gain by nurturing a group of people who can rebuild and affirm the extended family. Indeed, grandparents are the only group of people who can lead an extended family. That nurturing can only be done through sermons, classes, and small groups which emphasize how to minister without meddling. Many worthy attempts at intergenerational Sunday School classes and Bible study groups have met with failure, though courageous pioneers press on. Obviously, we are talking about strengthening the link between two, three, and even four generations which has, as we shall soon observe, geographical as well as emotional implications. Christensen (1991) offers an astute observation:

> The breaking of the bonds between generations is not ultimately an economic or political problem; rather, the fundamental reasons for the breaking of these bonds are cultural and spiritual. And in the estrangement of many grandparents from their grandchildren, we may detect the effects of the same forces and attitudes responsible for our national retreat from marriage and child-bearing and the upsurge in illegitimacy and divorce (p. 7).

### Facing the Empty Nest Syndrome

Sometimes we talk about the final years of parenting, but, of course, parenting never ends. Somehow it just turns into grandparenting as Christian adults in their fifties and sixties frequently find themselves engaged in both levels of leadership at the same time. But the mobility of modern America threatens close families, and the empty nest syndrome is a genuine period of struggle for middle and older adults. I bring it up here because how they handle it may very well determine the effectiveness of grandparenting. An old Yiddish proverb says, "Small children disturb your sleep, big children your life." In the book entitled *When Your Kids Aren't Kids Anymore*, Jerry and Mary White (1989) ask why parents don't let go, then offer a list of reasons: fear, vicarious living, anger, lack of trust, clinging, controlling, manipulating, among others.

They do not list loneliness, however, and that is a major factor in the empty nest syndrome. It's tough when the first child goes to college in another state, tougher when the last one leaves home to marry. The difficulty doesn't lessen when they live in the area for a few years, just enough to give the grandparents a good look at toddling grandchildren, then pull up and leave for a new job in Seattle. The sense of loss, the sheer agony of bond breaking, can often injure not only the relationship between the generations, but the relationship between the man and woman we call grandparents. All of a sudden they are alone looking at one another across the table. No more childish laughter fills the room; no more noisy teenagers need be told to turn down the radio or be home at a certain time; nobody's asking for advice. The nest is empty—the birds are gone.

Pastors and associate pastors in Christian education and related ministries are often too young to have experienced this very real crisis of adulthood. But that doesn't mean they can't understand it better and design effective ministries to help emerging grandparents relate better to each other now that they have more time to nurture that relationship. Along with all our struggles to redefine manhood, womanhood, and parenthood, and our countless books on marriage communication and child raising, we desperately need to help individuals in their fifties and sixties deal with this very real crisis of life.

### Forming Friendships with Adult Children

There is something special about calling your adult son or daughter your friend. It takes a bit of doing to move beyond the parent-child relationship to a peer level. But when adults in both generations achieve this, it brings immense reward. Deep are the agonies that emerge when grown children who should be friends have become alienated through criticism, controversy, geographical distance, or just plain neglect. The obvious impact on effective grandparenting is hardly obtuse—if you don't get along with your children, you're not likely to get much opportunity to get along with their children.

In fact, grandparent rights have become a major legal issue in a country torn apart by divorce and blended families. For example, if your son and daughter-in-law divorce and she takes the children to Connecticut, perhaps even blaming his irresponsible behavior on you, will you ever see them again? Edelstein (1991) addresses this issue, "In the past, parents completely controlled all matters of visitation and the courts refused to interfere. Since 1965, however, every state has enacted some kind of legislation addressing grandparent rights. That does not mean grandparents have an automatic right of visitation. In fact, each state stipulates who may petition for visitation of minor children, when and under what circumstances" (p. 40).

To be sure, churches need to understand prevailing grandparent rights in their own states. They may need to offer legal and ethical advice on these complex questions. But by God's grace it may be possible in most cases to preempt all that by helping older adults form and strengthen genuine friendships with their adult children.

## Serving as Substitute Parent

Be careful. When you least expect it, someone may walk up to you and say, "Mom, Dad, can I leave the kids with you for a few months while I try to get my life straightened out?" Support groups continue to grow across the nation for grandparents facing a second and unplanned parenthood. For many of them, the adjective "grand" has been removed. Unlike foster parents, grandparents who raise their natural grandchildren receive minimal federal or state support. The drain on finances, time, and energy presents a whole new problem in thousands of American families as grandparents—busy, working, active grandparents—reenlist to raise their grandchildren as they did their children.

At least part of the problem comes from illegitimate births in America. Fewer than 400,000 babies were born out of wedlock in 1970, but the ratio of such births rose from 11 percent in 1970 to 25 percent in 1987. Christensen (1991) not only notes the statistics but observes, "This surge in illegitimacy not only breaks ties to fathers, it also destroys or distorts links to grandparents" (p. 4). And, we might add, it creates the very real possibility of an additional parenting, or at least surrogate parenting, role falling to the grandparents.

But surrogate parenting is not defined merely by having your grandchildren actually in residence at your home. Two working parents living five miles away could create an immediate and obvious dependency on one or both grandparents. Interestingly, recent research indicates that surprisingly few grandmothers are available or willing to care for young children when mothers leave the home for paid employment. A study by sociologist Harriet Presser found that one-third of the grandmothers who do stay home to care for grandchildren are paid. To this phenomenon Christensen responds, "When large numbers of grandmothers watch their own grandchildren for pay, something strange—and deeply disturbing—is happening. When market attitudes intrude into the home, family ties lose something of their precious, unbought uniqueness" (Christensen, 1991, p. 5).

Busy grandparents will tell you of their delight when grandchildren visit—and their relief when they leave. What happens when they don't leave? What happens when they come day after day from seven in the morning till six at night? What happens when the exhausting task of overtime parenting becomes the lot of those who thought they had finally reached independence and well-earned rest? What does the church have to say to the thousands of grandparents who have been, willingly or unwillingly, thrust once again into the role of mom and dad? What do we build into our Christian education programs that offers any help for this strange but very real function of grandparenting?

## THE FUTURE OF GRANDPARENTING

In its April 1993 issue, *Scientific American* announced that by the year 2050, the number of people sixty-five and older is projected to expand to at least 65 billion, or about 20 percent of the planet's population. Tom Sine (1994) warns us, "We have raised our children to live in the world we grew up in. But that world no longer exists. We have programmed our Christian young, in our homes and churches, to expect to have everything economically that their parents have. And it simply isn't going to happen for most of them" (p. 5). Sine calls upon "graying Christians who hit the economy at a much better time [to] advance the money for the no-interest loans to set the next generation free. . . . As bleak as the outcome of the new demographic revolution seems, it is a revolution we can still win. But we have to wake up to what is happening in our world, and what will happen if we choose to ignore it" (1994, p. 6).

Sine entitled his article "Time to Start Dreaming—A Wakeup Call from the 21st Century." We have already noticed dramatic changes in grandparenting; Sine's emphasis on changing patterns of giving is only one of many. This last section of our chapter addresses some of those changes.

### Changing Images

We could substitute the words "styles" or "roles" for "images," but the outcome would be the same. Grandparents behave differently at the end of the twentieth century and into the twenty-first century than they have in the past, and there are some very good reasons for that. Families are smaller; many grandparents have a higher standard of living than their counterparts in the past; early retirement brings more leisure time to spend with grandchildren; and the most obvious, longevity makes it possible to live long enough to become grandparents and even great-grandparents.

Without delving into the intricacies of their research, we can summarize grandparenting styles discovered by Cherlin and Furstenberg (1992) in one of their own sentences: "Remote, companionate, involved: these styles of grandparenting seemed to capture the major variations in grandparent-grandchild relationships that were described to us in face-to-face interviews" (p. 70). In other words, grandparents as a whole exhibit varying levels of involvement in the lives of their grandchildren. Obviously, a significant factor here is geography, but social status is also important. Various anthropological studies indicate that greater independence of grandparents can actually lead to a greater emphasis on personal intimacy with the grandchildren. As these authors put it, "The new American grandparent wants to be involved in her grandchildren's lives, but not at the cost of her autonomy" (p. 190).

When we add this conscious or subconscious choice of style to the various roles we have discussed earlier, we see that grandparenting in the future is considerably more complex. In Lancaster County, Pennsylvania one can see hundreds of Amish farms in which the house has been added to again and again, making room for the expanding extended family. But in downtown Lancaster, or Harrisburg, or Philadelphia, complexity confronts us immediately. People who live longer, have more financial resources, greater mobility, and want a companionate role in their grandchildren's lives will be increasingly frustrated by divorce, blended families, increased mobility, and the difficulty of finding the right niche to exercise the grandparenting role.

## Changing Expectations

What do intergenerational ties provide? Or to put it another way, why bother with all this emphasis on grandparenting; why not just let it happen? Certainly one expectation is *greater autonomy*, as we have already noted several times. Despite the confusion of the Social Security system, which has always laid the ultimate burden of the support of any generation on those who follow it, modern grandparents do not want to rely on their children and grandchildren for economic security. The old line, "I never want to be a burden to you," now takes practical reality in the shape of IRAs, pension programs, and annuities.

Add to the expectation of autonomy the genuine hope and *need for emotional ties* between grandparents and grandchildren. Some sociologists refer to this as "sentimental currency," the joy of being loved and needed by one's grandchildren after the corporate world has decided to pass one by.

Third, we must mention the *anticipation of achievement* and the ongoing of the family contribution in a church, community, and culture. Though more obvious in sons and grandsons who carry the name, the ongoing impact in ministry as a grandfather gives his library to a grandson beginning seminary represents a very real and significant contribution to the kingdom.

### Changing Ministry Functions

When churches think about older adults, they commonly think about ways they can minister to those adults, certainly an important posture. But increasingly, they must think about ways those adults can minister in the church and to their own families. Many congregations provide for senior citizens by isolating them and entertaining them. And many older adults are content to let their congregations get away with such a poor excuse for ministry. Apart from their ministry at church as elders, teachers, officers, and a host of other important ministry roles, grandparents serve their grandchildren in ways for which no replacements can be found.

*Modeling:* Grandparents model life. If the spiritual and familial values of the top two generations are in line, children will soon catch on to the importance of a biblical lifestyle. Church attendance, Bible study, prayer, kindness, and a host of other behaviors and values may be taught by parents but can be reinforced with great impact by grandparents.

*Companionship:* Grandparents, especially those retired, have time to just hang out with their grandchildren. If both mom and dad work, or if dad's travel requires long periods of time away from home, grandpa and grandma can stand in at piano recitals, basketball games, and, one of the most important activities, taking the grandkids on vacation.

*Instruction:* Teaching is another important role. The Bible calls us to respect the accumulation of wisdom. By the time they reach later years, grandparents have more than just funny anecdotes of how life used to be. They can explain life as it should be to grandchildren forced to live in a very confused society.

*Financial Help:* This isn't always necessary; but when it is, and when grandparents can provide it, there is no reason why they should not assist with something as basic as clothing or perhaps even tuition for a Christian school or college.

## Changing Problems and Issues

As I write these paragraphs, I think of a grandparent in another state whose children are trying to cope with her meddlesome destruction of family unity. Presumably, through efforts to be accepted, and even respected, as family matriarch (she's a single mother who has become a single grandmother), she has resorted to lies and gossip in order to turn the heads and hearts of her children toward her—even if it means they must be turned against each other.

In today's complex society, the kind of loneliness and insecurity such a woman must feel leads us to understand, if not excuse, such behavior. Family structures have changed so fast that any sociological patterns today's grandparents may have learned from their own grandparents may likely be useless in this decade. What are some of the changing problems and issues?

*Staying in Touch:* Throughout all my wife's childhood and teen years, both sets of grandparents lived within fifteen minutes' driving distance from her home. They were always present at family gatherings. She could visit them virtually any time she wished. Local telephone calls provided communication between visits.

Now, grandparents could be thousands of miles away—accessible by phone, fax, or mail, to be sure. But somehow an Internet connection isn't quite the same as sitting on the porch of the old farmhouse sipping ice tea in which Grandma had just placed a mint leaf from her herb garden.

At first glance one might conclude that grandparents must bear the responsibility of staying in touch with their children and grandchildren—and they should. But when distance divides families, children will stay close to their grandparents only to the extent that their parents make that experience possible.

*Visitation Rights:* We have touched on this earlier, but perhaps it bears mentioning as American families continue to fragment. As Endicott (1994) reminds us:

> Limited rights presently exist for children born out of wedlock and their grandparents. Many states are now amending their laws to include children born out of wedlock in order to provide the children and grandparents equal protection.

These actions are to be filed in the state and county where the parent raising the child resides (p. 191).

She goes on to suggest ways grandparents can get around this problem without fighting the legal system for long agonizing months and even years. Personal requests made in love and graciousness often succeed better than a stern letter from an attorney on law firm stationery. Face-to-face meetings are considerably better than telephone conversations in matters like this. Compromise is always important, since such volatile emotional situations rarely can give both parties all they wish. Finally, the best interests of the child(ren) must be paramount in the thinking of all adult parties.

*Coping with Heartbreak:* Declining years bring regret along with the rest, and pain along with the peace. Could we have done more for our children? And if so, can we make it up with attention to our grandchildren? In one sense, the answer to both questions might be yes, but the second may never be pushed over the will of the parents. If you saw that episode of "All in the Family" in which Archie Bunker takes his grandson to be baptized against the wishes of his atheist son-in-law, you can never forget the combination of sincerity and stupidity marking that event. As long as the grandchildren have parents, the grandparents have no prominent parenting role. Advice may be given cautiously and graciously, but no one is under obligation to follow it. That's a tough posture when you have been accustomed to telling your children what to do for nearly two decades, but it is a mark of grandparental maturity to step away and allow your children to raise their children.

Someone has said, "There is no grandparenting university." Grandparents in your church probably learned how to be parents the hard way and achieved widely varying levels of success at that crucial role. Now they are thrust into a new one which requires all the help they can get. Christian educators who minister to grandparents and thereby strengthen families dare not make it a sterile exercise in demographics and sociological procedures. Perhaps it is best done in those now common, yet still crucial, small-group ministries that informally lead folks to see themselves in the Scripture and respond in biblical patterns. Informality—what grandparents do best—may very well be the key to their importance. Charlie Shedd (1976) puts it this way:

Seminaries, graduate schools, Bible colleges, summer camps, weekend retreats—they've done their good. A lot of it maybe.

Yet when it comes to theology in its purest form, can anything surpass this?

"My grandmother makes me think that God is her best friend."

And then she added this profound word (I thought it profound for a high school senior):

"I hope I can know Him that way too."

Wouldn't that be wonderful for all of us? And especially for our grandchildren (p. 138).


## For Further Reading

Bengtson, V., and Robertson, J. (Eds.). (1985). *Grandparenthood.* Beverly Hills, CA: Sage Publications. Two sociologists bring together a group of some fifteen scholars to explore this increasingly popular issue. Though the book adopts a secular approach, it does not ignore nor diminish the role of religion and values. Includes a chapter entitled "Christian Perspective on the Role of Grandparents."

Brubaker, T. (Ed.). (1990). *Family relationships in later life.* Newbury Park, CA: Sage Publications. One hesitates to use the word "unique" in describing a book, but this volume comes close. Noted for its variety, this fourteen-chapter book treats such subjects as "Sibling Interaction in Later Life," "Widowhood," and "Variations Among the Elderly in Black, Hispanic, and White Families."

Cherlin, A., and Furstenberg, F. (1992). *The new American grandparent.* Cambridge, MA: Harvard University Press. If one were to own only one secular book on the subject, this would probably be it. Of particular interest is the authors' treatment of grandparenting styles, which they group into three categories—remote, companionate, and involved. Four appendices describe the statistical approach to the study.

Endicott, I. (1994) *Grandparenting by grace.* Nashville: Broadman & Holman. The author, host of a family radio talk show in Seattle, is also the grandmother of twelve. The book is well organized and very easy to read, though perhaps overly anecdotal.

Kesler, J. (1993). *Grandparenting—The agony and the ecstasy.* Ann Arbor, MI: Servant Publishers. Taylor University's popular president identifies the unique position of grandparents in Christian families and challenges them to accept their special responsibilities.

# PART FOUR

# EDUCATION FOR THE FAMILY'S RELATIONSHIP TO SOCIETY

# NINETEEN

# HANDLING TELEVISION IN THE CHRISTIAN HOME
*Coleen Cook*

Television was introduced at the World's Fair in 1939. After seeing a demonstration, a *New York Times* reporter declared that TV would never be a serious broadcasting competitor because people would never have time to watch it. He failed to consider that people would make the time, and that the TV industry would do whatever it took to keep them watching. The average American has been glued to the screen three to four hours a day for the last several decades.

If today's Christian families use television in some way (and obviously most of them do), television influences them in some way. Whether it affects them positively or negatively is important to their personal spiritual growth and to the life of the church as a whole. Christian educators want to encourage our people to conform to Christ in both thinking and lifestyle. Can Christians use television and resist being conformed to the world it presents? If so, how can Christian leaders facilitate such "immunity" among Christian families in a TV-saturated culture? How can the church respond effectively to TV's influence?

As a former newscaster who saw television work from the inside out, I believe families need more insight into the forces that mold TV into what it is, and how TV molds us to some degree into what we are. We must recognize the shape that TV's influence can take in our lives as well as the reasons for its power over us.

Many viewers seem oblivious to what most television insiders readily admit—that TV has a limited capacity to reflect reality and considerable capacity for distortion. This is principally because TV is highly dependent on pictures to convey information. Its power is both enhanced and limited to the degree that it can change important ideas into video imagery. Pictures both shape and censor the content of news and entertainment.

Television is a mechanical makeover of reality. What we see on television is further distorted because it has been "digested" through a technical production process. The process of molding imagery and sound into a story or program always changes the nature of that story in some way. The emphasis on amusement and the drastic compression of events into an unreasonably short time period also distort TV's content. By nature, TV images are more emotional than informational, tipping the scales toward passion and away from reason. Since TV's focus is visual, cosmetic style and personality projection often triumph over substance.

Such factors are the "threads" of TV's tapestry. They exert a major influence over the content of programming. They are as much an influence (and in some cases a greater influence) on content as the human biases of TV's decision makers.

Many Christian leaders blame all the medium's shortcomings on the "anti-Christian" views of those who produce it. Human bias can certainly be a significant factor in TV programming; but if we recognize only this, educators will make little progress in helping Christians deal effectively with TV's influence. Christians must be taught not merely to second-guess TV producers, but to question the medium's ability to accurately depict reality.

Television presents a distorted picture of life, yet it powerfully influences thinking. According to former advertising executive and author Jerry Mander (1978), this is because TV doesn't just give us ideas, it determines how we will see those ideas and remember them in our minds. When a producer and a technology can determine our mental imagery, they wield great power over us. Too few have grasped the significance of this (pp. 240–245).

## THE BEHAVIOR TELEVISION PRESENTS

Our conscious and subconscious minds are filled with media-created, artificial imagery. What purpose do such images serve? Dr. George Gerbner, perhaps the foremost authority in America on the social impact of television, has actively searched for an answer to that question. His team conducted extensive research on the way television portrayed a variety of social topics, then contrasted such portrayals with more realistic, factually-grounded views. He then quizzed thousands of viewers about these subjects and about their viewing habits. His conclusion: the more time a person spent watching TV, the more his or her perceptions of life tended to reflect the televised view instead of a factually grounded view, regardless of how distorted, inaccurate, or stereotypical the televised view (Waters, 1982, pp. 136–138). We drink in TV illusions, unaware of how they influence us in dozens of ways.

Other evidence suggests that people actually act upon TV imagery as though it were reality. One federal study on television and social behavior concludes that television influences the way people develop human relationships, moral and ethical values, and family routines. Another study concluded that, along with other social factors, ". . . [television] may play a significant role in shaping behavioral life style . . ." (Networks, 1985, p. 11).

Viewers not only imitate the behavior of TV characters, but unconsciously regard many as "real." Christian author Tim Kimmel (1987) tells about an incident related to him by a friend in the pastorate: A woman in his congregation actually requested prayer in church for one of the couples on her favorite soap opera. Kimmel suggests that when Christians can't tell fiction from reality, society is in more trouble than we think (p. 153).

Christian educators should share the conclusions of such research with congregations, and encourage them to question the reliability of their own mental imagery. Such consciousness-raising efforts can help Christian families become aware of TV's influence.

## TELEVISION IMAGES AND MARRIAGE

In spite of such apparent ties between television and behavior, many continue to discount or underestimate TV's influence in the sexual revolution and in the mushrooming phenomena of divorce and remarriage. The shattered marriages of this generation and searching, disillusioned men and women of this age who drift from one romantic relationship to another suggest that many may be seeking after a "reality" they have been electronically conditioned to see. The current generation has learned "love" from countless hours of unrealistically presented sexual situations, male-female relationships, and marital roles. The imagery of these situations acts as a subconscious standard of what should be. Conflict and dissatisfaction result when real life does not measure up to a movie or soap opera plot.

Psychiatrist David Hellerstein (1987) found many couples gauging the success of their marriages by what they saw on TV. Such media-created expectations can cause marital disharmony. Real-life experience is bound to suffer in comparison, yet many couples seem unaware of this powerful influence on their expectations of each other. Hellerstein concludes that many American marriages now have three partners: two human and one electronic:

> Television has profound effects on married couples at their most intimate moments. It is deeply incorporated into their relationships and into their fantasies and dreams. . . . At worst, TV can be an escape from problems that desperately need to be dealt with directly. And an "affair" with TV watching can kill a marriage (p. 6).

Says California psychiatrist Dr. Pierre Mornell: "The images people see on TV are so unreal that they make working on a *real* marriage seem about as much fun as painting a battle ship" (Combs, 1987, pp. 147–148). Many counselors agree that the quick fixes suggested by many shows can unconsciously reinforce the impulse in real life to get out of a marriage fast if things don't go well.

People have always suffered from unrealistic expectations about life, but we now have a technology that can make fantasy look more real and appealing than reality itself. Christian counselors and pastors need to be particularly attentive to TV's influence in troubled marriages. Helping couples recognize the subconscious influence of television on marital expectations may contribute to a resolution of some problems.

Christian educators must remind people that the aim of the Christian life should be not to escape into the fantasy world that TV affords, but to live deeply and thoroughly for God in whatever real life circumstances we find ourselves. That is reality. Television is a false escape. A scriptural principle applicable to television for Christians is the Apostle Paul's admonition: "Do not conform any longer to the pattern of this world, but be transformed by the renewing of your mind" (Rom. 12:2).

## TELEVISION IMAGES AND CHILDREN

Children are even more vulnerable to the TV illusion because they have very little in terms of life experience with which to evaluate what they see. They are less able to call up other mental information or values to question the impressions TV leaves. Preschoolers especially absorb TV imagery like a sponge, with little or no capacity to distinguish fantasy from reality or interpret what they see beyond its face value. As one critic points out: "They are exposed to the whole world—as seen through the eyes of a TV screen—before they have developed the ability to understand and to cope with the larger society" (Skalka, 1983, p. 26).

In what ways does television change children? For one thing, *it turns them into adults before they are ready*. Children now carry many adult images in their minds which they consider to be real and something to model. Some surveys suggest that kids watch and prefer adult TV programs over children's programs (Kalter, 1988, p. 5). This isn't surprising, since it is hard for adults to insulate children from what they themselves watch.

Consequently, notes communications professor Joshua Meyrowitz (1988), children can no longer be shielded from social knowledge they are too immature to handle. Print communication allows for significant control over the information to which children have access, but TV has changed that (p. 5). Since we can't censor our children's viewing unless we censor our own, many children are now exposed to a confusing and mixed stream of immoral messages, political corruption, and a pseudo-worldview of fatalism and hopelessness before they are emotionally ready for it. Psychiatrist David Elkind (1985) warns that TV also thrusts premature adulthood on teens: "Teenagers now are expected to confront life's challenges with the maturity once expected only of the middle-aged, without any time for preparation" (p. 2).

A second way *television changes children is through the behavior it models*. We know that children copy and emulate what they see on TV. Someone else's view of life becomes a subliminal part of the child's mind. For example, because so many programming themes revolve around power and conflict, TV may make a significant contribution to encouraging sibling rivalry.

Children also copy what they see modeled in the home. However, the important job of modeling behavior is now shared with or, in some cases, delegated to television. The subtle risk in this is that children will be more influenced by an artificial illusion than with real life experience in the family sphere. As our children watch, they often learn the opposite of what we as parents may wish. Communications Professor Jay Rosen of New York University notes that TV wants to sell children on a way of life that their parents may not want for them, and subsequently sets up a conflict between parental views and the false worldview that television presents so convincingly (Kalter, 1988, p. 11).

The problem may be particularly critical in the first five years of life when, experts tell us, the core of a child's personality is formed. Since during these years children are the most demanding, it is also the most tempting time to use TV as a babysitter. Nielsen figures show that those under five now watch TV an average of about twenty-eight hours a week (Nielsen, 1990, p. 8); this means that those most vulnerable to television spend a significant amount of time in the most critical developmental phase of their lives learning "reality" from a medium that has a serious problem presenting it.

The problem is not confined to the under-twelve crowd. Researchers who studied TV's effect on ethnic attitudes of more than 1,000 New York City high school students found that many teens regard TV as both a learning tool and an accurate reflection of the real world. One in four agreed that "TV shows what life is really like," and that "people on TV are like real life"; 40 percent agreed that they learned a lot from the tube (Lichter, 1988, p. 6).

Christian parents must realize that even the more wholesome programs convincingly present unrealistic expectations of life to kids of all ages. The quickly resolving plots, instant gratification, and simplistic solutions all foster an unnatural, unbalanced view of the real world (Cook, 1993, pp. 202–209).


## TELEVISION IMAGES AND MATERIALISM

Television not only fosters an illusory view of life but also encourages unrealistic expectations in the material realm. From the moment we are born, Americans are bombarded with and indoctrinated by sales appeals—mostly from TV. The tube is the greatest instigator of the "I-could-be-happy-if-only" syndrome in America, the best of all preachers of the gospel of materialism, and the major perpetrator of our fundamental underlying cultural assumption that products are the solution to all our problems.

Products in America are sold by deliberately creating discontent where there previously was none by linking what we don't need with what we emotionally crave. Advertisers sell by exploiting our fears, our loneliness, our self-doubt, and our desire to compete.

The significance of TV advertising is especially paramount to Christians. The very nature of television, which thrives on creating discontent for the sake of commercial prosperity, flies in the face of such biblical commands as "you shall not covet" (Exod. 20:17) and "be content with what you have" (Heb. 13:5). We see tragic side effects of endlessly absorbed commercial messages in many ways, not the least of which is the incredible debt and financial pressures in which many families find themselves. "How to get out of debt and stay out of debt" ranks among the most popular topics now being offered at Christian conferences and seminars.

The Bible warns us about the seduction of money. Television did not create the love of money, but the principle preacher of prosperity to a culture immersed in hedonism and materialism is now the glimmering box that chatters and flashes material illusion at us for hours on end.

Christian families need reminding that our earning capacity never quite keeps up with our yearning capacity. Christian educators can help families by pointing out how ads fuel our material desires and distort reality by breeding discontent with our real-life situations. Educators can also help Christians realize that by allowing TV to determine what desires haunt our imagination, we have given it the power to decide, to a far greater extent than many realize, our very motives and pursuits in real life. We must give families a greater awareness of how commercials work to enslave them to artificial need and, in both a material and spiritual sense, leave them less than free.

## TAMING THE TV TYRANT

Screenwriter Loring Mandel (1995) insists that society has been reshaped by television but, like the spinning of the earth, many are unaware of it because they can't feel it (p. 7). Christian educators can heighten awareness and encourage Christians to deal with television. One way is to help them *develop a conscious aware-*

*ness of the "TV tapestry"*—the nature of the camera and editing process, the artificially shortened format, the emphasis on emotion, cosmetic considerations, and the other factors that manipulate content. Once viewers develop an awareness of the biases inherently woven into the television fabric, they can consciously unravel the illusion themselves. Author and communications professor Neil Postman (1985) suggests, "no medium is excessively dangerous if its users understand what its dangers are" (p. 161).

A second way Christians can respond to television is to cultivate mental immunity to its messages. We can't isolate ourselves and our children from all that TV pervasively imposes. In fact, in trying to do so we may make them more susceptible. Author and seminary professor David Augsburger (1973) points out, "Separate a young [person] from all contact with evil; and when he is suddenly faced with the opportunity, he has little power to refuse it. It is not the sterile safety of perfectly pure surroundings that we need, but inner resistance. Inner immunity to evil" (p. 39). Both kids and adults need to cultivate inner immunity to "mediated" imagery by learning to doubt its validity.

One way to do this is to argue with the television set. I have a friend named Peter who talks back to his TV. He shouts, argues, and ridicules whatever he suspects is false or contrary to Christian values. The set may not be listening, but I suspect his kids are. I think he also listens to himself. Arguments with the tube may not change TV, but they may prevent the TV from changing us. I have been told by those familiar with formerly Eastern bloc cultures that some children raised where TV was merely a tool of the state exhibit a deep distrust of it because their parents have encouraged that. Even in the free world, teaching a certain amount of healthy skepticism is desirable.

A third way to respond to the illusion is to *strengthen the quality of family life*. Robert Coles, an author, psychiatrist, and expert on children, notes:

> What children do with television psychologically, depends on the quality of their own lives—the quality of their family life. A child who is having a rough time of it personally—whose parents, for instance, are mostly absent, or indifferent to him or her, or unstable—will be much more vulnerable to the emotional and moral power of television. . . .

Coles concludes that a stable family life with a healthy code of moral values modeled by parents will help provide what he calls "a persisting immunity to the influence of various shows" (Children, 1987, p. 29).

Christian educators can also help to motivate their people to *use television less—and differently*. Families must look for ways to escape into reality more often. Church leaders can aid the consciousness-raising effort by forming classes and support groups about television designed to develop discerning viewers.

Television's influence presents a challenge for the church because it has conditioned a visually oriented generation. One way to meet this challenge is through drama. If we want to succeed as Christian educators in a TV-saturated culture, we must look for ways to "visualize truth" to the television generation. Willow Creek Community Church and others like it are dealing effectively with TV's societal transformation through the use of contemporary drama to teach biblical truth. Services feature contemporary skits which clone TV situation comedies and dramas in the style that their audiences are used to, yet deliver biblical truth and serve as sermon illustrations. (For information on contemporary drama resources for the church, contact Willow Creek Community Church, 67 East Algonquin Road, South Barrington, Illinois 60010). The church can learn something from successful social "preacher" and TV producer Norman Lear, who notes, "People accept information more readily when they're being entertained" (American, 1991, p. 1).

The job of the Christian educator is not just to convince families to watch less TV, but to help them see through its illusions. Viewers must begin to understand that TV is only a tiny window on a very large and complex world, its images only fragments of a much bigger reality. TV speaks powerfully, but incompletely.

Television will not go away. There is much we cannot change about it, so we must learn to live with it and respond to it appropriately. Christians can charge networks with the sin of caring only for ratings and profits, but some blame also lies at our doorstep if we never try to understand and put into perspective what we see. Christian educators must help families grasp that TV offers a stream of highly manipulated, technological illusions that are sometimes fun to watch, but not an accurate blueprint for living.

We began this chapter by describing a reaction to the first public TV display held in 1939. Someone else who witnessed an early demonstration of TV was author E.B. White. Unlike the *New York*

*Times* reporter, White prophetically declared that television would be the test of the modern world, either an "unbearable disturbance" or a "saving radiance" by which we would stand or fall. More than fifty years later, it seems that TV is an "unbearable disturbance" more often than a "saving radiance." We need to look at this technology in a different, more discerning light. The willingness of Christians to learn to "see" TV differently, to decipher its illusions, and to escape its unreality may make a critical difference between whether or not the "unbearable" disturbance becomes a more manageable one for all of us.

## For Further Reading

Boice, J. (1994). *Mind renewal in a mindless age.* Grand Rapids: Baker Book House. Boice's premise suggests that millions of people drift through life manipulated by television. He recommends the development of a biblical worldview through which the Christian can exercise discipline in handling all modern media.

Cook, C. (1992). *All that glitters: A news-person explores the world of television.* Chicago: Moody Press. An in-depth examination by a TV industry insider of how television distorts reality, why it is powerful, the nature of its impact on society, and how individuals can better cope with its influence.

Mander, J. (1978). *Four arguments for the elimination of television.* New York: Quill. A classic work on the nature of television, why it inherently deceives and is not reformable. The author advocates its elimination and builds a compelling case.

Muggeridge, M. (1977). *Christ and the media.* Grand Rapids: William B. Eerdmans Publishing Co. A satirical, insider's look at the weakness and nature of TV from a Christian perspective by one of Great Britain's best known journalists and TV personalities.

Postman, N. (1985). *Amusing ourselves to death: Public discourse in the age of show business.* New York: Penguin Books. A communications professor explores how television addicts culture to entertainment and show business demands, to the detriment of rational public discourse and reasoned public affairs.

# COPING WITH VIOLENCE IN CONTEMPORARY SOCIETY
*Kerby Anderson*

Growing up used to be less traumatic. Just a few decades ago, children worried about such things as a flat tire on their Schwinns and hoped that their teachers wouldn't give too much homework.

How life has changed. A 1994 poll found more than half the children questioned said they were afraid of violent crime against them or a family member (Adler, 1994, p. 44). This is not an irrational fear based on a false perception of danger. Life has indeed become more violent and more dangerous. Consider the following statistics:

- One in six youths between the ages of ten and seventeen has seen or knows someone who has been shot (*Newsweek*/Children's Defense Fund Poll, 1994).
- The estimated number of child abuse victims increased 40 percent between 1985 and 1991 (National Committee for Prevention of Child Abuse, 1994).
- Children under eighteen were 244 percent more likely to be killed by guns in 1993 than they were in 1986 (FBI Uniform Crime Report, 1993).
- Violent crime has increased by more than 560 percent since 1960 (Bennett, 1993, p. 2).

The innocence of childhood has been replaced by the very real threat of violence. Kids in school try to avoid fights in the hall, walk home in fear, and sometimes sleep in bathtubs in order to protect themselves from stray bullets fired during drive-by shootings.

Even families living in so-called "safe" neighborhoods are concerned. They may feel safe today, but there is always a reminder that violence can intrude at any moment. Polly Klaas and her family no doubt felt safe in Petaluma, California. But on October 1, 1993, she was abducted from her suburban home during a sleep over with two friends. If she can be abducted and murdered, so can nearly any other child.

A child's exposure to violence is pervasive. Children see violence in their schools, their neighborhoods, and their homes. The daily news is rife with reports of child molestations and abductions. War in foreign lands along with daily reports of murder, rape, and robberies also heighten a child's perception of potential violence.

It's a scary world, and today's children are exposed to more violence than any generation in recent memory. An article in *Newsweek* magazine concluded:

> It gets dark early in the Midwest this time of year. Long before many parents are home from work, the shadows creep up the walls and gather in the corners, while on the carpet a little figure sprawls in the glow emanating from an anchorman's tan. There's been a murder in the Loop, a fire in a nightclub, an indictment of another priest. Red and white lights swirl in urgent pinwheels as the ambulances howl down the dark streets. And one more crime that never gets reported, because there's no one to arrest. Who killed childhood? We all did (Adler, 1994, p. 49).

## VIOLENCE IN THE MEDIA

Violence has always been a part of the human condition because of our sin nature (Rom. 3:23). But modern families are exposed to even more violence than previous generations because of the media. Any night of the week, the average viewer can see levels of violence approaching and even exceeding the Roman Gladiator games.

Does this have an effect? Certainly it does. The Bible teaches that "as a man thinks in his heart, so is he" (Prov. 23:7). What we view and what we think about affects our actions.

Defenders of television programs say that isn't true. They contend that televised imagery doesn't make people violent, nor does it make people callous to suffering. But if televised imagery doesn't affect human behavior, then the TV networks should refund billions of advertising dollars to TV sponsors.

In essence, TV executives are talking out of both sides of their mouths. On the one hand, they try to convince advertisers that a thirty-second commercial can influence consumer behavior. On the other, they deny that a one-hour program wrapped around the commercials can influence social behavior. Obviously there is a contradiction, especially when we have so much documentation regarding the harmful effects of violence in the media.

So, how violent are the media? And what impact do media have on members of our family? Let's consider the evidence.

### Violence in the Movies

Ezra Pound once said that artists are "the antennae of the race." If that is so, we are a very sick society judging by the latest fare of violence in the movies. The body count is staggering: 32 people are killed in *RoboCop* and 81 killed in the sequel; 264 are killed in *Die Hard 2*; and the film *Silence of the Lambs* deals with a psychopath who murders women and skins them.

Who would have imagined just a few years ago that the top grossing films would be replete with blood, gore, and violence? No wonder some film critics now say that the most violent place on earth is the Hollywood set.

Violence has always been a part of moviemaking, but until recently, really violent movies were only seen by the fringe of mass culture. Violence now has gone mainstream. Bloody films are being watched by more than just punk rockers. Family station wagons and vans pull up to movie theaters showing R-rated slasher films. And middle America watches these same programs a few months later on cable TV or on video. Many of the movies seen at home wouldn't have been shown in theaters ten or twenty years ago.

The brutal imagery of movies should concern all of us. Even if the appalling assault on our senses is not concern enough, we should at least wonder if these visual images contribute to an increasingly dangerous society.

Nevertheless, most Americans show an ambivalent attitude toward violence. Apparently there's a contradiction between our

257

walk and our talk. We talk about the potential danger of violence in the media. One Gallup poll, for example, shows that 40 percent of Americans think movie violence is a "very great" cause of real violence and an additional 28 percent see it as a "considerable" factor (Plagen, 1991, p. 48). However, many of those same people who express concern will nevertheless stand in block-long lines to see the latest *Terminator* or *Die Hard* or Stephen King film.

Movie violence these days is louder, bloodier, and more anatomically precise than ever before. When a bad guy was shot in a black-and-white Western, the most we saw was a puff of smoke and a few drops of fake blood. Now the sights, sounds, and special effects often jar us more than the real thing. Slow motion, pyrotechnics, and a penchant for leaving nothing to the imagination all conspire to make movies and TV shows more gruesome than ever.

Movie thrillers used to emphasize the deductive powers of the investigator. These have now given way to plots about police investigators or action heroes with quick fingers who track down villains who have become increasingly psychotic and demonic.

Children especially confront an increasingly violent world with few limits. Do movie theaters really turn away children for being under age? Moreover, what is to prevent a child from buying a ticket for a PG-rated film and then walking into an R-rated film? And any child can turn on a cable movie or pop a video into the VCR and watch violent movies at home.

Children are seeing increasingly violent films at younger and younger ages. Purdue University researcher Glenn Sparks surveyed five- to seven-year-old kids in suburban Cleveland. He found that 20 percent said they'd seen *Friday the 13th* and 48 percent had seen *Poltergeist* (Plagen, 1991, p. 51).

### Violence on TV

Children's greatest exposure to violence comes from television. TV shows, movies edited for television, and video games expose young children to a level of violence unimaginable just a few years ago. The average child watches 8,000 televised murders and 100,000 acts of violence before finishing elementary school (Johnston, 1994). That number more than doubles by the time he or she reaches age eighteen.

A recent study claims that television is "considerably more violent" today than it was just two years ago. A study by the Washington-based Center for Media and Public Affairs found that television violence increased "across the board" for cable and broadcast networks alike in both fiction and nonfiction programming (Jensen, 1994).

Network executives disputed the study because it looked at all programs, including news and promotional ads, rather than focusing on just the content of network programming. But their criticism actually makes the point. The totality of TV programming affects families and especially young children.

The violent content of TV includes more than just the twenty-two-minute programs sent down by the networks. At a very young age, children view a level of violence and mayhem that in the past may have only been seen by a few police officers and military personnel. TV brings hitting, kicking, stabbings, shootings, and dismemberment right into homes on a daily basis.

The impact on behavior is predictable. Two prominent Surgeon General reports in the last two decades link violence on television and aggressive behavior in children and teenagers. In addition, the National Institute of Mental Health issued a ninety-four-page report entitled, "Television and Behavior: Ten Years of Scientific Progress and Implications for the Eighties." They found "overwhelming" scientific evidence that "excessive" violence on television spills over into the playground and the streets ("Warning," 1982, p. 77). In one five-year study of 732 children, "several kinds of aggression—conflicts with parents, fighting and delinquency—were all positively correlated with the total amount of television viewing" (Mann, 1982, p. 27).

Long-term studies are even more disturbing. University of Illinois psychologist Leonard Eron studied children at age eight and then again at eighteen. He found that television habits established at the age of eight influenced aggressive behavior through childhood and adolescent years. The more violent the programs preferred by boys in the third grade, the more aggressive their behavior, both at that time and ten years later. He therefore concluded that "the effect of television violence on aggression is cumulative" (Bogart, 1972-1973, p. 504).

Twenty years later Eron and Rowell Huesmann found that the pattern continued. Their researchers found that children who watched significant amounts of TV violence at the age of eight were consistently more likely to commit violent crimes or engage in child or spouse abuse at thirty (Plagen, 1991, p. 51).

They concluded "that heavy exposure to televised violence is one of the causes of aggressive behavior, crime and violence in society. Television violence affects youngsters of all ages, of both genders, at all socioeconomic levels and all levels of intelligence" (Plagen, 1991, p. 51).

Since that report in the 1980s, MTV has come on the scene with even more troubling images. Adolescents already listen to an estimated 10,500 hours of rock music between the seventh and twelfth grades. Now they also spend countless hours in front of MTV seeing the visual images of rock songs that depict violence, rebellion, sadomasochism, the occult, drug abuse, and promiscuity. MTV reaches 57 million cable households, and its video images are even more lurid than the ones shown on regular TV (Robichaux, 1993). Music videos filled with sex, rape, murder, and other images of mayhem assault the senses. And MTV cartoons like "Beavis and Butt-Head" assault the sensibilities while enticing young people to start fires and commit other acts of violence (Rosenthal, 1993). Critics count eighteen acts of violence in each hour of MTV videos (Powell, 1985).

**The Danger of Viewing Time**

Confronted with such statistics, many parents respond that their children aren't allowed to watch violent programs. Such action is commendable, but some of the greatest dangers of television are more subtle and insidious. It now appears that just watching television for long periods at all can manipulate one's view of the world.

George Gerbner and Larry Gross, working at the Annenberg School of Communications in the 1970s, found that heavy TV viewers live in a scary world. "We have found that people who watch a lot of TV see the real world as more dangerous and frightening than those who watch very little. Heavy viewers are less trustful of their fellow citizens, and more fearful of the real world" (Gerbner & Gross, 1976). They defined heavy viewers as those adults who watch an average of four or more hours of television a day. Approximately one-third of all American adults fit that category.

They found that violence on prime-time TV exaggerated heavy

viewers' fears about the threat of danger in the real world. Heavy viewers, for example, were less likely to trust someone than light viewers. They also tended to overestimate their likelihood of being involved in a violent crime.

If this is true of adults, imagine how much TV violence affects children's perceptions of the world. Gerbner and Gross (1976) say, "Imagine spending six hours a day at the local movie house when you were 12 years old. No parent would have permitted it. Yet, in our sample of children, nearly half the 12-year-olds watch an average of six or more hours of television per day." This would mean that a large portion of young people fit into the category of heavy viewers. Their view of the world must be profoundly shaped by TV. Gerbner and Gross therefore conclude: "If adults can be so accepting of the reality of television, imagine its effect on children. By the time the average American child reaches public school, he has already spent several years in an electronic nursery school."

Television violence affects both adults and children in subtle ways. While we may be oblivious, we should not ignore that growing body of data that suggests that televised imagery does affect our perception and behavior.

## VIOLENCE IN THE SCHOOLS

Just a few decades ago, school disciplinary problems centered on such things as chewing gum, running in the halls, talking in class, and an occasional fistfight during lunch recess. Students were respectful of teachers and each other. Few problems surfaced. And when problems did arise, teachers and principals could implement swift and effective punishment. How times have changed!

Not only do students attack one another, they assault teachers in record numbers. Each month 1,000 teachers require medical attention because of in-school assaults. An additional 125,000 teachers are threatened (Williams, 1994, p. 27A).

As recently as 1985, only 1 percent of Americans considered violence in schools a major problem. Less than ten years later, however, 18 percent now believe that violence is a major school problem ("Violence in the Schools," 1994, p. 1A).

Schools have become another venue for violence, and the educational process suffers. "Learning is compromised in schools that are not safe; our children deserve an education that is not compromised," acknowledged Education Secretary Richard Riley. He noted that parents want "some sense that schools are getting the help they need to end the violence."

A recent Gallup survey commissioned by Phi Delta Kappa found that violence in schools was the greatest concern of American parents. They listed such things as fighting, violence, and gangs as serious problems. They also listed "lack of discipline" as another important issue in the schools ("Adults in Poll," 1994).

Many factors leading to this increased violence fall outside schools' control: increased use of drugs and alcohol, growth of youth gangs, easy availability of weapons, the breakdown of the family, school lacking the discipline authority they once had, and increased portrayal of violence in media.

It is perhaps inevitable that violence outside of school would eventually make its way into the school. Street gangs and violence on the street could only be kept out of schools for so long, especially when halls and classrooms have become the new gangland battlegrounds. Approximately 135,000 children bring guns to school every day (Baehr, 1991, p. 21).

Not surprisingly, the most favored solution proposed by parents polled was "stronger penalties for student possession of weapons." Some other solutions proposed included: training for school staffs, more vocational or job training, drug or alcohol abuse programs, values and ethnic education, and education to reduce racial and ethnic tensions.

Media violence has spilled out into the streets; violence in the streets has spilled into the schools. But violence has also been coming from another source: the home. Domestic violence has been increasing for decades, and this may be the most disturbing trend of all.

## VIOLENCE IN THE HOME

The front door of many homes hides dark, violent secrets of domestic violence. The stories told in counselor's offices, police stations, and shelters for battered women only confirm our greatest fear that violence against a spouse or against children is more common than most of us want to acknowledge.

Unambiguous social statistics are often hard to come by, and this is certainly the case when considering domestic violence. In the aftermath of the revelations of O.J. Simpson, most news-magazines ran different (and often conflicting) cover stories on domestic violence. *Time* magazine stated that 4 million American women are assaulted by "domestic partners" each year. *Newsweek* magazine, however, put the number of women beaten by "husbands, ex-husbands and boyfriends" at 2 million a year. Each number was based on a reputable sociological study, even though their conclusions differed by a factor of two (Adler, 1994, p. 44).

Domestic violence usually goes on for years—undetected by neighbors and unrevealed by the victim. Sadly, the predictable progression of violence usually escalates over time. Sometimes the pattern of violence ends—in murder. There is less disagreement about these numbers. The FBI's Uniform Crime Report lists about 1,400 women a year killed by husbands or boyfriends (Adler, 1994, p. 56–57).

Ironically, the women often most in danger are those seeking to put an end to abusive relationships. "Experts warn that two actions most likely to trigger deadly assault are moving out of a shared residence and beginning a relationship with another man" (Blackman, 1994, p. 21). Often the very documents that are supposed to protect women (divorce decrees, arrest warrants, court orders of protection) spawn renewed and intensified violence.

Still these laws and court decisions do make a difference. The overall rate of women killed by husbands or boyfriends has dropped by 18 percent since the late 1970s, while the rate among blacks has dropped 41 percent since 1976 (Urschel, 1994, p. 11A). Granted there are more instances of domestic assaults reported, but this is no doubt due largely to the fact that heightened awareness has led to increased reporting. The murder rate, however, provides the truest indicator we have and it shows a positive trend.

Part of the reason is new laws. The number of laws dealing with domestic violence has grown exponentially in the past twenty years. In 1976, only one state had laws dealing with domestic violence. Now they have been adopted in nearly all states (Urschel, 1994, p. 11A).

## The Cycle of Domestic Violence

There is no place so violent as home. Spouse abuse, child abuse, rape, incest are all more prevalent there than anywhere else. In the privacy of the home—whether cramped apartments or spacious mansions—family members are pummeled and abused by husbands, wives, fathers, mothers, uncles, and boyfriends. Violence committed by someone expected to be a guardian is the ultimate betrayal.

Often the chain begins with wife abuse. In 1992, the U.S. Surgeon General ranked abuse by husbands and partners as the leading cause of injuries to women in their childbearing years, ages fifteen to forty-four. Ninety percent of the children in violent homes are aware of what's going on (Koenig, 1994, p. A-1). Soon the children become a part of the chain and adopt violence as a part of their lives.

In a group therapy session for behaviorally disordered teens, one kid revealed how his father severely beat his mother. A half hour later, on a different topic, he spoke of his dreams of marriage and family. When asked what he would do if his wife disagreed with him, he said, "She'll agree after I smack her!" (Cirio & Tieman, 1993, p. 11D).

Unfortunately, this young man was learning a lesson from watching his father beat his mother. He learned that violence gets short-term results; it helps you get your own way.

Violence of course, hurts the other person. It prevents relationships from growing and instills fear rather than love. Violence numbs us to the pain of another person. But many children ignore those lessons. They just know that "She'll agree after I smack her!"

This is the hideous reproductive cycle of family violence. Like a garden weed, it reproduces itself, sending out seeds and runners multiplying violence as it goes. Studies of prison populations show that 90 percent of all inmates were abused as children (Grant, 1983, p. 21). Most rapists were sexually assaulted as children. Most violent criminals were raised in violent families.

Children raised in homes rife with domestic warfare believe violence is the way to solve arguments and are more prone to abuse spouses and children. James Dobson (1983) estimates that more than 60 percent of abusive parents were themselves abused as children (p. 154).

This is the grim ecology of the violent family. Richard Gelles, sociologist at the University of Rhode Island, documents the cycle: "The husband will beat the wife. The wife may then learn to beat the children. The bigger siblings learn it's OK to hit the little ones, and the family pet may be the ultimate recipient of violence" (Dolan, 1983, p. 18).

Domestic violence may send Mom to the hospital and Dad to jail, but its greatest impact may be on the next generation. The children are sent on a lifelong spiral of guilt, anger, and anxiety that usually surfaces in their families, thus completing the cycle of abuse.

A child loses a sense of trust and security when a loved one is beaten. Children commonly suffer feelings of guilt, helplessness, anger, fear, confusion, and low self-esteem. These might manifest themselves in class discussions or casual conversations. Caring adults should be sensitive to the subtle clues family members give to suggest that their home is a violent place. Compassion requires that we ask questions, follow up on comments, and get involved.

## SUGGESTIONS FOR COPING WITH VIOLENCE

The previous pages of discussion should certainly wake us up to the importance of addressing the issue of violence in society. This issue should concern us all. The Dallas ABC affiliate WFAA/Channel 8 convened a series of town meetings called "Project 8: Family First." When they asked citizens about their major concerns, they ranked them in the following order (Schultz, 1994):

1. Crime and violence
2. Lack of moral values
3. Drug and alcohol abuse
4. Absent parents
5. Sex on TV
6. Violence on TV
7. Our school system
8. Teenage sex
9. Racial prejudice
10. Child abuse

Notice how many of these concerns could be listed under the general category of "violence and the family." Yet the impact of violence on the church and family is more frequently ignored than explored.

Christians must address this issue of violence in our society. Here are a number of specific suggestions for dealing with violence.

1. Learn about the impact of violence in our society. This chapter should be a good first step in helping to educate you about the pervasive influence of violence in our society. Share this material with the pastoral staff, elders, deacons, and church members. Help them understand how important this issue is to them and their community.

2. Create a safe environment. Families live in the midst of violence. We must make our homes safe for our families.

A child should feel that his or her world is safe. Providing care and protection are obvious first steps. But parents must also establish limits, provide emotional security, and teach values and virtue in the home.

The world can quickly become a scary place for a young person. By limiting a child's exposure to violence and by keeping lines of communication open, parents can deal with fears and concerns as they arise and reassure their children.

3. Parents should talk to their children. When a tragedy occurs, children are curious and confused. Nothing should be too terrible for parents to discuss. We need not go into graphic details, but we should answer our children's questions.

When children are left to their own fears and fantasies, they become upset. Parents can calm and comfort their children with a more accurate perception of the world and its dangers.

4. Parents should limit the amount of media exposure in their homes. The average young person sees entirely too much violence on TV and at the movies. Set limits to what your children watch, and evaluate both the quantity and quality of their media input (Rom. 12:2). Focus on what is pure, beautiful, true, right, honorable, excellent, and praiseworthy (Phil. 4:8).

5. Watch TV with children. One way to encourage discussion with children is to watch television with them. The plots and actions of the programs provide a natural context for discussion.

The discussion could focus on how cartoon characters or TV actors could solve their problems without resorting to violence. TV often ignores the consequences of violence. What are the consequences in real life?

6. Develop children's faith and trust in God. Children at an early age instinctively trust their parents. As the children grow, parents should work to develop their child's trust in God. God is sovereign and omnipotent. Children should learn to trust Him in their lives and depend upon Him to watch over them and keep them safe.

7. Discuss the reasons for pain and suffering in the world. We live in a fallen world (Gen. 3), and even those who follow God will encounter pain, suffering, and violence. Bad things do happen to good people.

8. Teach vigilance without hysteria. By talking about the dangers in society, some parents have instilled fear—even terror—in their children. Kids have been known to become hysterical if a strange car comes down their street or if someone they don't know looks at them.

9. Set a good example. Children learn by example. Parents who treat others with respect and dignity will model positive behavior to their children. Parents who are angry, disrespectful, and even violent model negative behavior.

Children should treat others as they would want to be treated (Matt. 7:12). Children should learn to develop the fruit of the Spirit (Gal. 5:19-24).

Parents should set firm guidelines and not tolerate violent behavior in the household. Children should learn that unkind, selfish behavior will not be tolerated at home or in school.

10. Work to establish broadcaster guidelines. TV or movie producers don't want to unilaterally disarm all the actors on their screens out of fear that viewers will watch other programs and movies. Yet many of these TV and movie producers would like to tone down the violence, but they don't want to be the first to do so. National standards would be able to achieve what individuals would not do by themselves in a competitive market.

Violence is the scourge of our society, but we can make a difference. We must educate ourselves about its influence and impact on our lives. Then we must apply the principles developed here.

## For Further Reading

Adams, C., and Fortune, M. (Eds.). (1995). *Violence against women and children.* New York: Continuum. Subtitled *A Christian theological sourcebook,* this work details the growing problem of spousal and child abuse in America. Of particular note is the section on the church's response.

Helfer, R., and Kewpe, R. (Eds.). (1987, rev. ed.). *The battered child.* Chicago: University of Chicago Press. These editors have put together a thorough textbook dealing with an American epidemic. It unfolds in four parts: context, assessment, intervention and treatment, and prevention.

Johnson, D., and Johnson, R. (1995). *Reducing school violence through conflict resolution.* Alexandria, VA: Association for Supervision and Curriculum Development. The authors introduce a conflict reduction approach which utilizes interrelated programs at both faculty and student levels. Emphases fall on negotiation and mediation.

Leehan, J. (1989). *Pastoral care for survivors of family abuse.* Louisville, KY: Westminster/John Knox Press. Much has been made in recent years of the lingering effects of dysfunctional family life and abuse on adults. This work describes the behavior of "survivors" and demonstrates the roles of family values and pastoral responses which can create a redemptive and healing atmosphere.

# TWENTY-ONE

# ABORTION—A BIBLICAL AND EDUCATIONAL PERSPECTIVE
*James A. Davies and Jerry Jenkins*

I'm forty-six years old. Last night, for the first time, I found out the names of my birth mother and biological father. He was in the army. On my birth certificate his age and residence are marked "unknown." She was sixteen. Unmarried. Alone, she carried my twin brother and me into the middle of the seventh month. We each weighed four and a half pounds at birth. The year was 1948. As I write this I wonder. If Beverly had become pregnant after the Roe v. Wade decision, would I have been aborted? I hope I can track Beverly down and tell her how grateful I am that she let me live.

Jim Davies,
Nov. 8, 1994

Educating families on the issue of abortion may be one of the greatest challenges facing the church.

This complex, ugly, emotional issue seems clear to people on both sides of the argument.

Many evangelicals do not want to talk or even think about abortion. They leave the fight to activists. They pray for those front-liners or send an occasional check to a pro-life organization. But they are not educated enough to defend their gut-level feeling that abortion is wrong. And they wonder why we need to dwell on something so distasteful.

Others hold that abortion's obvious abhorrence seems reason

THE CHRISTIAN EDUCATOR'S HANDBOOK ON FAMILY LIFE EDUCATION

enough to dwell on it. We believe that Satan (the thief) is the author of death ("The thief does not come except to steal, and to kill, and to destroy . . ." John 10:10a). We must realize that in this life-and-death battle we face the ultimate enemy. If ever there were a need to help people turn the light of Scripture on a subject they would rather not deal with, it is this one. Some view this an unpleasant task. But for the contemporary church, educating about abortion forms a vital concern.

Abortion is not just an American problem. From a global perspective, abortion has become the birth control of choice in several parts of the world. In many countries it is seen as a reasonable solution to population control. Christians worldwide need to be taught what the Bible says about the sanctity and sacredness of human life.

## THE EVANGELICAL POSITION

Entire books have argued the matter of the beginning of life. Some would have us believe that life begins at birth, not at conception. Thus the "terminating of a pregnancy," or the "elimination of a fetus (or fetal tissue)" is viewed as a medical procedure rather than the taking of human life. Pro-choice advocates need such clinical definitions to keep the truth about abortion from being known.

### The Sanctity of Life for the Unborn
Is the fetus a human being or not? That is the key question. Unfortunately, not a great number of biblical texts answer the query. Despite this limitation, key verses combine to teach several cardinal truths about the sanctity of the unborn's life.

Evangelical scholars have pointed to both Jeremiah and Paul, known and called by God for their life's work *while they were still in the womb* (Jer. 1:4-6; Gal. 1:15). Additionally, God is seen as *personally fashioning each individual in the womb* (Job 10:8-12; Ps. 139:13-16) and *considers the fetus fully human* (Job 3:11; Luke 1:39-44).

We find more definitive regard for the sanctity of unborn life in Exodus 21:22-25. In this covenant code law, two cases are presented. Case A refers to instances in which no harm occurs to either the mother or the prematurely born child (v. 22); Case B addresses penalties in which damage has come to mother and child or both (v. 23). It is enlightening to note that the passage, while referring to a fetus, uses the term "child," clearly showing that a human being is in view. Both cases describe an offense of a most serious nature: "he must pay as one deserving of death" (Kaiser, 1983, pp. 170–171).

God views the fetus as a human being with established value and worth. The value God sets on the unborn is clearly seen in Psalm 139:16: "Your eyes saw my unformed body" (*golem* refers to the embryonic stage of development). It was God who "knit me together in my mother's womb" (Ps. 139:13; cf. Job 10:18) and "knew me in my prenatal state" (Jer. 1:4-5; Job 33:4-6).

## The Sacredness of All Human Life

The Bible maintains that human life is unique. Four cornerstones form the foundation for this emphasis. (1) Humankind is different from plant, animal, and celestial life (1 Cor. 15:39-40); (2) Human life is made in the image of God (Gen. 1:26) and has an immaterial soul which will live for eternity (Mt. 10:28-29); (3) The unique sacredness of each human life is intensified by the fact that Christ died in order to purchase salvation for all who believe (Rom. 6:6-21); (4) Each believer is then commanded by God to live a life which brings greater glory to our Savior and King (1 Cor. 6:19-20).

Scriptural emphasis on the sanctity and sacredness of all human life causes evangelicals to believe that feticide is murder. Abortion is the willful ending of human life. Some allow abortions only when the fetus presents a danger to the life of the mother, while others maintain abortions should not be allowed.

Both viewpoints maintain that birth does not create life, it manifests a life already created. Evangelicals should believe that abortion is not just the termination of a pregnancy or the removal of prenatal tissue. Our concern is for the protection of human life from the womb through all of life. Based upon Scripture, each life, even that of an unborn child, is a unique, valuable, sacred creation in the sight of God.

## The Supreme Court Ruling

The pro-life advocate typically asks, if the fetus is not human life, what is it? They assume that pre-birthed humans have constitutionally guaranteed rights. Many fail to adequately understand

the basis the Supreme Court used in its now famous abortion rul-
ing of Roe v. Wade case (1973).

The decision was based on the right to privacy. The original ideas
came from the "search and seizure" laws that prohibited the state
from unwarranted entry into private homes. In the 1960s the court
began to apply "zones of privacy" to cases involving reproductive
rights (see Eisenstadt v. Baird, 1965). Justice Brennan wrote:

> If the right to privacy means anything, it is the right of the
> individual, married or single, to be free from unwarranted
> governmental intrusion into matters so fundamentally affect-
> ing a person as the decision whether to bear or beget a child
> (Woodward & Armstrong, 1979, p. 186).

During this time, evangelicals were broadly sympathetic to the
application of the privacy doctrine by the courts to the whole
arena of birth control. There was some sympathy by evangelicals
to the claim that such laws represented unwarranted governmental intrusion.

The court did not address the issue of whether or not an unborn child was a legal person with constitutionally guaranteed
rights. If evangelicals wish to reverse the decision on abortion,
from a legal standpoint, it is best argued on the basis of the
"search and seizure" privacy laws, not on the biblical fact that the
unborn is a prenatal human with potential viability.

## THE PRO-CHOICE STANCE

### Pro-Choice Rationale

*Woman's Freedom of Choice.* Likewise pro-choice advocates are
often mistaken about the basis of the court's decision. They maintain the court ruled that a woman has a constitutional right to "lib-
erty" or "freedom of choice." But claims to individual freedom of
conscience are no substitute for conformity to the will of God. The
pro-choice call for "a woman's right to control her body" reflects
not a responsible Christian attitude toward freedom but a secular-
ly informed individualism. Personal Christian freedom ends when
it infringes upon the rights of another. It is never an excuse or
cover for sin. Those who legitimately struggle for women's rights

must become more aware of accepting any rights which prevent the basic right-to-life of other, though yet unborn, human beings.

*An Individual Decision.* An abortion may take place behind closed doors, but it is seldom, if ever, a "private choice." Instead, legalized abortion has become a tool for the manipulation and exploitation of women. Boyfriends, husbands, and insistent parents beg and threaten to "do the sensible thing." Trusted professionals—physicians or social workers—often intimidate and coerce while promoting personal agendas (such as population control or personal financial gain). Sometimes they tell only partial truths. Many aborted women testify they were made to feel trapped and isolated. They experienced abortion not as an act of "choice," but as an act of despair; they felt it was their only alternative (Reardon, 1987, pp. 115–151).

*A "Safe" Procedure.* Pro-choice advocates would have us believe that abortion is a quick, simple, relatively pain-free procedure. Indeed, a woman can enter an abortion clinic pregnant in the morning and be back home or at work childless by lunchtime. Much is made of the safety and ease of this governmentally sanctioned, legal "procedure."

Of course one must ask, "Safe and easy for whom?" Surely an abortion is anything but safe and easy for the unborn child.

Most shocking to the uninitiated is the violence of an abortion. It is no simple procedure for mother or child. Depending on the stage of pregnancy, a saline solution might be injected directly through the abdomen, through the amniotic sac, and into the child to kill it. Then the dead child may be cut into pieces by increasingly larger surgical instruments that allow the abortionist better access and make it possible for the remains to be more easily removed, usually through suction.

If the abortion occurs earlier in the pregnancy, it can be accomplished by a D and C, the dilatation of the cervix and the curretage (cutting and scraping) of the uterus. This is by no means simple either, and most nonmedical people would be appalled to witness the process.

One can easily see why an abortion procedure contains significant medical dangers. Research conducted at eight major medical schools in the U. S. and in more than ten foreign countries shows that abortion was a dangerous risk to maternal mortality, perinatal fitness, congenital malformation, and future fertility (Grant, 1988).

In addition, countless stories of women who have suffered post abortion stress syndrome bear out the fact that an abortion can be devastating to the mother.

This is why Dr. Horton Dean, a respected gynecologist in private practice in the Los Angeles area, calls abortion "the greatest health hazard in America today"; "a national health disaster" (Grant, 1988, pp. 65–66). The procedure is a "risky business" (Grant, p. 67) according to Planned Parenthood. In spite of the risks, one should remember that no other area of medicine allows such an involved procedure to be done on a minor child without parental consent. Even more amazing, this is the *only* surgery legally protected from any sort of governmental regulation (Reardon, 1987).

*Every Child a Wanted Child.* Pro-choice advocates maintain that an unloved baby is better off aborted than living. But the question of a wanted child is best asked prior to intercourse.

Unfortunately the application of this ethically noble ideal—a world in which every person is loved and wanted—contains a serious abstract flaw. How do we attain the goal? By murdering unwanted children? Or by learning to want the ones we already have and will have?

But what about the victims of rape and incest?

This is the toughest and most tragic of circumstances, but again logic must come into play. A woman has been traumatized, and often these mothers are very young. Why should their lives be "ruined" by a pregnancy and then the birth of a child they didn't want? Must the victim be reminded of the crime every day of her life?

It's easy to pontificate on such matters until we wonder what we would do if a daughter, just barely old enough to menstruate, were impregnated by a criminal, perhaps a relative.

*A Plea for Compassion.* Compassion for the victim has led many to favor a pro-choice position. But dangerous icebergs float in these waters. The first is *selectivity.* The pro-choice position only selectively applies the ethic of compassion. Isn't murder a worse victimization than rape? To be deprived of life is even worse than to be deprived of virginity or freedom, is it not? Why should society show compassion to one victim but not the other?

The second iceberg is *relative values.* With the advent of biomedical research, laser surgery, macro-pharmacology, fiber optic scanning, prenatal testing, and DNA engineering, what values guide personal medical decisions? Since society lacks biblical absolutes, fearful horror stories have begun to emerge: fetal harvesting, women serving as breeders in surrogate motherhood programs, euthanasia, genetic manipulation in test tube baby experiments, infanticide, and more (Grant, 1988). Perhaps the child is an "unplanned accident" or genetically deformed. Perhaps it was not "meant" to be, but who should decide that? History is replete with examples of illegitimate or deformed children, or products of rape and incest, whose lives have benefited their families and society, and even brought glory to God.

*Unwantedness* is the third iceberg. The compassion argument assumes that no one wants a child resulting from rape or incest. Yet more than 10 percent of all married couples are childless. Many anxiously await adoption. The areas of adoption or parenting foster children are those in which evangelicals can significantly improve, especially with racially-mixed children.

**Necessary Sexual Activity**

Implicit within the pro-choice position is the hidden assumption that active sexual involvement is necessary to achieve "healthy living." Sexuality is one of the most powerful and subtle forces in human nature. But couples cannot fornicate their way to mental health.

A great percentage of human suffering is tied directly to sexual distortion, abuse, perversion, and frustrated relationships between men and women. Today's world promotes a sickness of heart and mind in the sexual dimension of life. Abortion contributes to this grand sexual sickness. It provides surgery to eliminate one outcome from recreational sex.

Scripture teaches the only healthy sexual relationships are found in a monogamous, committed relationship with a member of the opposite sex within the bounds of marriage. Many Christian teens have recognized this truth. Thousands have committed themselves to abstain from sexual acts before marriage. Over 200,000 teens recently signed cards pledging abstinence until marriage for a "Worth the Wait" rally in Washington, D. C.

Pro-choice advocates maintain that abortion is not a theological question. They see it primarily as a personal rights issue. A woman's freedom to control her body, the safety of an abortion procedure, privacy of the decision, and compassion for the plight of others are tenets of the system. The convenience of the mother is valued more than the continued existence and development of the life or potential life she carries.

## HOW TO TEACH ABOUT ABORTION

How can the church best teach about the sensitive issue of abortion? It is likely Christian educators cannot accomplish much by simply announcing an occasional seminar or optional workshop. Usually those who are already "with you" will attend. What else should be done?

### Sensitivity and Care

Abortion is an extremely emotional issue for many people. Great care and personal sensitivity are called for when addressing the topic. We must maintain biblical standards without compromise. But harshness and rigidity often drive people away from the truth.

Some Christians adopt a belligerent stance of condemnation as if to say, "We have the truth; we're better than you." Such moral arrogance is sin. We so antagonize people that we intensify their determinination to keep sinning. Sadly, such an attitude does not represent the compassion of Christ toward those who are lost or confused.

Christians are called to speak and act from a position of humble service rather than self-righteous power. The right-wing extremist who kills an abortion doctor or nurse is wrong. Such actions are a betrayal of basic Christian beliefs, not the way of love. It prostitutes the very principle he claims to uphold: the sanctity and sacredness of all human life. Thinking evangelicals find murder or fire bombing as abhorrent as abortion.

Early church belief and practice on abortion provides much illumination for the contemporary Christian. It furnishes a paradigm for avoiding and opposing abortion, war, and any other affronts to the sanctity of human life. The earliest Christian ethic (from Jesus to Constantine) can be described as "a consistent prolife ethic." But "a weakness of the early saints was their apparent preoccupation with conviction and condemnation to the near exclusion of compassion and forgiveness" (Gorman, 1982, pp. 90, 94). Many are repeating that error today.

## Teaching About Abortion

*General.* The church should encourage its membership to think and act Christianly about the abortion issue. This includes consistent teaching in a number of general concerns.

1. We must upgrade our passion concerning the fact that God loves every person. Every human being, no matter how wrong the views or despicable the behavior, is a person for whom Christ died. We dare not equate repugnant actions with the value of a person. Because God loves, all individuals should be treated with respect and dignity.

2. Let us remember that many pro-choice activists and some pro-life advocates have lives gripped by the power of sin. Often we have no idea of the kinds of influences to which they have been subjected. If we truly understand human sin nature, only God's grace makes good possible. Therefore, be compassionate and considerate to others. Opportunity to practice genuine forgiveness toward people whose activities are repulsive provides Christians with healthy lessons about God's forgiveness for our sins.

3. We need to build significant interpersonal relationships and support into any action plan. People grow best when attracted to environments described as warm, supportive, and loving. Encouragement and praise impacts in greater ways than condemnation and rebuke.

4. Some are especially called by God to take an activist position. The church should affirm those involved in proper civil disobedience, prenatal and legal counseling, foster parenting, and political influencing. This call to action should emcompass providing both for the needs of illegitimate children and relieving the suffering of women in difficult circumstances. We can't just talk the truth; we have to be the truth.

5. Activate the power of prayer. Little prayer is an affront to God. Time in individual and corporate prayer for the "silent holocaust" of abortion should become a mainstay in many of our churches. Throughout history significant prayer has changed both cultures and human lives.

*Specific.* Four specific areas should be addressed throughout the church Christian education program. All age groups need instruction in the following truths:

1. Teach the sacredness of human life (Ps. 139:13–16). All human life is precious. It is a unique, valuable commodity. Christ destroyed the hierarchy surrounding the relative value of different kinds of people. He removed all such differentiations. The born and unborn, viable and nonviable, the "normal" and the "abnormal" are all of value from a Christian perspective

2. Train believers to recognize the Lord's legitimate claim on our lives and bodies (1 Cor. 6:19-20). Christians do not belong to themselves. We are bought with a price. We are to glorify God with our lives and bodies, including our sexual practices. According to the Bible, this is our reasonable service of spiritual worship.

3. Instruct regarding the appropriateness of seeking joy, pleasure, peace, and justice (Phil. 4:8). Many Christians have foggy thinking in these arenas. Deep abiding contentment, ultimate pleasure, and true peace and justice are best sourced in God. This viewpoint stands in sharp contrast to that espoused by our humanistic and materialistic culture. John Piper's *Seeking God: Meditations of a Christian Hedonist* (Multnomah, 1987) is a good sourcebook in this area. He makes it clear that abortion is a by-product of a pleasure-seeking and excessively individualistic culture.

4. Unfortunately, part of the painful educational process may involve reading about, seeing pictures of, or perhaps even viewing a video of an actual abortion procedure. Some resources are as tastefully done as possible, but there is no getting around the fact that such are not for young children or the faint at heart.

Despite apathy and the complex challenges associated with the subject of abortion, it falls to church leaders to educate their charges and hold them accountable to the point of decision and action.

Abortion is not a pleasant topic. Some believers want nothing to do with it. But when properly educated in the light of Scripture, they can better decide their level of involvement in the cause. They may never feel led to engage in public demonstrations or to participate in Operation Rescue. But they can be equipped to state their positions with friends and neighbors. They can pray for people on the front lines. They can know where and how to invest in the cause as God directs them.

## ACTION INITIATIVES

Christian leaders can take a number of specific actions on the abortion issue. The following provide a representative list. Select those which best appeal to you.

### Parents and Family
1. Talk about the sanctity and sacredness of all human life.
2. Share how ultimate joy and happiness is found not in selfish pursuits but in giving.
3. Encourage your teenager's friends to come to your home. Get to know them. Share your opinion/story and why it is important to you.
4. Regularly spend family time with service projects that help others and affirm the highest Christian ideals. Talk about why you do it.
5. Expose your teenager to positive heroes and role models.
6. Discuss whether it is right for Christians, in a pluralistic society, to impose their beliefs on others.
7. Consider involvement as foster care parents or adopting a racially mixed child.
8. Volunteer to work in a teen counseling center or church nursery.

### Schools and Community Organizations
1. Counsel at a school clinic.
2. Volunteer to speak in health or sex education classes.
3. Challenge teens to articulate the reasons behind their decisions.
4. Sponsor discussion nights when parents and teenagers talk about important topics.
5. Promote awareness of "Worth the Wait" campaigns and that thousands of teens have chosen to make the chastity-until-marriage pledge.
6. Volunteer to tutor unwed mothers and single mothers.
7. Become a mediator for reconciliation between the girl and her family/parents.
8. Serve as weekend counselors at a home for unwed mothers.
9. Promote values and abstinence-centered sex education.

## Congregational and Denominational

1. Sponsor a congregational mentoring program during pregnancies.
2. Provide families with conversation questions in the worship bulletin. (See Appendix A for samples.)
3. Represent the evangelical position to local community groups and leaders.
4. Teach the value of all human life from the pulpit, in Sunday School classes, and in the youth group.
5. Teach the importance of a "Worth the Wait" choice. Honor youth who make the pledge the same way we recognize athletics and academics.
6. Make ethics and value-centered teaching a central core of the youth program.
7. Participate in proper civil demonstrations and activities.
8. Train counselors in all areas of needs: prenatal, post delivery/abortion, adoption, grief, post-partum depression, and personal worth.
9. Develop specialized recovery groups to deal with post-traumatic abortion stress syndrome. (The best counselors are often people who have gone through this themselves.)
10. Sponsor homes for unwed mothers.
11. Develop a complete adoption network including medical, emotional, spiritual, and legal aspects.
12. Establish a tutoring program for unwed mothers.
13. Teach and practice the importance of loving people who take a pro-choice position.
14. Sponsor mediator training.
15. Become active to pro-life political movements.
16. Establish a formal church/denomination position paper. Have copies readily available. (See Appendix B for an example.)
17. Expose church attenders to people who have marched, picketed, or counseled.
18. Provide current resource lists of curricula and training materials on abortion.
19. Practice church-wide love, care, forgiveness, and acceptance of pregnant teenagers and women who have aborted.

## APPENDIX A: 20 DISCUSSION QUESTIONS
## RELATED TO ABORTION

1. Is the nature of the fetus a matter of opinion?
2. What is a human being?
3. Is an infant a human being?
4. What distinction is there between *being* a human being and *functioning* as a human being?
5. Why is the fetus only a potential person?
6. Is abortion murder because it kills potential persons?
7. A person's genetic code begins at conception; why then is the fetus not an actual person?
8. In what ways is a fetus not part of the mother?
9. Do the fetus and the adult differ in kind or in degree?
10. Are the differences between an adult and a fetus morally relevant?
11. Does viability make a fetus human?
12. Does dependence on another make a nonperson?
13. Is it true that viability depends on time and place while personhood does not?
14. Is it foolish to claim to know when human life begins?
15. Is humanness ultimately a theological question?
16. If life is sacred in the abortion clinic, why not also on the battlefield?
17. Isn't murder a worse victimization than rape?
18. Who has reproductive freedom?
19. Is abortion good, evil, or neutral?
20. Is the status of the fetus the crux of the argument?

Partially adapted from Kreeft, P. (1983). *The Unaborted Socrates.* Downers Grove, IL: InterVarsity Press.

## APPENDIX B: CHURCH POSITION PAPER
## ON BEHALF OF THE UNBORN

**Conception.** Human life is created and sustained by God from beginning to end. The fetus is human life, God's handiwork in the womb. Human life is a unique, precious commodity, separate from all other forms of life.

**Incarnation.** For Jesus to become incarnate, to become truly human, entailed His participation in the full range of human experience from conception through death. Jesus' humility in the Incarnation dignified humanity and the unborn child. Every conception and every pregnancy is a unique, unrepeatable event.

**Neighbor Love.** Christianity introduces a moral responsibility to the unborn, who must be treated with the same kind of self-denying, sacrificial love as other human beings. St. Basil was correct in recognizing that making arbitrary distinctions between stages of fetal development to permit abortions is inconsistent with Christlike love.

**Enemy Love.** Enemies must be treated with self-denying, nonretaliatory love. The Gospel supplies the power to transform hatred into love. The fetus or the abortion doctor are not our enemies but neighbors to be loved.

**Justice.** We seek to civilly defend the rights and provide for the needs of the helpless, the innocent, and the poor.

**Peace.** Christian refusal to support abortion should manifest an attitude of nonviolence. Peacemaking demands removing all forms of hostility toward others, including the unborn.

**Quality of Life.** For Christians to introduce distinctions between human lives is a serious error. Christ has removed all such differentiations. He destroyed the hierarchy of the relative value of different kinds of people. The born and unborn, viable and nonviable, the "normal" and the "abnormal" are all of value from a Christian perspective.

Adapted from Gorman, M. (1982). *Abortion and the Early Church.* Downers Grove, IL: InterVarsity Press, pp. 96–99.

## APPENDIX C: SELECT RESOURCES and ADDRESSES

American Rights Coalition
P.O. Box 487
Chattanooga, TN 37401
800-634-2224

- Referral for abortion malpractice

Americans United for Life
1343 South Dearborn Street
Suite 1804
Chicago, IL 60601
312-786-9494

- Legislation & political dimensions

Bethany Christian Services
901 Eastern Ave., NE
Grand Rapids, MI 49503-1295
616-459-6273
Helpline: 800-BETHANY

- National adoption, pregnancy counseling, foster care
- Educational products division provides resources and videos worldwide

Care Net (a ministry of the
Christian Action Council)
109 Carpenter Dr., #100
Steerling, VA. 20164
703-478-5661

- National network for Crisis Pregnancy Centers
- Referrals and training
- Outstanding post-abortion Bible study groups

Crisis Pregnancy Center Ministry
(a division of Focus on the Family)
8605 Explorer Dr.
Colorado Springs, CO 80920
719-531-3400

- National network, refers to local centers
- "Heart Link" newsletter
- Benevolent resources and helps for CPCs

Feminists for Life
733 Fifteenth St, NW, Suite 1100
Washington, D.C. 20005
202-737-3352

- Pro-life Christian feminists

National Right to Life
419 Seventh St., NW, Suite 500
Washington, DC 20004
202-626-8800

- Nation's largest pro-life group
- Works to protect life from abortion, infanticide, and euthanasia

| | |
|---|---|
| Project Reality<br>Box 97<br>Gulf, IL 60029<br>708-729-3298 | • Abstinence education curriculum for the public schools<br>• Statistical information on the validity of abstinence |
| Teen Aid<br>East 723 Jackson<br>Spokane, WA 99207<br>509-482-2868 | • Detailed and comprehensive public school curricula available in a module format for church youth groups |
| Why Wait?<br>Josh McDowell Ministry<br>Box 1000<br>Dallas, TX 75221<br>214-907-1000<br>800-222-JOSH | • Learning positive reasons to say "no" to sex outside of marriage |
| Worth the Wait<br>Box 228822<br>Denver, CO 80222<br>303-843-9000 x 810 | • Goal: to bring sexual abstinence to over 10 million teens by 1996. Presented as a positive choice. Worldwide. |

**For Futher Reading**

Glenn, D. (1981). An exegetical and theological exposition of Psalm 139. In J.S. and P.D. Feinberg (Eds.), *Tradition and testament: Essays in honor of Charles Lee Feinberg*. Chicago: Moody Press. Good analysis of the passage.

Gorman, M. (1982). *Abortion and the early church*. Downers Grove, IL.: InterVarsity Press. Historical treatment focusing on the church's position on abortion from the time of Christ to Constantine.

Grant, G. (1988). *Grand illusions: The legacy of planned parenthood*. Brentwood, TN: Wolgemuth & Hyatt. Documents the results of Planned Parenthood's policies and practices.

Kaiser, W.C., Jr. (1983). *Toward Old Testament ethics*. Grand Rapids: Zondervan Publishing House. Excellent discussion of Exodus 21. Verse 22 does not refer to miscarriage as many modern versions maintain. The Hebrew word for miscarriage is not used here.

Kreeft, P. (1983). *The unaborted Socrates.* Downers Grove, IL: InterVarsity Press. Thought-provoking book using the Socratic method.

McDowell, J., and Day, D. (1987). *Why wait?* San Bernardino, CA: Here's Life Publications. Promotes the benefits and reasons for abstaining from premarital sexual involvement.

Newbigin, L. (1989). *The gospel in a pluralist society.* Grand Rapids: William B. Eerdmans Publishing Company. This book presents an intelligent argument on how to present a confident announcement of the Christian faith without sounding arrogant.

Reardon, D. (1987). *Aborted women—Silent no more.* Westchester, IL: Crossway. Provides assessment of the various groups in the abortion issue. Those who defend the right to abortion can be separated into two groups: mild followers and active. The active group encourages abortions and can properly be called pro-abortion. This group includes population control advocates and individuals who make money by profiting on abortions. They advance their "cause" by encouraging abortion among selected classes of women. Pro-abortionists have clearly dominated the abortion movement and are responsible for much of the manipulation and exploitation of women today. Pro-choice advocates form the second group. They perceive abortion as a right which should not be limited. But extreme actions are not typical of the majority.

Selby, T., with Bockman, M. (1990). *The mourning after: Help for the postabortion syndrome.* Grand Rapids: Baker Book House.

Woodward, B., and Armstrong, S. (1979). *The brethren: Inside the Supreme Court.* New York: Simon and Schuster. The book provides a fascinating, behind-the-scenes discussion of the formal and informal interplay, political, and interpersonal power struggles among the Burger Court justices during the Roe v. Wade decision.

# TWENTY-TWO

# THE CHURCH AND CHILD CARE
*Barb Alexander*

At the close of the twentieth century, the church in America faces a rapidly changing society in which we are all but forced to keep up a head-spinning pace of life. Spiraling costs of living, burdensome for the single parent as well as the two-career family, in many instances lead to lifestyles that require the use of a growing community service: day care. The entrance into the workforce of large numbers of mothers continues to create this need, and it is one ministry the church would do well to consider seriously if it wishes to be relevant.

Scenario One: Tom and Julie Simms are a two-career couple with two children of preschool age. Tom commutes from the suburbs to a large midwestern city; Julie works part time at a business in a nearby town. During the time Julie spends at work, her children are cared for at a day-care center near her workplace. She expects to return to full-time work once the children are in school and extended care all day.

Scenario Two: Kathy Jones, a single mother of three, works a full-time job during the day and does in-home sewing parttime in the evenings and on weekends to make ends meet. Her regular expenses include paying for the full-time day care of one preschooler and the before- and after-school care for her two school-aged children.

Scenario Three: Brian and Rebecca Nelson have two preschool-aged children whom Rebecca cares for at home. With Brian gone long working hours, Rebecca welcomes the Mother's Day Out program at a neighborhood church, where she can leave the children for a morning while she enjoys time with friends, unhurried shopping, or just a good book.

## UNDERSTANDING THE PROBLEM

The above scenarios, while fictitious, represent thousands of homes across the country—homes in which lives are touched in some fashion by the late twentieth-century social phenomenon called "day care." Record high U.S. divorce rates (Warren, 1994, p. 1) have forced many single parents to find some type of quality child care for their offspring, and two-career couples often find themselves with similar problems. "In 1993, 54 percent of mothers with children younger than three, and 64 percent of those with children ages three to five, were in the civilian labor force." (*The State of America's Children Yearbook 1994*, p. 29) In 1990, 6.5 million children under age five were cared for by someone other than a parent; of those, 64.5 percent were cared for in family child-care homes and child-care centers (*The State of America's Children Yearbook 1994*, p. 31).

*The Church Law & Tax Report* of May/June 1992 states that "churches currently provide between one-third and one-half of all child care," and that parents of preschoolers "prefer church-provided child care" (p. 2). Yet behind these front-page facts a quiet trend is emerging: "large numbers of women are leaving the workplace and making sacrifices required to stay at home while their children are young" (Dobson, 1994, p. 3). So with all these facts in mind, what kinds of child-care ministry can the church prayerfully consider?

## MOTIVATIONS FOR CHILD-CARE MINISTRY

Throughout the Old Testament one encounters God's favor toward the "fatherless," and encouragement to His people to be gracious toward them. Psalm 10:14 declares God to be "the helper of the fatherless," and Psalm 82:3 enjoins our defense of the "cause of the weak and fatherless." In Deuteronomy 24:19-22, God commands the Israelites to leave part of their harvest for the fatherless to glean, in order that "the Lord your God may bless you in all the work of your hands." Half of James' "pure religion" definition focuses on care for the fatherless and widows. Surely today one could consider children whose fathers or parents are absent much or all of the time as the "new" fatherless. To them we can apply the age-old principles of God's care and concern for such children.

There are other good reasons for a church to contemplate a child-care ministry. Among them are the following:

## Stewardship

Good stewardship of the Lord's property should appeal to many of your church members. Facilities that sit vacant or infrequently used throughout the week could be put to good use. The church's tax exempt status, space, equipment, insurance, and utilities make it a ready place for a child-care ministry. Its location in the heart of the community is an advantage as well (Reed, 1985, pp. 7–8).

## Evangelism

Winning children and families to Christ can be a natural by-product of a well-run, Christ-centered, child-care ministry. The director of a center in Fort Lauderdale says, "Children go home singing and reciting the Word of God they are taught in the school, thus reaching many families. Opportunities for ministry include visiting family members in the hospital, counseling, and touching a child or parent who is seeking a listening ear and an understanding heart" (Yeary, 1994, p. 25). Outreach can also come through non-churched families attending church functions or programs put on by the child-care center (Seaton & Rothaar, 1991, p. 6).

## Christian Values/Education

Children of church members and outsiders can receive a wealth of biblical input on a daily basis. Teachers "committed to growing in their own faith and love" can relate God's Word to "the routines of the daily program," and thus "contribute to the development of the whole child" (Seaton & Rothaar, 1991, p. 118) in a way that a non-Christian center cannot.

## Parent Education/Pastoral Care

Some churches set up "programs and study groups for parents of children in the weekday program" which offer "help with parenting skills as well as fun and fellowship within the circle of the church family" (Reed, 1985, p. 20). Speakers are invited to address topics of interest at meetings which may also be attended by church members, thus bridging the gap between families of the congregation and families of the weekday center (Seaton & Rothaar, 1991, p.12), and increasing the likelihood of ministering to the latter in a pastoral capacity.

## Outlet for Church Members

Those within the church who desire to give of their time will find a multitude of activities for which to volunteer in a child-care ministry setting—being "Grandmas" and "Grandpas" to the children; helping with meals or snacks; one-on-one reading times; or helping the support staff with their daily loads. Again, this all contributes to the main goal of the center, whether Christian education, evangelism, or whatever the congregation has determined.

## Community Relations

The very need for a certain aspect of child-care ministry in a community calls for serious consideration on the part of the church seeking relevancy to society. Whether an infant-care program, a day care for nearby office complex workers (*Child Care and Christian Education—A Policy Statement*, 1987, p. 2), or a once-a-week, half-day program to give stay-at-home moms a break, meeting such community needs will build more bridges to welcome the world into the church.

## OPTIONS FOR INVOLVEMENT

There are a multitude of programs from which to choose in becoming involved in a child-care ministry. Such options include:
1. Play Groups and Parent Cooperatives—Parents get together to share informally while their children play together, the parents often caring for each others' children on a rotating basis.
2. Mother's Day Out/Drop-in Care Programs—The church is open for children to be cared for while moms take time off. This gives relief from a demanding preschooler while it affords socialization for the child. Wishing to minister to the

growing body of stay-at-home fathers, some churches may title it "Parent's Day Out." Whatever its title, it can offer structured lessons or just playtime, and be run by volunteers or paid staff. "Drop-in Care" usually extends over more hours throughout the week than "Mother's Day Out," which tends to run once or twice a week only.

3. Nursery/Preschool—Normally a morning program for two, three, or five mornings a week, it can be part of a full-time day-care center as well. Children who attend are usually three or four years of age, although some centers include two- and five-year-olds as well. The planned curriculum ordinarily includes structured group times, free play, and a snack. An excellent preschool can be a major drawing factor for young families in the community, who often advertise for such a well-run program by word of mouth.

4. Family Day-care Coordinator—The church coordinates and provides "training for a network of family day-care homes, where people care for one to six children in their own homes" (Collins & Freeman, 1989, p. 26)

5. Day Care Center—This service is usually open at least nine or ten hours per day to serve working parents of preschoolers, and includes playtimes, snacks, lunchtime, afternoon nap, and so on. Some centers also offer occasional field trips.

6. Before/After School Care—School-aged children are supervised during non-school hours, often receiving the benefits of recreation, snacks, and perhaps even tutoring or homework help. There is a growing supply of curricula for this type of ministry.

7. Special Needs Child Care—"Children who are deaf, blind, mentally retarded, or have some other handicapping condition can be helped to full and rich lives by a quality child-care program" (Freeman, 1987, p. 15).

8. Emergency/Sick Child Care—Sick children are cared for in the church when regular caregivers cannot care for them.

9. Subsidized Care—HEAD START is the best known example of the church housing a program supported by government funds. This must be entered into with great forethought, as government monies are not permitted to support a center which teaches religion in any way (*Church Law & Tax Report*, 1992, p. 2).

10. Day Camp—The church sponsors a summer (or holiday) program of activities for children of working parents, who may take advantage of the program for their choice of hours, days, and weeks.

11. Church Co-op—"A cluster of churches may go together in order to support and sponsor a quality early childhood program for their community" (Seaton & Rothaar, 1991, p. 13). This allows for churches with greater resources to minister to congregations in poorer neighborhoods.

12. Housing a Non-profit Community Program—Such a group may contract to use church space, in which case the church forfeits its voice and influence in the particular purpose of the program. Yet it may be the right course to take if there is a community need and church members are too busy to get actively involved.

13. Resource and Referral—A church can be a focal point where families may gain information about quality child care in that community. Resource and referral centers may have lending libraries (toys or teaching materials), sponsor workshops for parents or other child-care providers, supply substitutes for local child-care programs, or help community families in their search for quality child care.

14. Advocacy—The church, whether or not it has a weekday child-care ministry, may inform itself of government legislation or community policies that affect families with young children. Then, armed with that knowledge, it may encourage its members to speak out for passage of regulations which can benefit such families.

## PREREQUISITES FOR INVOLVEMENT

In order for a child-care ministry to function effectively, it must have a proper foundation. The decision to have a child-care ministry must be bathed in much prayer. The enemy of our souls would like nothing better than to snatch as many little lives as possible and keep them and their families in his grasp. A church-based, child-care ministry could be a major effort to the contrary. Here are some major factors to be considered as a church enters the arena of child care.

## Sense of Mission

A "congregation must want and support the program," and they "must feel called to be partners in this ministry" (Seaton & Rothaar, 1991, p. 117). In order to present a united front in support of child care, the church must work through its ideas concerning the care of a child by someone other than its mother. Some would argue that sponsoring a child-care program in the church indicates that the church encourages mothers to work. However, mothers were in the work force long before churches took up the mantle of child care; and there are other community needs (ministries to divorcees, for example) which the church attends to without necessarily supporting the cause behind the need. The church can minister to moms at home through a mother's day out program and thus encourage stay-at-home moms. Whichever program it chooses, while caring for the already existing needs of children in the community, the church can communicate clear scriptural teaching about values (Hunter, 1986, p. 32).

By providing a variety of services, the church can support families who value mothering at home, struggling two-parent families, and single parents desirous of spending more time in child care. The church should choose qualified individuals to be part of a study committee to draw up a mission statement that will clearly express the purpose for the child-care ministry and its relationship to the church (Seaton & Rothaar, 1991, p. 40). The committee should also develop the goals and objectives of the program in the light of its mission.

## Knowledge of Community Needs

In conjunction with drawing up a mission statement, this study committee/task force set up by the church should conduct a thorough study of community needs to determine which type of child-care ministry is most appropriate (Reed, 1985, p. 20). Various kinds of surveys in the neighborhood and within the church will provide "conservative data which will demonstrate whether a potential mission exists" (Seaton & Rothaar, 1991, p. 16).

## Knowledge of What It Takes

Running a quality child-care center in a church requires a wide variety of resources. These include adequate indoor space, safe outdoor play area, sufficient bathroom facilities, equipment and storage, and office space. A trained and dedicated staff must be hired, and "basic requirements of health, fire and safety" must also be met (Freeman, 1987, p. 20). Many states have licensing regulations which must be adhered to in the setup and ongoing operation of the church's child-care program.

### Church-wide Consensus

The congregation *must* be "at one" with the purposes of the child-care ministry, and "view the weekday program as a part of the church's total plan" (Reed, 1985, p. 27). An informed vote of the membership at a congregational meeting is advisable, depending on church polity. There will most likely be tensions down the road between Sunday and weekday staff which will be easier to resolve knowing that the entire church decided to engage in this ministry.

### Commitment to Communication

Once the center is up and running, the congregation should be kept abreast of events in the weekday program and how it benefits the church. Church bulletins, slide presentations, artwork displays, open house, and special program nights exemplify avenues of communication that will help the church understand and feel a bond with its child-care ministry (Seaton & Rothaar, 1991, p. 122). These approaches are reminiscent of efforts to promote missions within the church, and rightly so; for this outreach, so very "Jerusalem" in its location (Acts 1:8), is indeed a missionary one.

### Building Relationships

Once a church has discerned the will of God in the establishment of a child-care ministry, it will take ongoing effort to maintain a good relationship between the church and the center. Organizing "a children's council with all programs for children represented," dedicating weekday teachers along with Sunday School teachers on Dedication Sunday, as well as other ideas for continual communication (Norton, n.d., p. 3) will all contribute to maintaining a healthy relationship between the two entities.

## DRAWBACKS TO CONSIDER

As with any serious consideration to engage in a new ministry, both sides of the picture must be clearly in view. The child-care operation of a church will face difficulties that could conceivably affect the smooth running of this outreach.

### Finances

In church child care, "a good program neither makes money nor costs a church money." It basically breaks even and takes in enough to defray the cost of teachers' salaries and training, equipment, supplies, and parent night speakers (Reed, 1985, p. 46). Since it may require one to three years of operation to attain financial independence, it is more likely that the center, at least initially, will lean on the church, rather than the reverse.

### Time

It requires much time and effort to set up and run an effective board to be responsible for the child-care center. It is also time-consuming to acquire licensing by the state, to keep up church facilities under constant use, and to undergo frequent evaluations as to the quality and effectiveness of the program.

### Staff Turnover

In 1991–1992, the annual turnover rate for child-care teaching staff was 26 percent (*The State of America's Children Yearbook 1994,* p. 30). In the last decade, church child-care programs experienced a devastating 42 percent annual turnover rate (Freeman, 1987, p. 6). Since many believe that anyone can teach young children, such workers are often underpaid and denied many benefits. A church can educate parents as did the director of Trinity Lutheran Preschool in Moorhead, Minnesota. In her commitment to elevating staff salaries, she saw no families leave her program after she educated parents and then raised the rates ("Child Care Information Exchange," 1991, p. 46). Hiring quality staff and paying them attractive wages will be a continuing concern.

### Church/Center Relationship Stress

Even if the center gets off to obvious success, expect that over time, problems will develop between Sunday and weekday programs, usually along the lines of responsibility for equipment and finances, how to utilize the same space, and "who has the final say on the child-care program" (Norton, n.d., p. 3). Coexisting as partners in the work of the Lord will take continual prayerful effort.

## High Standards to Maintain

"For many parents, because a center is housed in a church, there is an assumption that it will reflect the highest of church values" (Norton, n.d., p. 5). Parents' expectations of a church-based, child-care center are higher than those for a commercial facility (*Child Care and Christian Education—A Policy Statement,* 1987, p. 3), anticipating that Christian values will be transmitted through the Christian staff members (Reed, 1985, p. 28). Thus a church's child-care ministry has an unwritten reputation to maintain, through a quality program which undergoes annual evaluation and through state licensing renewal, if applicable.


## CONCLUSION

The church today, whether urban or suburban, large or small, stands before an open door into the child-care arena. Whether or not the ranks of mothers working outside the home swell or subside in the years to come, some kind of church-based, child-care program could prove a powerful instrument, ministering to the church's own members as well as drawing in outsiders.

And as the church has historically discovered, relevancy demands being in touch with the community it desires to reach. The church that seriously ponders its mission to its "Jerusalem" should prayerfully consider a child-care program as a distinct and privileged possibility of service.


## For Further Reading

Freeman, M. (Ed.). (1987). *Helping churches mind the children.* New York: All Union Press. An abbreviated resource for use in setting up a child-care center in a church. A full-page sample community survey is included, as well as an extensive chapter dedicated to listing helpful resources for many areas relative to the field.

Freeman, M. (1991). *Partners in family child care.* New Orleans: National Council of Churches of Christ in the USA. Discusses why and how churches can be involved with home day-care centers. Helpful resources are listed after each topic.

Reed, M., (1985). *The church-related pre-school.* Nashville: Abingdon Press. A step-by-step guide to setting up and running a church-sponsored child-care center. Two excellent chapters give thorough attention to working with teachers and parents.

Seaton, K., & Rothaar, L. (1991). *Early childhood ministry and your church.* Minneapolis: Augsburg Fortress. Covers start-up and maintenance of a church-run early childhood ministry. Includes sample forms and goes into helpful detail. Good for someone new to the field.

Steele, D., et al., (1992). *Congregations and child care: A self-study.* New York: National Association for the Education of Young Children. A workbook-style publication to aid in self-evaluation of a church-related child-care program. When a church completes this self-study, its program can be recognized by the Ecumenical Child Care Network, an arm of the National Council of Churches' Child and Family Justice Office.

TWENTY-THREE
# DEALING WITH SEX-EDUCATION
# PROGRAMS IN PUBLIC SCHOOLS
*Lory and Bruce Lockerbie*

As evangelical Christians, we believe that human beings are created in the image of God; we are "fearfully and wonderfully made" (Ps. 139:14). Furthermore, God in His wisdom made us male and female and commanded us to "be fruitful and increase in number" (Gen. 1:28). Reproduction is in His plan. Thus, for biblically-obedient parents of children, the burden "to bring them up in the training and instruction of the Lord" (Eph. 6:2) includes teaching children about human sexuality.

We must teach our children not only about their sexuality but also about their moral responsibility—to themselves, to others, and to God. The question facing Christian parents is this: *How can we best give our children a clearly biblical message, that sex and sexuality are gifts of God to be enjoyed in a morally responsible manner?*

For parents of children in secular schools, another question arises: *How can we prepare them for any mixed or wrong messages that would turn sex into something either unwholesome or meaningless?*

## WHY THE CONFLICT?

Since the end of World War II, Planned Parenthood and other social agencies have challenged schools to offer comprehensive instruction in human sexuality and sexual practices. Now the Federal government has also entered the sex-education controversy, promoting the need to limit further spread of the AIDS epidemic through explicit sexual instruction and condom distribution.

Many persons—including one self-identified as "a liberal Jewish carpenter," as well as religious conservatives—have come forward to oppose any intrusion of secular values upon a highly sensitive and sacramental topic (Budnick, 1994, p. 4). In particular, they oppose the demystifying of sex and the parallel assumption that abortion is a legitimate form of birth control by means of "pregnancy termination"—a favorite euphemism. If sex education must be taught, these advocates call for curricula promoting abstinence only (Portner, 1994, p. 5).

Yet, in spite of claiming their rights to discuss sex with their children *as* and *when* and *how* they wish, too few parents have been exercising those rights—or at least doing so very well. By default, therefore, many have left their children ignorant and unprepared for the consequences.

Advocates of sex education in schools have been able to win gradually and incrementally precisely because they could shame the opposition with accusations of prudery, ignorance, and unrealistic expectations, all enemies of progressive behavior (Dressler, 1994, p. 4). According to a Rolanda/SEICUS 1994 survey, more than 20 percent of teens advocate that sexual intercourse be experienced by age sixteen (Marriott, 1994, p. 71).

But most curricula in sex education deliberately avoid that which makes human sexuality different from animal mating or plant pollenization: the moral dimension. Instead, such curricula assume that cold, clinical, but graphic information is enough to equip a child to make appropriate ethical—if not strictly moral—choices.

Because, with other biblical Christians, we hold that the "body is a temple of the Holy Spirit" (1 Cor. 6:19), we are convinced that no parents can either ignore the reality of their children's need to know about sex nor abdicate their responsibility in favor of the schools. All parents, believers or not, are obligated to inform and instruct their own children about physical development, normal sexual desire, and moral responsibility.

We further believe that the Bible imposes upon the church a mandate to support Christian parents as they seek to bring up their children in godly nurture. Therefore, the local church must play a part in the Christian education of its youth regarding sexual responsibility.

We believe that schools calling themselves Christian must rein-

force sound teaching about sex at home and in church, not merely for the sake of imparting information but for shaping whole
and mature disciples of Jesus Christ.

From this perspective—as persons committed to a biblical understanding of the human body and its health—we contribute
this chapter.

## A NEW ERA

As grandparents ourselves, we look back to our own youth and
remember how naive and underinformed we were about "the
birds and the bees." Most of our friends were just as blissfully ignorant. How times have changed! Today, our grandchildren face
moral and physical conditions more frightening—and at the same
time, more hopeful—than anything their parents or grandparents
could imagine. The environment they inhabit is both worse and
better than ours was at their age.

It is worse for all the obvious reasons. Today's children are
growing up in a society that has all but eliminated the possibility
of innocence. At an ever earlier age, a young child is force-fed the
fruit from the Tree of the Knowledge of Good and Evil; his or her
eyes are opened to see and be corrupted by what she sees. One
sixth-grader in Lory's public school, upon learning that he was
about to begin a unit of study on the reproductive system, told his
teacher, "We don't need this course; we have cable TV."

In popular culture, assumptions about early sexual activity and
promiscuity are prevalent. A generation ago, TV host Jack Paar, of
the "The Tonight Show," uttered the phrase "water closet" and was
rebuked by his network; today, every sitcom reverberates with toi-
let humor, and every well-adjusted character is represented as
being in a sexual relationship with somebody, most often without
benefit of marriage.

Finally, the single greatest change since our own childhood has
been the broadening social acceptance of sexual perversions as
legitimate "lifestyles," especially by the apostate church. Homosexuality and lesbianism were once universally condemned on
biblical grounds; now these behaviors have advocates and even
champions in almost all but the most fundamentalist denominations.

## MAKING OUR POINT

Today's children know far more about sex than we did at their age. A familiar quip puts it well: "These days when a father says, 'Son, I think it's time we have a little talk about sex,' the reply is apt to be, 'O.K., Dad, what did you want to know?'"

But if these general social conditions are worse than when we were young, far better is the honest and direct approach some evangelical Christian parents and families, pastors and churches, teachers and schools, are now taking toward the gift of human sexuality and its proper, biblical stewardship. The inclusion of this chapter in this book is evidence.

Today's schoolchildren, especially those enrolled in public schools, are bound to receive formal instruction in human sexuality as part of the mandated curriculum in health education. Yet headlines such as "AIDS Curriculum: Fighting Words/Shapers of Teachers' Guidelines Are Hostile and Exhausted" (Dillon, 1994, p. B1) have caused many parents uneasiness when they think about their children's sex education classes. So we must commend parental vigilance; but we believe a calm approach can be adopted in most instances, one which balances legitimate public health concerns with the Christian family's inculcation of biblical virtues, supported by the witness of the church.

## TEACHING SEX EDUCATION RESPONSIBLY

In most schools—whether public or not—whatever health curriculum exists is still taught by the regular classroom teacher, who must add to her general knowledge and methodology the special knowledge of the human body. In these instances, the topic of health is often glossed over because of the teacher's lack of professional preparation. In some schools, a nurse offers health instruction as part of her duties; in others, a physical education teacher moves from the gym to the classroom. We believe that parents should encourage their public school boards to hire and appoint health professionals, trained in health science, to teach a full curriculum of health education, including human sexuality.

Only a few schools in America are as enlightened as the Three Village Central School District, Setauket, New York, a Long Island public school district where Lory has worked for twenty-five years. A registered nurse and certified teacher of health education, she and her colleagues offer a full program in elementary through secondary grades that covers all systems of the body, including the reproductive system. Lory's classes through third grade meet once a week for thirty minutes in her classroom, dedicated to the purpose; grades four through six meet weekly for forty-five minutes. We urge parents to call upon their board of education for a fully-funded health program with academic integrity.


## "GROWING HEALTHY"

The "Growing Healthy" curriculum that Lory has been teaching to elementary schoolchildren is a broad-based approach to teaching youngsters about the wonders of the human body. The early grades are devoted to establishing a good understanding of the body as a super machine. Instruction in self-respect and awe for how we are made start early. Young children learn to appreciate and understand the body systems and how they work together to function as a unit. Total health can only be achieved if mind, body, and emotions are balanced.

The curriculum is comprehensive over the elementary years, including good nutrition, dental hygiene, bicycle safety, fire prevention, anti-smoking lessons, drug and alcohol awareness and resistance, and all the other familiar and expected topics. But by far the most eagerly anticipated unit is reserved until near the end of the sixth-grade year, a twelve-week period devoted to coeducational instruction and titled "Introduction to Puberty" (Friedman, 1992/93).


## "INTRODUCTION TO PUBERTY"

As children come to understand that the body has nine systems, it is only natural that, approaching the end of their elementary schooling, they begin to focus on the body system central to this phase of their lives. Children aged eleven to sixteen are in a period of growth and development known as puberty. Within these years the pituitary gland located in the brain begins to trigger the production of hormones responsible for the dramatic and often troubling changes that preadolescent boys and girls experience. During these years, the body and the emotions begin to undergo a series of changes that ever so subtly result in the metamorphosis from young boys and girls to young adults.

We believe that, if they are adequately prepared intellectually and emotionally for these years, young people emerge into young adulthood with confidence and enthusiasm, knowing that what they have been experiencing is natural, normal, and intended to be a time for formation of attitudes and values for adult living.

The sixth-grade program called "Introduction to Puberty" approaches its topic in a sensitive, matter-of-fact way. The teacher allays most parents' concerns by assuring them that this is not a course in how to have sex, only in how the body's reproductive system functions. Following this period of parental information, with opportunities for them to view instructional materials—videos, filmstrips, leaflets, and lesson plans—students whose parents have given their permission are enrolled in the puberty course.

Next, the students themselves must be cautioned that this is not a sexy education course; it is a clinical study of the reproductive system, male and female, stressing personal respect and responsibility, including abstinence. The class is conducted professionally and with no self-consciousness whatever; yet because these are twelve-year old children, stern expectations are stipulated and demanded of them. For instance, no slang terms or street talk is permitted; no personal references to anyone else's body or behavior are tolerated. One violation exiles the offender from health class to the school library for the remainder of the three months.

Given these ground rules, children relax and appear to be comfortable when the content is presented in a straightforward manner without embarrassment.

We believe that the key to a successful sex education program is the experience and character of the health educator assigned to teach. This person must be knowledgeable and in control of an atmosphere potentially charged with awkward moments. Immature adults and prepubescent children can create an explosive environment. How unwittingly blessed a public school district is when its teachers of health education are persons of wide experience and spiritual depth.

Since every child matures at a different pace and every home situtation is different, students come to Lory's program from a variety of backgrounds and with many degrees of misinformation. She begins with the basics of puberty: the changes a person experiences within a broad time frame. When students have mastered the terminology of anatomy and physiology for both male and female systems—including such vocabulary as *uterus, placenta, umbilical cord,* and *vas deferens*—the course then focuses on the purpose of reproduction, describing conception, pregnancy, and childbirth to complete the unit.

Naturally, this program evokes many questions from students, best engaged when such questions are written anonymously on a card and answered directly in the following class. Students find this approach congenial and nonthreatening; as a result, they are comfortable writing what they might otherwise be too shy to ask a teacher or parent.

We observe that most parents are grateful for the course, especially those who share information and ideas openly with their children. In many instances, however, parents are themselves too bashful and uncomfortable to speak with their children, preferring that their offspring learn about reproduction accurately and in a better fashion than they did as children. Such parents are often relieved that the task has been appropriately handled in an academic setting.

We also observe that an elementary school puberty program serves as an effective stepping-stone into junior high school. Providing younger boys and girls an informed base enables them to accept and better understand the mysteries of nature and better appreciate the remarkable discoveries they are making about themselves.

The milieu in which Lory teaches is an utterly secular public school; nonetheless, this type of education—done appropriately—offers a desperately needed balance. In a society whose values are drifting and morals are being torn apart in every aspect, a strong base of knowledge can at least equip a child with the minimum needed to make choices that will govern his or her future. Of course, knowledge without moral content is dangerous; but so too, moralizing in a vacuum of ignorance can lead to unwise curiosity. So, better an informed preadolescent than a child deliberately kept from knowing "the facts of life."

## A DIFFERENT BALL GAME

What Lory describes in her elementary school offers an early practical approach to the ideal of sex education as a deterrent to sexual irresponsibility. Her students are, for the most part, curious twelve-year olds. Some of the girls have begun development and self-consciously wear a training bra, while many of the boys are prepubescent and silly.

But by junior and senior high school, the course in health education is "a different ball game," as one of Lory's colleagues puts it. By grade eight, sexual experimentation is common; by grade ten, a fumbling attempt at sexual intercourse is no longer rare; by grade twelve, multiple sexual relationships accompanied by pregnancy, abortion, and treatment for a sexually-transmitted disease—including testing for HIV and AIDS—are commonplace. In such an environment, the call for abstinence is in danger of being laughed out of the room; still, that message needs to be urged, especially in view of the continuing AIDS crisis. According to *Newsweek,* increasing numbers of youth are choosing to assert chastity and virginity as acceptable choices (Ingrassia, 1994, p. 59).

Typically, the teacher of a sex education course in junior or senior high school faces a problem analogous to a colleague who teaches driver's education: Both attempt to instill fundamental knowledge, hoping to inspire responsibility, and thereby save lives from destruction. The differences between teaching sex education and teaching driver's education are that one must qualify and receive a license to drive a car, and there are laws which, if disobeyed, will result in severe punishment. Not so with sexual activity; the challenge from society is, "Just do it!" Teenagers recognize these differences. Many are far more cautious behind the wheel of the family car than they might be in the back seat.

We believe that Christian parents whose teenager is enrolled in a public school's sex education class have a right to know the intent of the teacher, the nature of the course's content, and the tone of its presentation. A responsible teacher will avoid trivializing the course by using its potential for high interest to increase his or her own popularity by hints or claims of being a sexual sophisticate. The teacher will also avoid personal references or salacious assumptions; the teacher will respect the moral framework represented by any member of the class; and the teacher will earnestly advocate abstinence from sexual activity for whatever reasons can be validated, including the religious scruples of those who maintain them.

## SEX EDUCATION IN THE CHRISTIAN SCHOOL

We believe that an integral part of every Christian school's rigorous academic curriculum should be an equally rigorous presentation of instruction in health education. If the Christian school maintains that God indwells the body of each believer, then instruction in health should not exist merely as an elective opposite courses in keyboarding or photography but as a core course. At the very least, it should serve as a corollary to the serious study of the Bible.

We further believe that health education should be taught by someone deeply familiar with the Scriptures and able to explicate relevant biblical texts, relating them to the human physical and sexual condition. Whereas the public school curriculum can relate sexual respect and responsibility only in two dimensions—with oneself and toward another human being—the biblical approach within a Christian school ought to find as its starting point the human being's accountability to God, from which self-respect and respect for others lead to responsible behavior—including the decision to "flee from sexual immorality" (1 Cor. 6:12-20).

Furthermore, because the Bible is not reticent about sexual topics—whether in the Old Testament narratives, the Song of Solomon, or the New Testament's standards for Christian behavior—the teacher of sex education in a Christian school has ample material on which to draw, both as illustration and as precept.

## SEX EDUCATION IN THE CHURCH

Increasingly, some of the most forward-looking congregations have begun to include specific instruction in biblical sexuality in their Christian education curricula. Pastors offer prenuptial counseling that treats the nature of sex in marriage and the significance of a joyous and satisfying sexual relationship between husband and wife. As a result, more and more evangelical wives and husbands would seem to possess an enlightened understanding of what the Bible teaches about sex, to replace our generation's post-Victorian embarrassment and silence on the subject.

But we believe that the same sort of counsel and instruction is needed for preadolescents through single adults. Why can't a church offer a course for young people called "Getting to Know Me," taught by a health professional and introducing the young audience to the wonders of the human body? How about following such a course with a series on dating? Another on nutrition? Another on the dangers of addictions such as smoking, drinking, and drugs? Another on overcoming lusts and obsessions of all kinds?

## SEX EDUCATION IN THE CHRISTIAN HOME

We believe strongly in parental responsibility; therefore, we end this chapter in the Christian home.

How responsible about their sexuality are the children of Christian homes? Not very, McDowell and Hostetler's 1994 survey of almost 3,800 teenagers from thirteen denominations discloses. In fact, among professing teenage believers, pregnancy and abortion rates are not far different from the rest of American society.

It's easy to blame such bad news on the depraved moral environment that surrounds us, but perhaps a more pointed reason for the immorality of professing Christian teens originates at home. The fact is, even as some earnest Christian parents protest sex education in their children's schools, they neglect to fill the void at home; worse, some permit the void to be filled by tolerating indiscriminate television viewing or listening to corrupting music. Even Christian parents can be guilty of the charges of indifference, neglect, or timidity.

If, because of inadequate biblical teaching, Christian parents are ashamed of their own sexuality, they will project on their children feelings of guilt whenever curiosity is stimulated or desire aroused. If, on the other hand, parents address sexuality as normal—indeed, as God-given and therefore holy—they will also be able to address natural sexual urges and even lust in biblical terms, finding room for God's grace instead of assuming condemnation.

We believe that such instruction can best be given by God-fearing parents whose children learn from them by means of a double authority: First, the example of loving adults whose own healthful living demonstrates warmth and affection for each other; second, by those parents' strong reliance upon the precepts and promises of God's Word.

Such instruction should begin simply, gently, without drama, and should flow, as much as possible, from natural circumstances. When an older child watches a parent change her baby brother's diaper and asks about the infant's anatomy, the parent should not dismiss the questions nor invent facetious answers but directly respond with the simplest kind of reply and explanation. The older child will accept the parent's response and know that her brother is formed differently from herself because God made boys different from girls. Later on, she will learn from her parents the reason for that difference.

We believe that parents must teach what the Bible says about love and mutual respect. Jesus Christ taught that all revealed Scripture hangs on what He called "the first and greatest commandment" and the second like it: "Love the Lord with all your heart, soul, strength, and mind" and "Love your neighbor as yourself" (Luke 10:27). Loving God and loving others cannot be separated from respecting oneself. Therefore, "the Golden Rule" is the linchpin holding together this summons to holy living: "In everything, do to others what you would have them do to you" (Matt. 7:12).

While teenage promiscuity is fueled by our decadent culture, and peer pressure tells youth that "everybody's doing it," godly parents can be encouraged by such movements as "True Love Waits," an abstinence movement begun by the Southern Baptist Convention, which on July 29, 1994, brought 20,000 teenagers and more than 200,000 pledge cards to Washington, DC (Donovan, 1994, p. 4).

God's way is still best; parents who adhere to God's moral standards have reason to hope that their children will also.

**For Further Reading**

Dobson, J. (1989). *Preparing for adolescence.* Ventura, CA: Regal. A general overview of preadolescent physical and behavioral changes a girl or boy can expect and how parent and child can meet those changes.

Dobson, J., and Bauer, G. (1990). *Children at risk*. Dallas: Word. The well-known psychologist/broadcaster teams with the conservative advocate of "family values." Chapters 3 and 4, "Love and Sex" and "Questions and Answers," are particularly helpful.

Kilpatrick, W. (1992). *Why Johnny can't tell right from wrong*. New York: Touchstone. The Roman Catholic ethicist offers critique and counsel in hard-hitting chapters 3 and 4, "Sex Education" and "How Not to Teach Morality."

St. Clair, B., and St. Clair, C. (1993). *Talking with your kids about love, sex and dating*. Wheaton, IL: Victor Books. Advice from parents spread over twelve common-sense chapters.

# TWENTY-FOUR

# TEACHING THE TRUTH ABOUT HOMOSEXUALITY
*Mario Bergner*

Homosexuality, which is the proper term for sexual activity between members of the same sex both in males and females, is but one expression of fallen human nature. Almost as long as humanity has had to contend with its fallenness, it has had to contend with homosexuality. The Book of Leviticus, traditionally dated to the time of Moses around 1446 B.C. to 1406 B.C., mentions strong prohibitions against homosexuality (Lev. 18:22; 20:13). Aristophanes, the Athenian dramatist who lived sometime between 448 B.C. and 385 B.C., used homosexual situations as part of his comedic writings. The authors of the New Testament, writing in the latter half of the first century A.D., had no hesitations about addressing homosexuality (Rom. 1:26-28; 1 Cor. 6:9; 1 Tim. 1:10). "The Church Fathers universally condemned male homosexual behavior" (Wright, 1990, pp. 435–436). This is attested to in the Didache 2:2 as in the writings of John Chrysostom (Ho. in Gen., 43.4;) and Augustine (Conf., 3.8.15). One thing is certain, the ancients honestly and openly dealt with homosexuality.

Many years ago, as a young Christian man, I struggled with homosexual feelings. The culture pushed for a tolerance and qualified acceptance of homosexuality. The media exploited the medical community's speculations on the possibility of a biological bias toward homosexuality. Supposedly, it was only a matter of time before homosexuality was proven to be an innate condition like the color of my eyes. Consequently, it was assumed that homosexuality was unchangeable.

The church rarely addressed human sexuality and even less frequently mentioned homosexuality. There were only two polarized and prevailing views regarding homosexuality. The first claimed that it was contrary to the Bible and, therefore, condemned. The second suggested that the Bible was an antiquated document which did not apply to the modern expression of homosexuality. This view condoned it. Both views denied the reality of sexual healing and redemption for the homosexual. The culture, media coverage of medical findings, and the church all failed to tell me the truth about homosexuality.

## HOMOSEXUALITY IS CHANGEABLE

Medically, homosexuality is changeable. Since the advent of psychology, the medical community has consistently reported successful treatment of this problem. Listed here are six doctors who, as part of their psychological or psychiatric practices, have treated homosexuals and written books about changing homosexuality: Dr. Jeffrey Satinover, *Homosexuality and the Politics of Truth* (1995); Dr. Joseph Nicolosi, *Reparative Therapy of Male Homosexuality* (1991); Dr. Gerard van den Aardweg, *On the Origins and Treatment of Homosexuality: A Psychoanalytic Reinterpretation* (1986); Dr. Irving Bieber, et al., *Homosexuality: A Psychoanalytic Study of Male Homosexuals* (1988); Dr. Ruth Tiffany Barnhouse, *Homosexuality: A Symbolic Confusion* (1977); and Dr. Lawrence Hatterer, *Changing Homosexuality in the Male: Treatment for Men Troubled by Homosexuality* (1970). In 1992, the National Association for Psychoanalytic Research and Therapy of Homosexuality (NAPRTH), (16442 Ventura Blvd. #416, Encino, CA 91436), was formed. This group exists to advance the field of treatment for homosexuality.

The most recent medical research seeking to find a biological basis for homosexuality has centered on three areas of concentration: (1) psychoendocrine research (Doner, 1988; Mayer-Bahlburg, 1990; Mayer-Bahlburg, 1991); (2) brain structure studies (Swabb and Hofman, 1988; Swabb and Hofman, 1990; LeVay, 1991) and (3) genetics (Bailey and Pillard, 1991; Bailey and Pillard, 1993; Hamer, 1993). All researchers agree that even if a biological marker were found in all homosexual people, such a correlation would not imply causation. They are quick to point out that behavior is variously determined. They uphold a healthy respect for the complexity of human sexuality and the many known and unknown factors that contribute to sexual development.

Biological studies of human sexual orientation are hotly disputed within the medical community. In 1993, Dr. William Byne and Dr. Bruce Parsons published a comprehensive critique of these studies in the journal *Archives of General Psychiatry*. Much of the push to find a biological basis for homosexuality comes from the influence of the politically active gay community on the medical community. For a comprehensive study on the politicization of medical research seeking to find a biological basis of homosexuality, see Satinover's book mentioned above.

No conclusive evidence for a biological basis to homosexuality has been found. Most researchers state that if such evidence were found, it would merely be a predisposing factor and not a causative one. From a Christian perspective, a predisposing biological factor contributing to the possible development of homosexuality in a person correlates to the biblical view that sin dwells in the flesh (Rom. 7:18). We all have a predisposing fleshly nature that motivates all our behaviors toward sin—including our sexuality. However, the Good News is that, through regeneration and the exercising of our wills in concert with God's will, we need not be slaves to the sinful impulses that motivate our behaviors, sexual or otherwise.

## HOMOSEXUALITY IS REDEEMABLE

Biblically, homosexuality is one of the sins from which Jesus died to redeem us. Probably the most hopeful word about the redemption of homosexuality is found in 1 Corinthians 6:9-11. There homosexuality is listed among other sins, including drunkenness, adultery, slander, and thievery. But the word of hope comes in the first half of verse 11, which says, "and such were some of you." This implies that Paul proclaimed redemption to persons in the first century afflicted with homosexuality.

Paul's threefold "method" for ministering such redemption is found in the second half of verse 11—"but you were *washed,* you were *sanctified,* you were *justified* in the name of the Lord Jesus

Christ and by the Spirit of God." Being washed is related to the preparation and experience of baptism. In baptism, the new Christian willingly lets go of his or her old life by dying to it, even as Jesus died on the cross, and then rises to a new life apart from the old one, even as Jesus rose from the dead. Being sanctified is the process by which a person, after being converted, embarks on the lifelong journey of becoming holy, even as Jesus was holy. This process of sanctification could also be called "identification with Christ." Sanctification and growth in holiness is the pathway to Christian maturity (the goal of personal healing). Finally, being justified means knowing not only that one is forgiven of sins, but also that, because God no longer looks on our past sins, we are free from shame and guilt.

## THE GOSPEL MINISTRY OF REDEMPTION

This threefold order of redemption can only be properly operative in a church whose ministry is modeled after that of Jesus in the Gospels. This order of ministry, like the order of redemption, is threefold. The first is teaching; the second, preaching; and the third, healing. The Bible attests to this order in Matthew 9:35, which reads, "Then Jesus went through all the towns and villages, *teaching* in their synagogues, and *preaching* the good news of the kingdom, and *healing* every disease and sickness." This verse bridges the first and second sections of Matthew's Gospel. The first is about Jesus teaching, preaching, and healing. The second is about Jesus' disciples teaching, preaching, and healing.

### Understanding Redemption
Teaching the truth about homosexuality begins with an understanding of the process by which a person struggling with this problem receives sexual redemption in Christ. Repentance from all sin, including sexual sin (homosexual or otherwise) is a good beginning. The redemptive process is a combination of discipleship and pastoral care.

Discipleship follows conversion and regeneration in Jesus Christ. Identification with Jesus is the personal goal in the Christian life; all healing is an outgrowth of that goal. Our union with Jesus, who is the image of God, restores the image of God in us as male and female (Gen. 1:27), our true identity. Biblically, there is no such thing as a homosexual *per se,* only males and females who engage in homosexual behaviors. Renouncing one's identity as "gay or lesbian" and embracing one's identity as the male or female bearer of God's image is part of the sexually redemptive process for the homosexual. Additionally, teaching the basics in Christian spirituality, such as Bible study, personal devotions, and loving others through service are central aspects of discipleship.

Pastoral care, when born out of discipleship, enables a person to examine himself or herself before God. The Christian struggling with homosexual issues must face the gender confusion preventing him or her from realizing true identity in Jesus. Inevitably, gender confusion is rooted in broken relationships with significant others of both sexes. Healing these broken relationships begins with applying the Cross of Christ to forgive sin in self and others. After forgiveness is applied, one must deal with the wounding and shaping effects these relationships have had on the personality. Ongoing pastoral care is necessary to help a person come free from unhealthy attitudes, emotions, and behaviors rooted in these past relationships.

**Recognizing Sin**

Teaching on homosexuality also entails lovingly addressing the popular cultural beliefs that homosexuality is an innate condition. The published material within the medical community documenting the changeability of homosexuality is helpful. If homosexuality were innate, then it could not be changed. Again, the biological studies in this area are inconclusive and are not seeking a causative factor but a predisposing one. However, if medical evidence for a biological factor influencing the development of homosexuality were found, then the same medical technology that discovered such a factor could be employed in finding a medical treatment for homosexuality.

Preaching the truth about homosexuality begins with biblically-based sermons that place homosexuality in the category of all other sins, focus on the redemptive work of Christ, and employ a sound exegetical usage of the original biblical languages. Perhaps the greatest damage done to the right handling of God's Word in regard to homosexuality is poor scholarship. Such scholarship argues that homosexuality was rejected in biblical cultures because it was related to homosexual rape (Sodom and Gomorrah); it was insincere and unloving sexual behavior committed by heterosexuals (Rom. 1); or it is really male prostitution (1 Cor. 6:9 and 1 Tim. 1:10).

John Boswell's book, *Christianity, Social Tolerance, and Homosexuality* (1980), offers an example of such work. According to Boswell, the acceptance of homosexuality is a culturally determined phenomenon. He asserts the Bible does not speak to the possible positive cultural contexts for homosexuality. Such a positive context, in Boswell's view, treats homosexuality as an innate orientation and encourages committed monogamous same-sex unions. For this reason homosexuality ought to be accepted as a viable sexual alternative for all Christians. According to Boswell, the Greek word translated homosexual (*arsenokoitai*) in Pauline passages exclusively referred to active male prostitutes, and not to homosexuality in general.

In 1984, D. F. Wright published a definitive scholarly work establishing that "homosexual" is the correct translation for *arsenokoitai*. Wright reasons that Paul, being a Greek-speaking Jew, would have been familiar with the Old Testament in its Greek translation, the Septuagint (LXX). Therefore, Paul would have used the same Greek word the LXX uses for homosexual in the Levitical passages for his New Testament references—which he did. Another such scholarly work refuting Boswell was published in 1986 by Dr. Richard B. Hays in *The Journal of Religious Ethics.*

Healing homosexuality is inextricably linked to instructional preaching. When a church teaches the medical truth about the changeability of homosexuality and preaches the biblical truth about God's desire to redeem homosexuality, then it adopts a position to pray for the healing of homosexuals who desire to change.

### Finding Help

Ministries that equip the Body of Christ to extend redemption and healing for homosexuality include Pastoral Care Ministries (PO Box 1313, Wheaton, IL 60189-1313); Redeemed Life Ministries (PO Box 1211, Wheaton, IL 60189-1211); Desert Streams Ministries (12488 Venice Blvd., Los Angeles, CA 90066-3840); Regeneration Ministries (PO Box 1034, Fairfax, VA 22030-1034); and a host of others, many of which operate under the umbrella of Exodus International (PO Box 2121, San Rafael, CA 94912).

Small groups focusing on sexual redemption in Christ, such as

Andrew Comiskey's Living Waters Program (available through Desert Streams Ministries), are a good source of ongoing healing and pastoral care for the Christian struggling with homosexuality. Additionally, both Pastoral Care Ministries and Redeemed Life Ministries offer week-long and weekend seminars ministering personal and sexual redemption in Christ. Regeneration Books (PO Box 9830, Baltimore, MD 21284-9830) publishes a quarterly mail order catalog offering the most comprehensive list of books on the subject of redemption for the homosexual. I recommend Leanne Payne's, *The Broken Image* (1981), Andrew Comiskey's, *Pursuing Sexual Wholeness* (1989), and Mario Bergner's, *Setting Love in Order* (1995).

## THE DELICATE BALANCE OF TEACHING, PREACHING, AND HEALING

Today we have at least three types of inadequate shepherds within the church who violate the delicate balance of teaching, preaching, and healing.

### Inadequate Shepherds

The first includes those who only preach and teach but do not minister healing. I encountered such shepherds in the Bible-believing churches of my youth. Although they knew the truth, they were not equipped to apply the biblical redemptive triad "washed, sanctified, and justified" to my broken sexuality. In fact, they only preached sermons on the condemnation of the homosexual. Never did I hear a message on the redemption of homosexuals.

The second type includes those who neglect the lost condition of the homosexual altogether. They hold that homosexuality is not sin. They ignore the medical truth about the changeability of this condition and do not preach the biblical incompatibility between homosexuality and Christianity. Without the truth, they offer neither healing nor redemption to those struggling with this problem.

The third type is probably the most dangerous. They know redemption from homosexuality is a biblical reality. But they are caught up in church structures bonded to the second group of shepherds. They suggest that in order to be an inclusive church, we have to honor the "traditional liberal" viewpoint on this subject. What they call "tradition" the Apostles and Church Fathers called "heresy." This third group builds bridges to the second group, afraid to say to them, "You are outside the biblical world view and therefore outside the church. Integrating homosexuality and Christianity is heresy." In one context they affirm the ministry of redemption for the homosexual; in another they make room for "gay Christians."

## Historical Models

John, Paul, and Polycarp are our models in such matters. They all knew not to build bridges with persons who corrupted the truth. John refused to dialogue or tolerate the gnosticism of Cerinthus in the first-century church. Church Father Irenaeus, a disciple of Polycarp, wrote in *Against Heresies,*

> John, the disciple of the Lord, going to bathe at Ephesus, and perceiving Cerinthus within, rushed out of the bath house without bathing exclaiming, "Let us fly, lest even the bathhouse fall down because Cerinthus, the enemy of the truth is within" (p. 476).

Likewise, Paul commanded the Corinthian believers to expel the immoral brother (1 Cor. 5:9). (However, this expulsion is for a redemptive purpose. Second Corinthians 2: 5-11 indicates the one who is expelled is to be restored and comforted should he seek forgiveness.) Additionally, Polycarp, John's disciple, refused to dialogue and tolerate the gnostic Marcion in the second century church.

> Polycarp himself replied to Marcion who met him on one occasion, and said, "Dost thou know Me?" "I do know thee, the first-born of Satan." Such was the horror which the apostles and their disciples had against holding even verbal communication with corrupters of the truth (Irenaeus, A.D. 182–188, p. 476).

Cerinthus, the immoral man in 1 Corinthians 5, and Marcion all claimed to be Christians. Neither John, Paul, nor Polycarp engaged in dialogue with such men. From both medical and biblical viewpoints homosexuality is a changeable condition. The medical answer to homosexuality is treatment through psychological and psychiatric means. The biblical answer to homosexuality is redemption through being washed, justified, and sanctified in Jesus Christ.

The congregation that wants to minister effectively to persons struggling with homosexuality must uphold the biblical triad of teaching, preaching, and healing. This entails speaking the truth in love to misguided Christians within the church who wrongly tolerate modern-day gnostics asserting homosexuality is compatible with Christianity. Just as John, Paul, and the early Church Father Polycarp spoke out against those who corrupted the truth, so too we must speak out against those who corrupt the truth about the healing and redemption of homosexuals. We may even need to disassociate ourselves from such people. Moreover, as a church we must be equipped to properly minister sexual redemption in Christ to all Christians who struggle homosexually. Only then can the Gospel ministry of teaching, preaching, and healing be preserved. Only then will the truth be told about homosexuality.

### For Further Reading

Bergner, M. (1995). *Setting love in order.* Grand Rapids: Baker Book House. The author's personal account of his struggle with homosexuality and reflections on what must be in order to live the redeemed life.

Payne, L. (1995). *The broken image.* Grand Rapids: Baker Book House. A thoughtful examination of the roots of homosexuality with the clear hope of healing.

Pieper, J. (1966). *The four cardinal virtues: Prudence, justice, fortitude, temperance* (Richard and Clara Winston, Trans.). Notre Dame, Ind.: University of Notre Dame Press. An important book (the author has written other related ones as well) dealing with the virtues. In our individualized culture many will, even in the church, question the need for living the virtuous life. Pieper clearly shows the importance of virtue in Christian ethics and life.

Satinover, J. (1995). *Homosexuality and the politics of truth.* Grand Rapids: Baker Book House. The author documents how homosexuality has moved from beng considered an aberration a generation ago to simply an alternative lifestyle.

# CONCLUSION

During the turbulent days of post World War II America, Al Scalpone penned the memorable line "The family that prays together stays together." The slogan was used in the Roman Catholic Family Rosary Crusade of that era. Through the campaign and its slogan we hear concerns about the strength of the family and its survival midst the pressures of American culture. This is a simple reminder, from fifty years ago, that in every age the people of God must constantly consider how families can be strengthened as places of service, rest, nurture, and worship.

In putting together this volume, we sought people who had firsthand involvement and interest in the areas they were addressing. Thus, in reading the viewpoints of such authors of passion and concern, you may have felt that they were vying with each other to "sell" their particular issues. This was intended, but it points to a larger problem in so many contemporary approaches to the family. We have a better grasp of the parts than the whole. However, in the long run, the church will not be served well if we simply politicize "the family" and demand attention be given to our worthy agendas whether they be special needs children, single parents, or the effects of media on the family.

In this volume we find the wise and seasoned words of exceptional practitioners. The ideas suggested have been tried and refined and reflect some of the best approaches to family life education available today. However, we would like to suggest some additional areas that need research and attention in this vital area of family life education and ministry.

• *The virtues.* Family life has a way of showing what we are made of. There are virtues (e.g., fidelity, patience, forgiveness) foundational to our joyful living and healthy family life which need to be part of any comprehensive spiritual formation/family life education program. In contemporary family-oriented books— the current volume is not an exception—the virtues necessary for family life do not receive as much attention as more psychologically oriented issues like interpersonal communication. We need to give the virtues far more attention in our research and teaching on family life.

• *Gender issues.* A refreshing aspect of this volume is that it is not overburdened by confusing "family life education" with an indoctrination in gender roles. Evangelicals have wasted time and resources in trying to define and promulgate precise "gender roles" for family members. This approach has proven unworkable and has largely been set aside, but ignoring gender differences is not what is needed either. We need clear biblical research, by those who understand what is truly feminine and masculine, which can help us embrace this part of our identity.

• *Role of children.* Jesus showed compassion for children, those who can so easily become the victims of a society racing to meet its agenda. The church needs to understand the genuine ministry of children in our midst and how they fare in our culture. In a society where value comes from "what we produce" it is easy to view children as only having a "potential value." As Christians we need to look carefully at the way our culture often devalues children.

Finally, with these caveats aside, we want to extend our thanks to our contributors. They were able to write simply and clearly about what they have found to work in educating families and strengthening "the ministry of the family." The next step is up to you. May your church community be blessed as you implement their family life helps.

# REFERENCES

Abbott, T. (1974). *Ephesians and Colossians*. In The International Critical Commentary. Edinburgh: T & T Clark, 1897, reprinted.

ACSI Directory, 1994. Whittier, CA: Association of Christian Schools International.

Adler, J. (1994, July 25). The numbers game. *Newsweek*, pp. 56-57.

———. (1994, January 10). Kids growing up scared. *Newsweek*, p. 44.

Adults in poll count violence as schools' biggest concern. (1994, August 26). *Dallas Morning News*, p. 8A.

*American Family Association Pass Along Sheet.* (1991).

Anderson, R., and Guernsey, D. (1985). *On being family*. Grand Rapids: William B. Eerdmans Publishing Co.

Augsburger, D. (1973). *A risk worth taking*. Chicago: Moody Press.

Axelson, J. (1993). *Counseling and development in a multi-cultural society*. Pacific Grove, CA: Brooks/Cole.

Baehr, T. (1991, December). *Religious Broadcasting*, p. 21.

Bailey, J., and Pillard, R. (1991). A genetic study of male sexual orientation. *Archives of general psychiatry*.

———. (1993). Heritable factors influence sexual orientation in women. *Archives of general psychiatry*, p. 59.

Balswick, J., and Balswick, J. (1989). *The family: A Christian perspective on the contemporary home*. Grand Rapids: Baker Book House.

Bane, M.J. (1976). Marital disruption and the lives of children. *Journal of Social Issues*, 52(1).

Barna, G. (1993). *The future of the American family*. Chicago: Moody Press.

———. (1990). *The frog in the kettle*. Ventura, CA: Regal Books.

———. (1991). *User friendly churches*. Ventura, CA: Regal Books.

———. (1992). *Baby busters: The disillusioned generation*. Chicago: Northfield Publishing.

Barnhouse, R. (1977). *Homosexuality: A symbolic confusion*. New York: Seabury Press.

Baum, S. *Gifted but learning disabled: A puzzling paradox*. (Eric Digest No. E479) Reston, VA. The Council For Exceptional Children, (Eric Clearing House On Handicapped and Gifted Children), pp. 1–2.

Baum, S., and Owen, S. (1988). High ability/learning disabled students: How are they different? *Gifted Child Quarterly*, 32, 321–326.

Beiber, I. (1988). *Homosexuality: A psychoanalytic study of male homosexuals*. Northvale, NJ: Jason Aronson.

Bengston, V., and Robertson, J. (Eds.). (1985). *Grandparenthood*. Beverly Hills, CA: Sage Publications.

Bennett, W. (1990). *The de-valuing of America: The fight for our culture and our children*. New York: Simon and Schuster.

———. (1994). *The index of leading cultural indicators*. New York: Simon and Schuster.

———. (1993, March). *The index of leading cultural indicators*. Washington: Empower America/Heritage Foundation, p. 2.

Bergner, M. (1995). *Setting love in order*. Grand Rapids: Baker Book House.

Blackman, A., et al. (1994, July 4). When violence hits home, *Time*, p. 21.

Bloom, A. (1988). *The closing of the American mind*. New York: Simon and Schuster.

Bogart, L. (1972-1973, Winter). Warning: The Surgeon General has determined that TV violence is moderately dangerous to your child's mental health. *Public Opinion*, 504.

Boswell, J. (1980). *Christianity, social tolerance, and homosexuality*. Chicago: University of Chicago Press.

Brestin, D. (1988). *The friendships of women*. Wheaton, IL: Victor Books.

Briscoe, J. (1980). *Thank you for being a friend*. Grand Rapids: Zondervan Publishing House.

Brooks, A. (1989). *Children of fast track parents*. New York: Penguin.

Brown, B. (1991). *When you're mom no. 2: A word of hope for stepmothers*. Ann Arbor, MI: Servant Publications.

Brubaker, T. (Ed.). (1990). *Family relationships in later life*. Newbury Park, CA: Sage Publications.

Budnick, B. (1994). We need to restore sanity to sex education. *AmericanTeacher*, 79(4).

Buttry, D. (1988). *Bringing your church back to life: Beyond survival mentality.* Valley Forge: PA: Judson Press.

Byne, W., and Parsons, B. (1993). Human sexual orientation: The biological theories reappraised. *Archives of general psychiatry.*

Capehart, J. (1992). *Becoming a treasured teacher.* Wheaton, IL: Victor Books.

Carnegie Council on Adolescent Development, cited in Barbara Vobejda, (1992, December 10). Home alone: Glued to the TV. *The Washington Post.*

Cassuto, U. (1972). *A commentary on the book of Genesis.* Vol. 1. Jerusalem: The Magnes Press, first Hebrew ed., 1944; first English ed., 1961, reprinted, 1972.

Cavalletti, S. (1983). *The religious potential of the child.* New York: Paulist Press.

Chandler, R. (1991). *Racing toward 2000.* Washington, D.C.: Family Research Council.

Cherlin, A., and Furstenberg, F. (1992). *The new American grandparent.* Cambridge, MA: Harvard University Press.

Child Care and Christian Education—A Policy Statement (1987), The United Methodist Church.

Children and TV: Big Family Role, (Summer/Fall 1987). *Media and Values.*

Choun, R., and Lawson, M. (1993). *The complete handbook for children's ministry.* Nashville: Thomas Nelson Publishers.

Christensen, B. (1991, March). The grandparent gap. *The family in America* (3).

Cirio, P., and Tieman, J. (1993, December 1). Violent behavior is learned behavior. *St. Louis Post-Dispatch*, p. 11D.

Clapp, R. (1993). *Families at the crossroads: Beyond traditional and modern options.* Downers Grove, IL: InterVarsity Press.

Clements, M. (1993, December 12). What we say about aging. *Parade.*

Clendinning, B., Jr. (Ed.). (1971). *Family ministry in today's church.* Nashville: Convention Press.

Collins, K., and Freeman, M. (1989, July-August) Starting a child-care program in your church. *The Christian Ministry.*

Combs, N. (October 1987). Is your love life going down 'the tube? Condensed from *Redbook*, reprinted in *Reader's Digest.*

Comiskey, A. (1989). *Pursuing sexual wholeness,* St. Marys, FL: Creation House.

Conroy, D., and Fahey, C. (1985). Christian perspective on the role of grandparents. In V. Bengston, and J. Robertson (Eds.), *Grandparenthood* . Beverly Hills, CA: Sage Publications.

Cook, C. (1993). Television's impact on your kids. In J. Jenkins (Ed.), *Families: Practical advice from fifty experts.* Chicago: Moody Press.

Coontz, S. (1992). *The way we never were.* New York: Harper-Collins Publishers.

Cox, A. (1990). *Structures and techniques.* Cambridge, MA: Educator's Publishing Service.

Cromartie, M. (1993, September 13). The virtue man. *Christianity Today*, p. 31–33.

Cullen, P. (1990). Stepfamilies: The growing majority. *Marriage and family*, 73(5), 18–21.

Curran, D. (1983). *Traits of a healthy family*. Minneapolis: Winston Press.

Curry, A. (1993). Mentoring and discipleship. In K. Gangel and J. Wilhoit (Eds.), *The Christian educator's handbook on adult education*. Wheaton, IL: Victor Books.

Daniel, E. (1984). *The ABC's of VBS: How it can work for you*. Cincinnati: Standard Publishing Co.

Davis, Jr., C. (1982). *Ministering to mobile families*. Nashville: Broadman Press.

De Moss, R. G. (1992). *Learn to Discern*. Grand Rapids: Zondervan Publishing House.

Dettoni, J., and Dettoni, C. (1992). *Parenting before and after work*. Wheaton, IL: Victor Books.

Dillon, S. (1994, October 24). AIDS curriculum: Fighting words/shapers of teachers guidelines are hostile and exhausted. *The New York Times*.

Dobson, J., and Bauer, G. (1990). *Children at risk*. Dallas: Word Publishing.

Dobson, J. (1994, August). *Focus on the Family Newsletter*.

———. (1983). *Love must be tough*. Waco, TX: Word Books.

Dockery, K. (1993). *When a hug won't fix the hurt*. Wheaton, IL: Victor Books.

Dolan, B. (1983, September 5). Private violence. *Time*, p. 18.

Doner, G. (1988). Neuroendocrine response to estrogen and brain differentiation in heterosexuals, homosexuals and transsexuals. *Archives of sexual behavior*, 17, 57–75.

Donovan, C. (Ed.). (1994) *Washington Watch*, 5(9).

Dressler, J. (1994). Kids need frank, honest information. *American Teacher*, 79(4).

Durfield, R., and Durfield, R. (1991). *Raising them chaste.* Minneapolis: Bethany House.

Edelman, M. (Winter 1995). Cease fire! stopping the gun war against children in the United States. *The Chicago Theological Seminary Register*, 85(1).

Edelstein, S. (1991, January). Do grandparents have rights? *Modern Maturity*, p. 40.

Eggebeen, D. (1988). Determinants of maternal employment. White preschool children: 1960–1980. *Journal of Marriage and the Family*, 50, 149–159.

Eisenham, T. *Big people, little people: A course for parents of young children.* Elgin, IL: David C. Cook.

Elkind, D. (1985, April). Teens in crisis: All grown up and no place to go. Focus *on the Family.*

Elliott, D. (1994, March 28). No market for grannies. *Newsweek,* p. 137.

Elmer-Dewitt, P. (1990, November 26). Why junior won't sit still. *Time*, p. 59.

Evans, A. (1990). *America's only hope: Impacting society in the 90s.* Chicago: Moody Press.

Everett, E., Sutton, C., and Sutton, J. (1993). Special education in Christian/fundamentalist schools: A commitment to all the children. *Journal of Research on Christian Education*, 2 (1), 67–73.

Falwell, J. (1992). *The new American family: The rebirth of the American dream.* Dallas: Word Publishers.

Farrell, W. (1994). Spouse abuse: A two-way street. *USA Today*, p. 15A.

FBI Uniform Crime Report. (1993).

Fisher, B, (1981). *Rebuilding:When your relationship ends.* San Luis Obispo, CA: Impact Publishers.

Ford, L. (1991). *A curriculum design manual for theological education.* Nashville: Broadman Press.

Fox, L.H., Brody, L., and Tobin, D. (Eds.). (1983). *Learning disabled gifted children: Identification and programming.* Austin, TX: Pro-Ed.

Frazier, S. (1994). *Psychotrends: What kind of people are we becoming?* New York: Simon & Schuster.

Freeman, M. (Ed.). (1987). *Helping churches mind the children.* New York: All Union Press.

Friedman, H. (1992/93). Three village central school district, Setauket, New York. *Sixth Grade Puberty Education Program.*

Friedrich, G. (Ed.). (1975). *Theological dictionary of the New Testament,* vol. 5 (G.W. Bromiley, Trans.). Grand Rapids: William B. Eerdmans Publishing Company.

Gangel, K. (1981). *Building leaders for church education.* Chicago: Moody Press.

———. (1989) *Feeding and leading.* Wheaton, IL: Victor Books.

Gangel, K., and Hendricks, H. (1988). *The Christian educator's handbook on teaching.* Wheaton, IL: Victor Books.

Gerbner, G., and Gross, L. (1976, April). The scary world of TV's heavy viewer. *Psychology Today.*

George Bush's "Grandfather thing": Hug, read, and listen. *Grandparent Times,* 3(1), 1.

Glenn, N.D. (1991). The recent trend in marital success in the

United States. *Journal of Marriage and the Family*, *53*(2), 261–270.

Gorman, M. (1982). *Abortion and the early church*. Downers Grove, IL: InterVarsity Press.

Grant, G. (1988). Grand illusions: The legacy of planned parenthood. Brentwood, TN: Wolgemuth & Hyatt.

Grant, M., et al. (1983, September 5). Child abuse: The ultimate betrayal. *Time*, p. 21.

*Growing healthy*. Topeka, KS: TEMCO (The Educational Materials Company), and New York: National Center for Health Education.

Hamer, D.H. (1993). A linkage between DNA markers on the X chromosome and male sexual orientation. *Science*, *261*, 321–328.

Hancock, L., and Gordon, J. (1995, April 3). The story rug is now full. *Newsweek*, p. 58.

Hatterer, L. (1970). *Changing homosexuality in the male: Treatment for men troubled by homosexuality*. New York: McGraw-Hill.

Hays, R. (1986). Relations natural and unnatural: A response to John Boswell's exegesis of Romans 1. *Journal of Religious Ethics*, *14*(1).

Hellerstein, D. (1987, September 26). Can TV cause divorce? *TV Guide*, p.4.

Hendriksen, W. (1957). *New Testament commentary*. Grand Rapids: Baker Book House.

Horn, W. (1993, July 14). *Education Week*, 26.

Hunt, S. (1992). *Spiritual mothering*. Wheaton, IL: Crossway Books.

Hunter, B. (1986, February 21) Breaking the tie that binds, *Christianity Today*.

Ingrassia, M. (1994, November 17). Virgin cool. *Newsweek, 124* (16).

Irenaeus. Against heresies. In A. Roberts and J. Donaldson (Eds.), *Ante-Nicene Fathers* (vol. 1, p. 476). Peabody, MA: Hendrickson Publishers.

Jensen, E. (1994, August 5). One-day study finds rise in violence on TV, but research method is disputed. *Wall Street Journal*.

Johnson, J. (1995, February 6). How churches can be truly pro-family. *Christianity Today*, pp. 33–37.

Johnston, J. (1994, March 20). Kids: Growing up scared. *Cincinnati Enquirer*, p. E01.

Kaiser, W. (1983). *Toward Old Testament ethics*. Grand Rapids: Zondervan Publishing House.

Kalter, J. (1988, July 29). How TV is shaking up the American family. *TV Guide*, pp. 4–12.

Keay, I. (1989). *Child of pain, children of joy*. Old Tappan, NJ: Fleming H. Revell.

Keshet, J. K. (1988). The remarried couple. In W.R. Beer (Ed.), *Relative strangers: Studies in stepfamily processes*. Totowa, NJ: Rowman and Littlefield Publishers.

Kimmel, T. (1987). *Little house on the freeway*. Portland, OR: Multnomah Press.

Kjos, B. (1990). *Your child and the new age*. Wheaton, IL: Victor Books.

Knowles, M. (1978). *The adult learner: A neglected species*. Houston: Gulf.

Koenig, A. (1994, August 28). Children often scarred forever by domestic violence. *Sunday News,* p. A-1.

Kornhaber, A. (1985). Grandparenting and the "new social contract." In V. Bengtson and J. Robertson (Eds.), *Grandparenthood.* Beverly Hills, CA: Sage Publications.

Kraft, V. (1992). *The influential woman.* Dallas: Word Publishing.

———. (1992). *Women mentoring women.* Dallas: Word Publishing.

Kreeft, P. (1983). *The unaborted Socrates.* Downers Grove, IL: InterVarsity Press.

Larson, J. (1986). *A church guide for strengthening families.* Minneapolis: Augsburg Publishing House.

LeBar, L. (1995). *Education that is Christian.* Wheaton, IL: Victor Books.

LeVay, S. (1991). A difference in hypothalamic structure between heterosexual and homosexual men. *Science, 253,* 1034-1038.

Lewis, C. S. (1948, August 14). Notes on the Way, *Time and Tide, 29.*

Lichter, S., and Lichter, L. (1988, Spring). Does TV shape ethnic images? *Media and Values.*

Mandel, L. (1986, May 11). How I'd save television. *Parade Magazine.*

Mander, J. (1978). *Four arguments for the elimination of television.* New York: Quill.

Mann, J. (1982, August 2). What is TV doing to America? *US News and World Report,* p. 27.

Marriott, M. (1994, October 17). Not frenzied, but fulfilled. *Newsweek,* pp. 70-72.

Maston, T.B. (1983). *The Bible and family relations*. Nashville: Broadman Press.

Mayer-Bahlburg, H. (1990/1991). Will prenatal hormone treatment prevent homosexuality? *Journal of child and adolescent psychopharmacology, 1*(4).

McDowell, J., and Hostetler, B. (1994). *Right from wrong*. Dallas: Word Publishing.

McDowell, J. (1987). *How to help your child say "no" to sexual pressure*. Waco, TX: Word Publishing.

McKay, B. (1991). *What ever happened to the family: A psychologist looks at sixty years of change*. Cleveland: United Church Press.

Meet cover director Lorrie Thoemke (1991). *Child Care Information Exchange, 9*(1).

Melville, K. (1988). *Marriage and family today* (4th ed.). New York: Random House.

Meyrowitz, J. (1988, January 15). Is TV keeping us too well-informed?" *TV Guide*, p. 4.

Miller, D.R. (1994). *Counseling families after divorce*. Waco, TX: Word Publishing.

Minirth, F., Newman, B., and Warren, P. (1992). *The father book*. Nashville: Thomas Nelson Publishers.

Mitchell, A. (1991, February/March). When 6 x 7 = 47. *Parents of Teenagers*, p. 14.

National Committee for Prevention of Child Abuse. (1994).

Networks voice views on violence research," (1985, Fall). *Media and Values*.

*Newsweek*/Children's Defense Fund Poll. (1994, January).

*Nielsen Report* (1990).

Norton, M.P. Weekday/day care: Need and opportunity. Article #5, with children, United Methodist Church.

Olson, R., and Leonard, J. (1990). *Ministry with families in flux*. Louisville: Westminster/John Knox Press.

Ornstein, R., and Thompson, R. (1984). *The amazing brain*. Boston: Houghton-Mifflin.

Papernow, P. (1984). The stepfamily cycle: An experimental model of stepfamily development. *Family relations, 33*.

Payne, L. (1995). *The broken image*. Grand Rapids: Baker Book House.

Perkins, J., and Tarrants, T. (1994). *He's my brother.* Grand Rapids: Baker/Chosen Books.

Perkins, S., and Rice, C. (1993). *More than equals: Racial healing for the sake of the gospel*. Downers Grove, IL: InterVarsity Press.

Piper, J., and Grudem, W. (1991). *Recovering biblical manhood and womanhood: A response to evangelical feminism*. Wheaton, IL: Crossway Books.

Plagen, P. (1991, April 1). Violence in our culture. *Newsweek*, pp. 48, 51.

Popenoe, D. (1988). *Disturbing the nest*. New York: Aldine De Gruyter.

Porter, C., and Hamel, M. (Eds.). (1992). *Women's ministry handbook*. Wheaton, IL: Victor Books.

Portner, J. (1994). Grassroots warriors waging battle over sex-ed curriculum. *Education Week, 14*(6).

Postman, N. (1985). *Amusing ourselves to death: Public discourses in the age of show business*. New York: Penguin.

---

Powell, H. (1983, December) Ministry through day care, *Church Administration*.

Powell, S. (1985, October 28). What entertainers are doing to your kids. *US News & World Report*.

Ranieri, R.F. (1987). *The blended family: A guide for stepparents*. Liguori, MO: Liguori Publications.

Reardon, D. (1987). *Aborted women—silent no more*. Westchester, IL: Crossway Books.

Reed, M.C. (1985). *The church-related pre-school*. Nashville: Abingdon Press.

Robichaux, M. (1993, February 9). MTV is playing a new riff. *Wall Street Journal*.

Roehlkepartain, J. (Ed.). (1993). *Children's ministry that works*. Loveland, CO: Group Books.

Rosemond, J. (1989, April). Is your child hyperactive? *Better Homes and Gardens*, p. 38.

———. (1994, September). Your attention, please. *Hemispheres*.

Rosenthal, P. (1993, October 11). MTV is playing with fire. *Los Angeles Times*.

Ross, A. (1988). *Creation and blessing*. Grand Rapids: Baker Book House.

Sargent, L. (1991, March/April). Learning differences. *Christian Parenting Today*.

Satinover, J. (1995). *Homosexuality and the politics of truth*. Grand Rapids: Baker Book House.

Scanzoni, L., and Scanzoni, J. (1988). *Men, women and change: A sociology of marriage and family* (3d ed.). New York: McGraw-Hill.

Schaefer, R. (1988). *Racial and ethnic groups*. Glenview, IL: Scott-Foresman.

Schaller, L. (1990, September 26). Where's the family going? *The Lutheran*.

———. (1985). *The multiple staff and the larger church*. Nashville: Abingdon Press.

Schreur, J., and Schreur, J. (1994). *Family fears*. Wheaton: Victor Books.

Schroeder, I. (1987, Autumn). The sources of male/female differences and their implications for Christian nurture. *Christian Education Journal, 8,* 73–84.

Schultz, Margaret. (1994, January 25). Focus on the family brings hope. *Fort-Worth Star Telegram*, p. 1.

Seaton, K.L., and Rothaar, L.L. (1991). *Early childhood ministry and your church*. Minneapolis: Augsburg Fortress.

Sine, T. (1994, April/June). Time to stop dreaming. *OMS Outreach*, *93* (2).

Skalka, P. (1983, Spring). Take control of your TV, *Friendly Exchange*.

Springer, I. (1990, December). What every grandparent should know. *AARP Bulletin, 31*(2).

Staff (1992, May/June). Federal assistance to church-operated child care centers. *Church Law & Tax Report*.

Stafford, T. (1991, September 16). The old-age heresy. *Christianity Today*, p. 30.

The state of American's Children 1994 (1994). Washington, D.C.: Children's Defense Fund.

Stellway, R.J. (1990). *Christiantown*. New York: Haworth Press.

Stigers, H. (1976). *A Commentary on Genesis*. Grand Rapids: Zondervan Publishing House.

Stinnett, N., Chesser, B., and DeFrain, J. (Eds.). (1974). *Building family strengths: Blueprints for action*. Lincoln, NE: University of Nebraska Press.

Stonehouse, C. (1993). Learning from gender differences. In K. Gangel and J. Wilhoit (Eds.), *The Christian educator's handbook on adult education*. Wheaton, IL: Victor Books.

Sutton, J. (1991). Understanding mildly disabled students in Christian schools. *Balance* (Bob Jones University), *12*(3), 4.

Swaab, D., and Hofman, M. (1990, December 24). An enlarged suprachiasmatic nucleus in homosexual men. *Brain Research, 537*(1-2), 141-148.

Sweet, J.A., and Bumpass L.L. (1987). *American Families And Households*. New York: Russell Sage Foundation.

Sylwester, R., and Cho, J. (1992/1993, December/January). What brain research says about paying attention. *Educational Leadership, 50*(4), 71-75.

Townsend, J. (1991). Interview.

Townsend, J. (1991). Untitled Paper. Elgin, IL.

United States Statutes, 1974.

Urschel, J. (1994, June 30). Yes. there's spouse abuse, but . . . *USA Today*, p. 11A.

Violence in the schools. (1994, September 2-5). USA Snapshot. *USA Today*, p. 1A.

Wagner, C. Peter. (1984). *Leading your church to growth*. Ventura, CA: Regal Books.

Wallerstein, J., and Kelly, J. (1975). The effects of parental divorce: Experiences of the preschool child. *Journal of the American Academy of Child Psychiatry*, 14.

———. (1977). Divorce counseling: A community service for families in the midst of divorce. *American Journal of Orthopsychiatry*, 47(1).

Wallis, C. (1994, July 19). Life in overdrive. *Time*.

Walvoord, J., and Zuck, R. (Eds.). (1983). *The Bible knowledge commentary, New Testament*. Wheaton, IL: Victor Books.

Walvoord, J., and Zuck, R. (Eds.). (1985). *The Bible knowledge commentary, Old Testament*. Wheaton, IL: Victor Books.

Warning from Washington. (1982, May 17). *Time*, p. 77.

Warren, E. (1994, August 14) Children have refuge above rancor. *The Chicago Tribune*, sec. 2.

Washington, R., and Kehrein, G. (1993). *Breaking down the walls: A model for reconciliation in an age of racial strife*. Chicago: Moody Press.

Waters, H. (1982, December 6). Life according to TV. *Newsweek*.

Weber, J. (1994, June 6). When kids just can't pay attention. *Business Week*.

Wender, P. (1987). *The hyperactive child, adolescent, and adult—Attention deficit disorder through the lifespan*. New York: Oxford University Press.

Westoff, L.A. (1975, August 10). Two-time winners. *New York Times Magazine*.

Where have all the children gone? *Business Week*, (1992, June 29).

White, J. and White, M. (1989). *When your kids aren't kids anymore*. Colorado Springs: NavPress.

Whitmore, J. (1980). *Giftedness, conflict and underachievement.* Boston: Allyn and Bacon.

Whitmore, J., and Maker, J. (1985). *Intellectual giftedness among disabled persons.* Rockville, MD: Aspen.

Wiegand, J. Interview. Woodstock, IL.

Williams, W. (1994, August 25). Expensive incompetents won't fix schools. *Dallas Morning News,* p. 27A.

Willis, W. (1985). How to enlist volunteers. *Christian education profile.* Wheaton: Scripture Press Publications.

Winkler, H. (1991, April 14). *Chicago Tribune.*

Woodward, B., and Armstrong, S. (1979). *The brethren: Inside the Supreme Court.* New York: Simon & Schuster.

Wright, D. (1990). Homosexuality. In E. Ferguson (Ed.), *Encyclopedia of early Christianity.* New York & London: Garland Publishing.

Wright, D.F. (1984). Homosexuals or prostitutes? *Vigilae Christianae,* 38.

Wright, N. (1976). *Communication, key to your marriage.* Glendale, CA: Gospel Light Publications.

Wright, W. (1989). *Sacred dwelling: A spirituality of family life.* New York: Crossroad Publishing Company

Wyckoff, D.C. (1959). *The Gospel and Christian education.* Philadelphia: Westminster Press.

Yeary, O. (in press) Your school, daily stewardship. *Advance* (Assembly of God magazine)

# NAME INDEX

Ornstein, R., 201
Ortlund, R.C., 31
Owen, S., 193

Paar, J., 301
Papernow, P. 152–153
Parsons, B., 313
Pastoral Care Ministries,
  316–317
Patton, G., 194
Paul, 20, 24–25, 30, 32, 84,
  87–90, 113, 190, 227, 248,
  270, 313, 316, 318–19
Payne, L., 317
Pharoah, 26
Pillard, R., 312
Piper, J., 31, 278
Plagen, 258, 260
Planned Parenthood, 274
Polycarp, 318–319
Popenoe, D., 127–128
Porter, C., 86
Portner, J., 300
Postman, N., 252
Pound, E., 257
Powell, H., 260
Presser, H., 234
Professional Association of
  Christian Educators, 65
Promise Keepers, 71–72

Ranieri, R. 152
Reardon, D., 273–274
Redeemed Life Ministries,
  316–317
Reed, M., 289–290, 293–296
Richmond, G., 72
Riley, R., 262
Robichaux, M., 260
Rockefeller, N., 194

Rockford Institute Center, 231
Rockwell, N., 33, 229
Rodin, A., 194
Rodman, H., 184
Roehlkepartain, J.L., 184–185
Rose, R., 72
Rosemond, J., 203–204, 208
Rosen, J., 250
Rosenthal, P., 260
Rothaar, L., 289–290, 292–294

Samson, 38
Sarah, 38
Sargent, L.W., 202, 210
Satan, 270, 318
Satinover, J., 312–313
Satir, V., 128
Scalpone, A., 321
Scanzoni, L. and J., 13
Schaefer, R., 46
Schaller, L., 9
Schimmer, J., 7
Schreur, J. and J., 13
Schroeder, I., 84
Schultz, 265
Scaton, K., 289–290, 292–294
Shedd, C., 239
Sidey, H., 225
Simpson, O.J., 263
Sine, T., 235
Skalka, P., 249
Slaughter, J., 7
Smalley, G., 72
Solomon, 38
Sparks, G., 258
Spitz, M., 211
Spock, B., 7, 228
Springer, I., 28
Stafford, T. 229
Stellway, R., 127

# SUBJECT INDEX

# Editors

**Dr. Kenneth O. Gangel** (Ph.D., University of Missouri), after a distinguished career at Dallas Theological Seminary, is now executive director of the Toccoa Falls College Graduate Studies Division. A noted expert on Christian education and a prolific author, his many books include *Feeding and Leading*.

**Dr. James C. Wilhoit** (Ph.D., Northwestern University) is professor of Christian education at Wheaton College. His published works include a number of scholarly articles and books, including *Christian Education and the Search for Meaning*.

# Contributors

**Mrs. Barb Alexander** is preschool director at Aurora Christian School in Illinois.

**Mr. J. Kerby Anderson** is CEO of Probe Ministries in Dallas, Texas.

**Dr. Leith Anderson** is senior pastor at Wooddale Church in Eden Prairie, Minnesota.

**Dr. V. Gilbert Beers** is president of Scripture Press Ministries in Wheaton, Illinois.

**Rev. Mario Bergner** is an Anglican priest at the Church of the Resurrection and founder and director of Redeemed Life Ministries, both in Wheaton, Illinois.

**Dr. Beth Brown** is associate professor of educational ministries and administration at Denver Seminary.

**Dr. Samuel L. Canine** is chairman of the Department of Pastoral Ministries at Dallas Theological Seminary.

**Mrs. Jody Capehart** is a conference speaker and author making her home in Richardson, Texas.

**Mr. David Carder** is assistant pastor of counseling services at First Evangelical Free Church in Fullerton, California.

**Mrs. Colleen Cook**, a former TV news anchor, is a freelance writer living with her family in Marrero, Louisiana.

**Dr. James A. Davies** is professor of Christian education and dean of the Graduate School at Simpson College in Redding, California.

**Dr. Daryl Eldridge** is associate professor of foundations of education in the School of Religious Education at Southwestern Baptist Theological Seminary in Ft. Worth, Texas.

**Dr. Anthony Evans** is senior pastor of Oak Cliff Bible Fellowship and president of the Urban Alternative in Dallas, Texas.

**Rev. Jeffrey S. Gangel** is the campus pastor at Toccoa Falls College.

**Dr. Lynn Gannett** is assistant professor of Christian education at Dallas Theological Seminary.

**Mr. Jerry Jenkins**, former vice president for publishing and editor of *Moody* magazine, is writer-in-residence at Moody Bible Institute.

**Marlene Le Fever** is manager of ministry relations at David C. Cook Church Ministries in Colorado Springs, Colorado.

**Dr. Bruce Lockerbie** is chairman and CEO of Paideia, Inc., an educational consulting service based in Stony Brook, New York.

**Lory Lockerbie** is a health educator at William Sidney Mount Elementary School in Stony Brook, New York.

**Dr. David R. Miller** is school psychologist at University Christian School in Jacksonville, Florida.

**Dr. Brian Newman** is clinical director at the New Life Clinic in Richardson, Texas.

**Dr. Deborah Newman** is a clinical therapist at the New Life Clinic in Richardson, Texas.

**Mr. Dennis Rainey** is director of FamilyLife Ministries and co-host of a daily family radio broadcast originating in Little Rock, Arkansas.

**Mrs. Jane Schimmer** is academic language therapist at Trinity Christian Academy in Dallas, Texas.

**Dr. James R. Slaughter** is professor of Christian education at Dallas Theological Seminary.

**Prof. Clarence W. Wulf** is director of the School of Christian Education at Toccoa Falls College.